CHINA'S CHALLENGES IN MOVING TOWARDS A HIGH-INCOME ECONOMY

Other titles in the China Update Book Series include:

The titles are available online at press.anu.edu.au/publications/series/china-update

CHINA'S CHALLENGES IN MOVING TOWARDS A HIGH-INCOME ECONOMY

EDITED BY LIGANG SONG
AND YIXIAO ZHOU

Australian
National
University

PRESS

社 会 科 学 文 献 出 版 社
SOCIAL SCIENCES ACADEMIC PRESS (CHINA)

ANU PRESS

Published by ANU Press
The Australian National University
Acton ACT 2601, Australia
Email: anupress@anu.edu.au

Available to download for free at press.anu.edu.au

A catalogue record for this book is available from the National Library of Australia

ISBN (print): 9781760464523
ISBN (online): 9781760464530

WorldCat (print): 1263655300
WorldCat (online): 1263655305

DOI: 10.22459/CCMTHE.2021

Cover design and layout by ANU Press

Contents

List of figures

List of tables

Contributors

Joel Bowman, The Australian National University

Shawn Xiaoguan Chen, University of Western Australia

Cai Fang, Chinese Academy of Social Sciences

Haoran Hu, Shandong University

Kunwang Li, Nankai University

Jia Peng, Chinese Academy of Social Sciences

Wang Ruimin, Development Research Centre

Niu Sanyuan, Development Research Centre

Rao Sihang, Peking University

Ligang Song, The Australian National University

Sizhong Sun, James Cook University

Shao Ting, Development Research Centre

Wang Wei, Development Research Centre

You Wu, Beijing Technology and Business University

Liu Xin, Development Research Centre

Liu Xingshuo, Peking University

Yanchao Xu, Yunnan University

Libo Yin, Central University of Finance and Economics

Sheng Yu, Peking University

Deng Yusong, Development Research Centre

Liqing Zhang, Central University of Finance and Economics

Yixiao Zhou, The Australian National University

Acknowledgements

The China Economy Program (CEP) at the Crawford School of Public Policy in The Australian National University (ANU) acknowledges the financial support provided by BHP for China Update 2020. We thank the program support and editing assistance provided by CEP Project Manager Timothy Cronin, Crawford School of Public Policy, and our colleagues from the East Asia Forum (EAF) at ANU. This is the 20th volume in the China Update book series. China Update 2020 provides a platform for leading researchers on the Chinese economy to discuss various issues relating to the challenges and opportunities in China moving towards a high-income economy. We sincerely thank our contributors for their valuable contributions to this year's book. Thanks also go to ANU Press, notably Emily Tinker and Jan Borrie, for their expeditious publication of the book series every year. We thank the Social Sciences Academic Press (China) of the Chinese Academy of Social Sciences in Beijing for translating and publishing the Chinese version of the book each year—making this valuable research available to a wider readership.

1

Challenges and roadmaps for moving towards a high-income economy

Ligang Song and Yixiao Zhou

China's per capita income reached US$10,000 in 2019—an important milestone in measuring the significant improvement in wellbeing for 1.4 billion Chinese people resulting from the decades-long program of reform and development. In the same year, China's total gross domestic product (GDP) reached US$14.3 trillion, accounting for 16.4 per cent of global GDP according to World Bank estimates, which matches closely to China's share of about 18 per cent of global population. Along with the rise in per capita income and total GDP, the Chinese economy witnessed some fundamental changes in the pattern of industrialisation, continuing to move towards high value-added production, trade and investment, progress on innovation and technological change and large-scale poverty reduction. These changes reflect some key features associated with a new and more advanced stage of growth and development. These structural changes are expected to continue to deepen and will allow China to accomplish its goal of becoming a high-income economy, which is one marked by a level of per capita income above US$12,270.[1]

---

1   The World Bank classifies countries into low-income, lower middle-income, upper middle-income and high-income economies according to gross national income per capita (World Bank 2021).

Dynamic changes in moving up the ladder of development

China's consistent, rapid economic growth over four decades was made possible by a good combination of economic reform and opening (Lin 2013a) and its demographic structure (Cai et al. 2018). The strong incentive effects of reform and opening matched so well with China's abundant supply of labour (initially low skilled, then shifting towards highly skilled at later stages of development) during the high-growth period in explaining the fundamental pattern of China's economic development (Li et al. 2012). Some key development lessons can be learned from this experience.

First, China's pattern of economic growth has centred on the development of manufacturing industries, which for a consistently long period drew significant investment despite contraction in its share in total investment in recent years (Figure 1.1). Investments in industry created employment, facilitated the unprecedented scale of urbanisation, established a comprehensive manufacturing base and turned China into an international industrial powerhouse through deepened international integration and specialisation at the beginning, following the East Asian manufacturing-based growth model in the 1970s and 1980s, and later through participating in global production networks (Kojima 2000; Lin 2013b). The development of manufacturing has had positive externalities as expounded by Kaldor's growth laws, which say there is a strong positive correlation between the growth of manufacturing output and the growth of GDP, a strong positive correlation between the growth of manufacturing output and the growth of productivity in manufacturing, and a strong positive relationship between the growth of manufacturing output and the growth of productivity outside manufacturing (Thirlwall 2015). One empirical work using cross-provincial data from China has validated such growth laws in the Chinese context (Thirlwall 2011: 111).

Second, China's industrial sector development did not leave the development of the agricultural sector too far behind. In fact, China's agricultural sector has maintained record productivity growth throughout the reform period while going through its own transformation (Sheng and Song 2019). This allowed a continuously large number of migrant workers to move to the cities, while the rural sectors have become an important source of demand for industrial goods due to the steady rises in rural household incomes. The way in which industrial and rural development support each other through rural reform and urbanisation has led to rapid increases in income in both sectors, narrowing the income gaps between them. A significant change in government policy towards agriculture in 2005 saw for the first time in Chinese history the abolition of agricultural taxes, lessening the financial burden on farmers (Heerink et al. 2006), although much needs to be done to deepen rural reform, especially reforms of both leased and rural residential lands (Liu 2018). This is in sharp contrast to the experience of many developing countries, where industrial growth was achieved at least temporarily at the expense of rural sector development through policies of 'urban bias' (Pugh 1996), which eventually dragged down their overall development as a result (Lipton 2007).

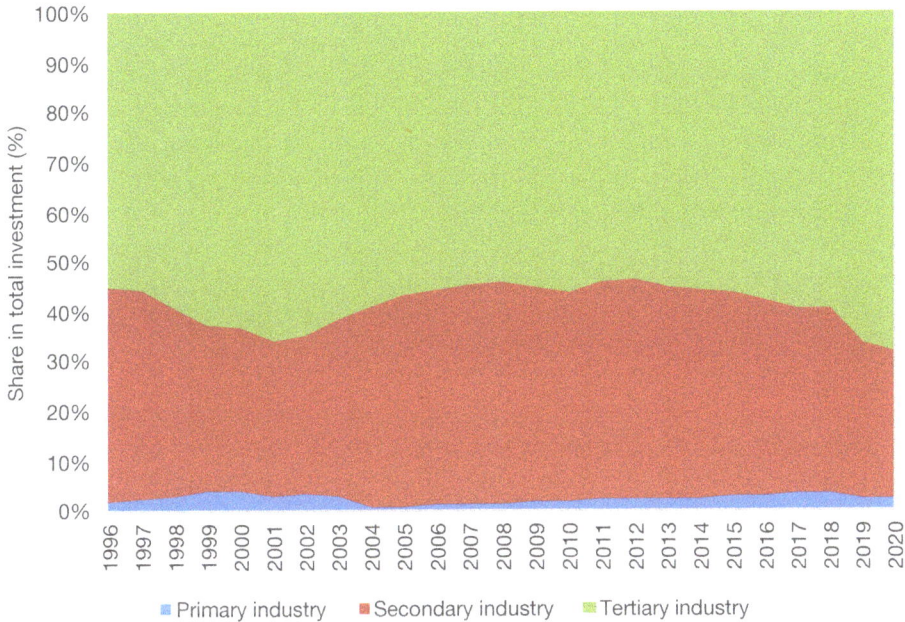

Figure 1.1 Fixed-asset investment in three types of industries as a share of total investment in China (1996–2020)

Source: Authors' construction using data from CEIC Database.

Third, infrastructure development in China has been a success story during the reform period. The massive investments in infrastructure by both government and the private sector—including in roads, bridges, railways, ports, air links, fast trains, large-scale water projects, electricity and gas—have paved the way for foreign investment and played an important role in enhancing the process of marketisation, which facilitates freer internal flows of goods, factors of production and ideas (Qin 2016; Song and van Geenhuizen 2014; Yu et al. 2012). The literature on the 'new economic geography' suggests that widening the market brings benefits in terms of increased competition and contestability in markets and, therefore, transportation infrastructure allows greater dissemination of knowledge and technology (Canning and Bennathan 2000). As Canning and Bennathan (2000: 2) pointed out:

> [I]f the takeoff in developing countries relies on a co-ordinated bout of investment, the public provision of risky, large scale infrastructure projects may provide a trigger for private sector investment and escape from a poverty gap.

The Chinese experience in infrastructure development supports this point. China is now on its way to building the so-called new infrastructure that will underpin its embrace of the digital economy (Meinhardt 2020).

Fourth, the periods in which China's rapid economic growth took place coincided with the periods in which globalisation processes were enforced or reenforced, marked by the transition from the General Agreement on Tariffs and Trade (GATT) to the World Trade Organization (WTO) in 1995. Under the auspices of the WTO, global trade and cross-border investment flows were accelerated and China became an important player in the process. The year 2021 marked the twentieth anniversary of China's accession to the WTO. Over the past 20 years, China has become the largest trading nation in the world through its deep integration with the global economy and domestic reforms in compliance with the requirements of the WTO (Drysdale and Hardwick 2018). By 2020, China had become the largest recipient of foreign direct investment (FDI), surpassing the United States, against a background in which global total FDI fell by 42 per cent due to the impact of the COVID-19 pandemic, according to the United Nations Conference on Trade and Development (UNCTAD 2021).

China had also become a big investor in overseas markets, with its total outflow of FDI reaching US$118 billion, making it the third-largest overseas investor after the United States and Japan in 2019. Although falling from its peak of outward investment reached in 2016, China's outward investment in the countries of the Belt and Road Initiative (BRI) continued to grow rapidly (to 11.7 per cent in 2019). China has made great efforts in opening its markets to foreign competition, deepening its domestic reforms, addressing issues such as intellectual property rights, state subsidies and market competition, and state-owned enterprise (SOE) reform to fully comply with the requirements of the WTO (Yu 2018; Zhou et al. 2019).

Fifth, the catch-up phase of China's economic development saw significant progress in innovation and technological change, underpinned by its human capital and increased capacity for innovative activities. China's spending on research and development (R&D) climbed 10.3 per cent to RMB2.44 trillion (US$378 billion) in 2020, as reported by China's National Bureau of Statistics (NBS 2021). According to the NBS report, R&D spending accounted for 2.4 per cent of China's GDP in 2020 (Figure 1.2). The report shows that, by the end of 2020, China had 522 'national key laboratories' and 350 'national engineering research centres' in operation; some 457,000 projects had been funded by the National Natural Science Foundation of China in 2020 and 3.6 million patents had been granted—up by 40 per cent from 2019. These developments allowed China to leapfrog its technological capabilities in several key areas, including digital technologies, as well as compelling it to pay more attention to the protection of intellectual property rights in the transition from technological imitation to innovation (Zhou 2014). According to the Global Innovation Index, which provides detailed metrics about the innovation performance of 131 countries and economies around the world,

China was ranked first in innovation performance for middle-income countries and fourteenth globally. The World Intellectual Property Organization (WIPO) reported that its China office received a record total of 1.54 million patent applications in 2018, ahead of the United States, Japan, South Korea and the European Patent Office (EPO). China recorded double-digit growth in 2018, while patent filings slightly dropped in the United States and Japan. More than 84 per cent of all patent filings in 2019 occurred in the intellectual property (IP) offices of China, the United States, Japan, South Korea and the EPO. China accounted for more than 40 per cent of the world total (Figure 1.3).

In lifting China's technological capabilities, both the public and the private sectors have been working more closely in making technological breakthroughs in areas such as new sources of energy, electric cars, aviation and space technologies and 5G networks. For example, by 2020, China had built the world's largest 5G network, accounting for more than 70 per cent of the global total and leading the world in terms of registered patents on key 5G technologies. China has attached great importance to the development of its '5G+ Industrial Internet' strategy, which has been emphasised in the central government's main working reports for four consecutive years. According to the China Academy of Information and Communications Technology, China has more than 1,100 5G+ Industrial Internet projects under construction, covering 22 industries, including cement, automobiles, petrochemicals, steel, mining and oil fields (Xinhua 2021b).

According to a report by China's Ministry of Industry and Information Technology, the quantity of industrial robots produced in 2020 increased by 19.1 per cent year-on-year (Xinhua 2021a). The real hope is that these developments in frontier technologies relating especially to the digital transformation of the economy could lead to economy-wide improvements in productivity. Such a transformation would have global implications in terms of new modes of industrialisation, new patterns of trade and cross-border transfers of technology, and new pattern of consumption.

Sixth, one of the damaging consequences of the so-called investment-driven model of growth is environmental degradation. China's decades-long industry-led growth path has been characterised by rapidly growing energy and emission intensities and increases in its global market shares of manufactured products and natural resources such as petroleum and minerals (Roberts et al. 2016; Zheng et al. 2020). Its carbon emissions and share in global emissions have constantly increased since the 1970s and noticeably accelerated after 2002, when the pace of its industrialisation accelerated. As a result, incremental carbon emissions have surged, with China surpassing the United States since 2007 to become the world's largest emitter of carbon dioxide. Given the scale, pace and trajectory of its industrialisation, China faces an enormous challenge for mitigation. Yet, it is clearly in the country's interests to do so given the high price it has been paying for environmental degradation. To confront this challenge, China has adopted a grand strategy that includes technological change and innovation, market price mechanisms, adjustments of industrial structure, the use of renewable energy and changes in consumption patterns, with a hope that low carbon growth can be generated (Jiang et al. 2013).

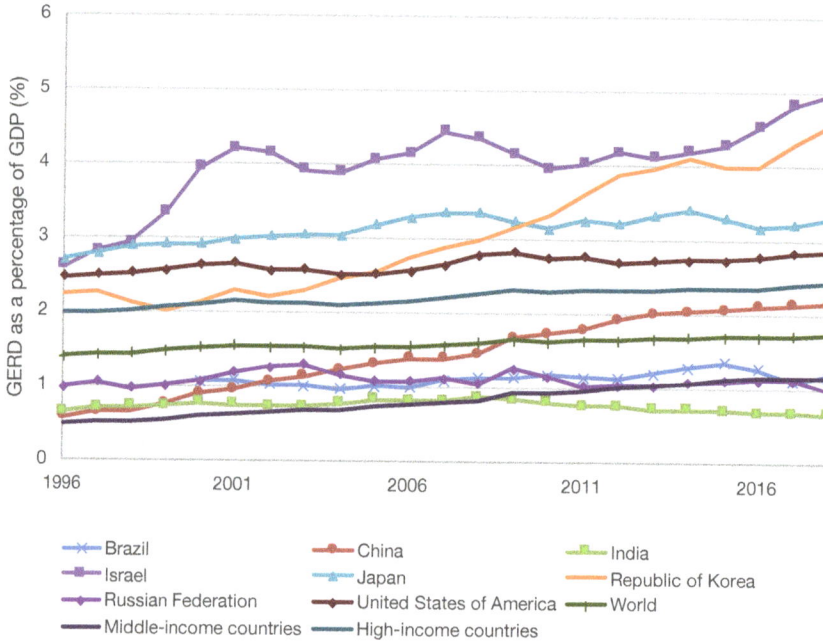

Figure 1.2a. R&D intensity in various economies, 1996–2018

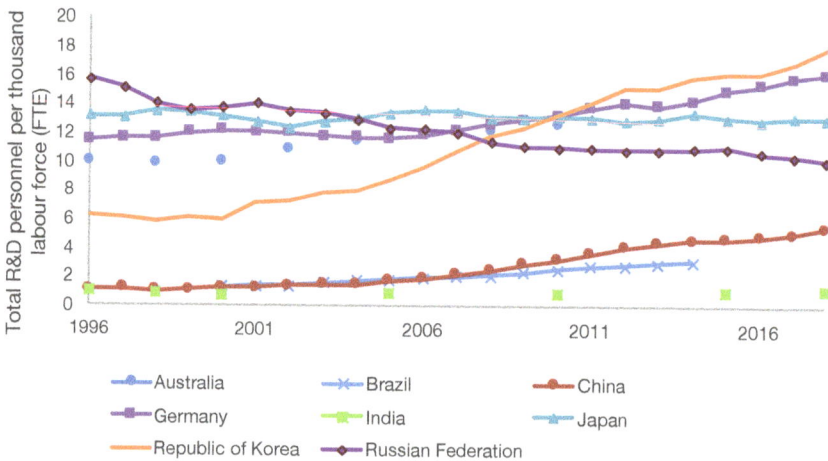

Figure 1.2b. R&D personnel intensity, 1996–2018

Figure 1.2 R&D intensity and R&D personnel intensity in various economies

Note: R&D intensity is R&D expenditure as a share of GDP (R&D intensity). R&D personnel intensity is Total R&D personnel per thousand labour force.

Source: Constructed from UNESCO data.

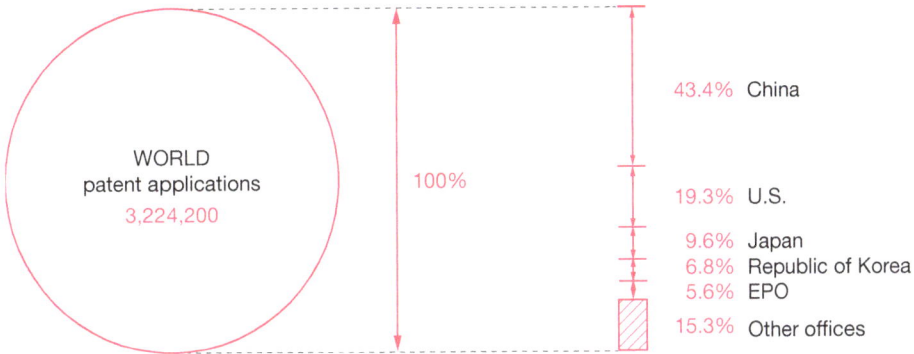

Figure 1.3 Major countries in patent applications in 2018
Source: World Intellectual Property Database website.

Finally, the modernisation drive has fundamentally changed the fabric of Chinese society. With rising income levels, China has created the world's largest middle class (Kharas 2017) and eliminated absolute property (Guo et at. 2019); its universal healthcare covers 93 per cent of the population, and its urbanisation ratio reached 62 per cent in 2020. With massive investment in education, China has substantially improved the literacy of its people through compulsory education and expanded levels of training. Its higher education sector has also begun to enter the global top university rankings (Fraumeni et al. 2019; Li et al. 2014). At the same time, its population is ageing (Figure 1.4).

> Because mortality will continue to decline and fertility will probably stay at a relatively low level, population ageing is likely to be an irreversible trend of long-term development rather than a historical event occurring at a particular time. (Zhao 2011: 296)

In summary, there have been three significant windows of opportunity for economic transformation in China in the past 40 years. China has successfully met the challenges of the first two and is yet to prove its success for the third. The first window was the historic opportunity to reform and open the economy in the late 1970s, which allowed China to decisively move away from the centrally planned system to embrace an open market economy that fundamentally unleashed all productive forces in creating wealth, leading to high economic growth and much improved standards of living. The second window of opportunity was China's accession to the WTO in 2001, which formally admitted China to the global trading system, allowing it to build a more rules-based market-compatible system with a high degree of interdependence with the rest of the world. China has since benefited enormously from globalisation and contributed to the improvement of global welfare while exerting strong competitive pressure on its trading partners in dealing with the enormous adjustment costs. The third window of opportunity is how China in the post-COVID-19 pandemic world will embrace digital technologies to transform its mode of economic growth and address the challenges of structural change, deglobalisation, an ageing population, income inequality, public sector debt and climate change. Success in addressing all the key challenges will hold the key for China to elevate itself to the status of a high-income economy.

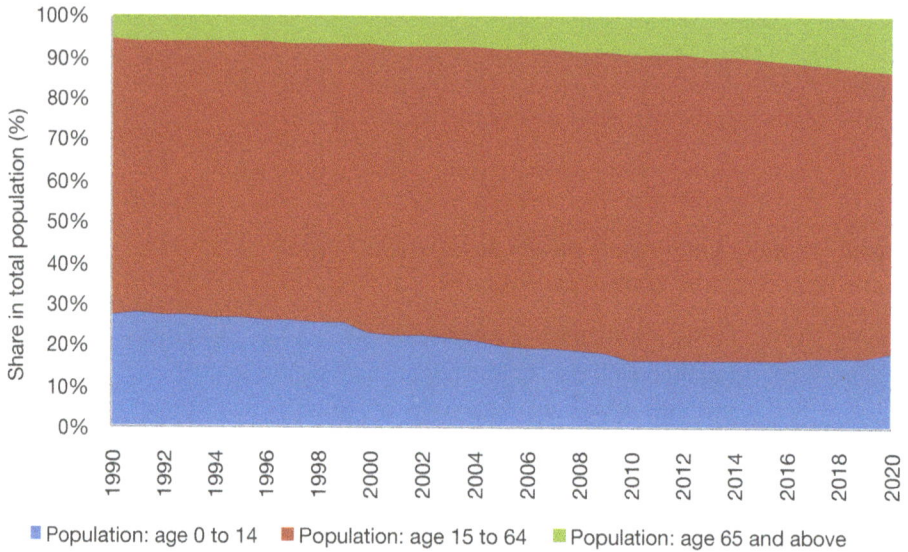

Figure 1.4 China's population by age group as share of total population, 1990–2020 (per cent)

Source: Authors' construction using data from CEIC Database.

At the same time, some longstanding structural problems remain, such as resource misallocation, inefficiency, high emission intensities, income inequality and lack of market-compatible institutions. In the Chinese context of a partially reformed system, these problems need to be addressed through broad-based supply-side reforms, institution-building and social changes to prevent China from falling into the so-called middle-income trap, where income growth stagnates and society loses momentum for growth and development resulting from the rising costs of production and an inability to keep pace with structural reform to produce more high valued-added goods through improved productivity and technological progress. Again, building market-compatible institutions is the key for securing long-term growth and development.

There is some urgency for this as China tries to avoid 'getting old before it gets rich' (Dollar et al. 2020). The pace of China's move towards an ageing society highlights the need to deepen its supply-side structural reforms, including reform of the family planning policy and its household registration system (*hukou*) and rural reforms. This concern is warranted considering economic growth has been decelerating in recent years—in part because of demographic change: there has been an absolute fall in China's working-age population since 2012, fertility rates continue to fall and its total population is expected to fall from 2025 (Bai and Lei 2020). Part of that growth deceleration is also due to the falling level of productivity in recent years. The Fourteenth Five-Year Plan, which will be implemented from 2021 with a new development strategy, aims to address these structural issues and to build a more mature market system while continuing to raise the level of per capita income and address the challenges of climate change and income inequality.

Maintaining growth amid the COVID-19 pandemic

The COVID-19 pandemic—a once-in-a-century event—began at a time when there were many uncertainties in the global economy, including the slowdown in China's economic growth. The global economy contracted by –3.5 per cent as a result of widespread lockdowns and severe disruptions to global supply chains. China became the only major economy to achieve growth, of 2.3 per cent, amid the onslaught of the pandemic in 2020, against the background of global economic contraction (IMF 2021). China's economy has recovered steadily, with employment and people's wellbeing effectively guaranteed as economic and social development have been better than expected. China's job market remained stable in 2020, with the surveyed unemployment rate in urban areas standing at 5.6 per cent—below the government's annual target of 6 per cent. In the same year, China's total GDP surpassed RMB100 trillion (equivalent to US$14.7 trillion), accounting for about 17 per cent of global GDP. This achievement ended the final year of China's Thirteenth Five-Year Plan (2016–20) on a positive note, despite the impact of the pandemic.

A roadmap to a high-income economy: The Fourteenth Five-Year Plan and the new strategy of 'dual circulation'

China's post-COVID-19 economic recovery coincides with the implementation of the Fourteenth Five-Year Plan—the economic and social development blueprint for the period 2021–25, as well as the long-term vision for China by 2035 (NDRC 2021). The vision proposes that China will realise 'socialist modernisation', become a 'socialist modern nation' and reach medium developed-economy status by 2035. The plan sets out the key priorities for the next five years for China's growth and development. Setting a long-term development goal is important for rebuilding the confidence of the Chinese people after the heavy blow dealt by the pandemic.

The five-year plan could be a watershed moment in China's economic development path, as policy goals move up a gear from 'comprehensively building a well-off society' to 'comprehensively building a modern socialist nation'. Policies in the plan aim to strengthen the underpinnings of the modern nation's long-term growth in a well-rounded approach, covering the economy and the market, governance and law, defence and security, culture and identify, science and technology, environment and health, participation in the global economy and governance. The plan has 19 chapters and 65 subchapters, sets out 20 main indicators of economic and social development and describes measures and initiatives, including 102 major engineering projects within the plan's five-year period. Local and sectoral plans fleshing out these targets in greater detail will be released throughout the year.

The plan covers several key themes, including: enhancing innovation and scientific research to provide strategic support to economic development and scientific and technological self-reliance; strengthening the domestic market, boosting domestic demand and deepening supply-side reforms under the 'dual circulation strategy'; deepening market reforms and enhancing coordination between the government and the market; prioritising rural development through the pull of urban development; optimising and promoting coordinated regional development and new urbanisation; developing China's cultural soft power; enhancing green, sustainable and low-carbon economic growth; further opening up to world markets, relying on the large domestic market to enhance international cooperation, promoting BRI cooperation and participating in the reform of global economic governance; improving people's living standards and their sense of achievement, wellbeing and safety, while responding to population ageing; establishing strategies for and coordinating development of national security; and strengthening national defence and military modernisation.

In the plan, the urgency of technological innovation is palpable. Chapters 2, 3 and 5 elaborate on the issue of innovation and technological progress. Because China's labour force peaked in 2011 and its society is ageing, the rate of entrepreneurial activity and innovation may slow, while labour costs, care responsibilities and demand for healthcare resources will add to the cost of operating the economy. Counteracting forces include continued technological progress, labour-substituting and augmenting automation and rising labour quality. For any country, technological progress can come from both domestic innovation and absorption of technological diffusion from abroad. As tensions in technological competition rise, China is compelled to rely more on domestic R&D. We therefore expect to see a rise China's R&D expenditure from this year.

Chapter 4 of the plan discusses developing China's domestic market and building a 'new development pattern', which centres on the 'dual circulation strategy' first articulated by President Xi in May 2020 as China began to plan its post-pandemic economic recovery. The dual circulation strategy aims to promote a stronger domestic market ('internal circulation') while continuing to strengthen China's international economic position ('external circulation'). Domestic circulation is the staple component of this strategy, while external circulation is the complement.

The establishment of this strategy reflects several considerations: increasingly uncertain international markets due to trade conflicts; global value chains becoming more regionalised and localised after the pandemic due to security concerns; rebalancing from export-driven to consumption-driven growth and raising domestic consumption and utility; and enlarging the domestic market and reducing unevenness in growth and incomes across regions. While China may be able to rely more on indigenous innovation to drive technological progress, declining access to international knowledge flows would be costly to any country, as innovation processes are becoming more interconnected and networked. Therefore, China will need a strategy to become more internationally connected to knowledge flows.

Overall, the Fourteenth Five-Year Plan reveals a strong resolution to overcome various challenges and, if successful, the capabilities learned would enable China to achieve high-income status sooner than expected.

Structure of this book

Against the above background, this book explores the challenges faced by the Chinese economy in the transition to a high-income economy, including agricultural development, financial reform, internationalisation of the renminbi, urbanisation, as well as topics related to innovation, corporate-sector development and market competition. China's growth experience has been full of exciting changes and important lessons about reform and structural change, and this year's *China Update* is again the way to gain insights into these.

In Chapter 2, Cai Fang and Jia Peng detail the relationship between China's status as an upper middle-income country and domestic trends in social mobility, particularly as these questions relate to China's ability to overcome the middle-income trap. Using cross-country data, the authors investigate the relationship between development stage, growth rate and social inequality, and examine the drivers of Chinese growth over the past 40 years of reform, detailing how these drivers have changed over time. They find that the primary drivers that sustained social mobility in decades past—namely, labour market mechanisms, massive internal migration and major structural economic reforms—are now inadequate as China has developed and low-hanging growth opportunities have attenuated.

The authors challenge the idea that rising problems of social mobility can be tackled solely through expansion of the economic pie. Instead, they argue that these issues must be additionally addressed via economic and social reforms, including progressive taxation and redistribution policies, as well as the mitigation of institutional obstacles, especially the *hukou* system. The authors conclude by offering policy suggestions aimed at enhancing social mobility and a more equitable sharing of developmental dividends. They suggest reform of basic social services provision to operate on de facto rather than de jure residence status, while additionally highlighting the central government's institutional responsibility to mitigate the costs of *hukou* reform to alleviate the associated externalities faced by local governments.

Considering China's increased dependence on the importation of agricultural goods to meet growing domestic demand, the authors of Chapter 3, Rao Sihang, Liu Xingshuo and Sheng Yu, investigate China's current and historical comparative and competitive advantages for 17 major crop and livestock products. Using global commodity-level agricultural trade data for the period 1978–2018, the authors calculate the revealed comparative advantage (RCA) and relative trade advantage (RTA) indices to compare China's relative advantages in the trade of certain commodities. They reveal a rapid decline in China's earlier comparative advantage for most agricultural products compared with the rest of the world, indicating that the rise in demand caused by population and economic growth has outpaced growth in agricultural output. With even further growth in food demand anticipated over the coming decade, the authors forecast future demand by commodity and calculate the overall bilateral complementarity coefficient for China and several important countries and regions to best determine potential sources of supply. Their findings indicate that it is in China's interest to import land and water-intensive goods to free up its own land and resources for products for which it possesses relative advantage.

The authors point out that there are more than 3.5 billion hectares of land suitable for agriculture throughout the world, but only around 1.5 billion hectares are being used effectively. If trade and investment relationships could be rearranged between China and the rest of the world based on their comparative competitiveness, global food supply would significantly increase. Therefore, rearranging agricultural trade between China and her trading partners could present a win-win strategy for China as well as for the world. Therefore, the concern that China's food demand will compete with demands from other developing countries, imposing greater pressures on global food supply, may be misplaced.

In Chapter 4, Wang Wei, Deng Yusong, Shao Ting, Wang Ruimin, Niu Sanyuan and Liu Xin detail the many achievements of China's urbanisation since the start of the reform and opening period more than 40 years ago. The authors describe a process in which the urbanisation level has steadily increased, urban patterns have been optimised, cities' overall competitiveness has been significantly enhanced and the system of urban governance has continually improved. Accompanying all these advances has been the steady improvement in residents' living standards. With its urbanisation rate at 60 per cent, China has now entered a new stage of urbanisation, characterised by the pursuit of high-quality development—a status that coincides with a new technological revolution.

Looking forward to 2050, the authors predict that China will enter the ranks of high-income countries and its industrial structure will undergo profound changes. With the transformation and upgrading of urban industries, cities in the future will focus on the requirements of high-quality development. The authors contend that China will need to continually improve the quality and efficiency of urbanisation to create an efficient, low-carbon and green urban development model, arguing that the creation and application of a new technological revolution present an opportunity for the high-quality development of Chinese cities. Their findings indicate that the huge domestic market potential and institutional dividends brought by the new round of reform and opening will be the drivers of the next stage of China's urbanisation.

Governments in China currently find themselves constrained by the necessary trade-offs between cutting tax rates to incentivise business investment and boost consumption and maintaining tax revenue to match its expenditure. To reconcile the tension, the authors of Chapter 5, Yanchao Xu and Shawn Xiaoguang Chen, propose a tax-neutral reform centred on the improvement of tax enforcement across firms, which are currently subject to misallocation and aggregate productivity losses. They examine the theoretical mechanisms sustaining such reform and empirically investigate its feasibility, finding that the underlying mechanisms rest on the positive feedback loop of 'lower tax rate = better tax enforcement and compliance = higher productivity = greater tax base = lower tax rate'. Based on county-level public financial data and industrial firm surveys during 2000–07, the authors use the abolition of agricultural taxes in 2005 as a 'quasi-natural experiment' to test key mechanisms. Using the estimates of key parameters, the authors roughly estimate the lower bound of the value-added tax rate cut able to sustain revenue-neutral reform.

In Chapter 6, Sizhong Sun explores aggregate innovation activities and their growth effects in China. Through examination of both inputs (including R&D) and outputs (including patents), the author reaches several conclusions with important implications for China's growth potential: first, innovation in China is on an upward trajectory, with little evidence of a slowdown in growth; second, innovation appears to promote economic growth in the long run at both the national and the industry levels; third, there is no short-run growth effect from innovation at the national level. Considering the growth effect of innovation and the increasingly binding resource constraints faced by China, innovation will likely play a more important role in China's future economic growth.

Analysis of the financial health of Chinese companies provides important clues for understanding the trajectory of the Chinese economy and is useful for assessing the effectiveness of government policies affecting business and corporate activity. With previous analyses of the state of China's corporate sector indicating a general decline in profitability and an increase in corporate leverage since the Global Financial Crisis, in Chapter 7, Joel Bowman seeks to provide an update on more recent developments in the sector through an examination of official survey data supplemented by granular data derived from the financial statements of more than 3,700 nonfinancial companies listed on the Shanghai and Shenzhen stock exchanges. The author finds that more recent declines in corporate profitability have been primarily driven by the private sector, even as private firms maintain higher levels of profitability than state-owned firms.

The findings show that major drivers of this trend include a squeeze on less-regulated credit caused by reforms aimed at reducing risk in the financial system, and the private sector's greater exposure to a global slowdown in manufacturing and trade. This has been felt particularly acutely by export-oriented manufacturing firms, affected by relative economic sluggishness in advanced economies and by the US–China trade dispute. After examining the status of corporate leverage and the special challenges faced by the real estate sector, the author details recent government measures aimed at easing financial conditions for small firms, while acknowledging the challenge of achieving these aims in practice.

Developed in the context of economic globalisation and low domestic land and labour costs, processing trade became an important source of China's growth, industrialisation and employment. In Chapter 8, Kunwang Li and Haoran Hu examine the impact of policies aimed at transforming and upgrading processing trade in China, the implementation of which began in 2003. The authors use Chinese customs and industrial panel data for the period of 2000–06 to empirically test the impact of transformation and upgrading policies for processing trade on enterprise productivity by use of the double-difference method.

Their findings indicate that these policies have contributed to resource misallocation and have had a net negative effect on productivity. As the policies explicitly promote the transfer of processing trade from the dominant eastern regions of China to the west and centre, the eastern regions endowed with natural geographic and logistical advantages have been most negatively impacted, disturbing production efficiency and original resource allocation. Given that these policies are aimed at cultivating private firms, the authors find that foreign-owned and joint-venture firms engaged in processing trade with imported materials have been especially negatively affected by the policies' crowding-out effects acting as a drag on production efficiency. They find that processing trade has exhibited a steady downward trend since 2000, but product structure has improved. Nonetheless, the authors caution that industrial policy should be orientated towards efficiency to avoid creating new distortions.

In Chapter 9, Liqing Zhang, Libo Yin and You Wu analyse bilateral offshore renminbi exchange rate returns in an augmented uncovered interest rate parity regression to assess the offshore renminbi's safe-haven characteristics. To explore the issue, the authors evaluate the relationship between the bilateral exchange rate returns on the offshore renminbi against major global currencies and BRI currencies, as well as global risk factors. The empirical results of their study indicate the following: first, the offshore renminbi exhibits safe-haven characteristics, which exist in certain major currencies and some national currencies in the BRI regions; second, the safe-haven characteristics of the offshore renminbi underlying some national currencies in the BRI regions are relatively weak compared with major currencies; third, the above-mentioned features possess time-varying characteristics, and the hedging values of the offshore renminbi are more prominent in extreme cases. The related results provide important references for asset allocation, hedging strategy arrangements and even the prevention of systemic risk in global financial markets.

References

Bai, C. and Lei, X. (2020), New trends in population aging and challenges for China's sustainable development, *China Economic Journal* 13(1): 3–23. doi.org/10.1080/1753 8963.2019.1700608.

Cai, F., Garnaut, R. and Song, L. (2018), 40 years of China's reform and development: How reform captured China's demographic dividend, in R. Garnaut, L. Song and F. Cai (eds), *China's 40 Years of Reform and Development: 1978–2018*, 5–28, Canberra: ANU Press. doi.org/10.22459/CYRD.07.2018.01.

Canning, D. and Bennathan, E. (2000), *The social rate of return on infrastructure investments*, The World Bank Policy Research Working Paper 2390, Washington, DC: The World Bank. doi.org/10.1596/1813-9450-2390.

Dollar, D., Huang, Y. and Yao, Y. (eds) (2020), *China 2049: Economic challenges of a rising global power*, Washington, DC: Brookings Institution Press.

Drysdale, P. and Hardwick, S. (2018), China and the global trading system: Then and now, in L. Song, R. Garnaut and F. Cai (eds), *China's 40 Years of Reform and Development: 1978–2018*, 545–74, Canberra: ANU Press. doi.org/10.22459/CYRD.07.2018.27.

Fraumeni, B.M., He, J., Li, H. and Liu, Q. (2019), Regional distribution and dynamics of human capital in China 1985–2014, *Journal of Comparative Economics* 47(4): 853–66. doi.org/10.1016/j.jce.2019.06.003.

Guo, Y., Zhou, Y. and Liu, Y. (2019), Targeted poverty alleviation and its practices in rural China: A case study of Fuping county, Hebei Province, *Journal of Rural Studies*. doi.org/ 10.1016/j.jrurstud.2019.01.007.

Heerink, N., Kuiper, M. and Xiaoping, S. (2006), China's new rural income support policy: Impacts on grain production and rural income inequality, *China & World Economy* 14(6): 58–69. doi.org/10.1111/j.1749-124X.2006.00045.x.

International Monetary Fund (IMF) (2021), *World Economic Outlook Update*, January, Washington, DC: IMF. Available from: www.imf.org/en/Publications/WEO/Issues/ 2021/01/26/2021-world-economic-outlook-update.

Jiang, P., Chen, Y., Geng, Y., Dong, W., Xue, B., Xu, B. and Li, W. (2013), Analysis of the co-benefits of climate change mitigation and air pollution reduction in China, *Journal of Cleaner Production* 58: 130–37. doi.org/10.1016/j.jclepro.2013.07.042.

Kharas, H. (2017), *The unprecedented expansion of the global middle class: An update*, Global Economy & Development Working Paper 100, February, New Delhi: Brookings India. Available from: hdl.handle.net/11540/7251.

Kojima, K. (2000), The 'flying geese' model of Asian economic development: Origin, theoretical extensions, and regional policy implications, *Journal of Asian Economics* 11: 375–410. doi.org/10.1016/S1049-0078(00)00067-1.

Li, H., Li, L., Wu, B. and Xiong, Y. (2012), The end of cheap Chinese labor, *Journal of Economic Perspectives* 26(4): 57–74. doi.org/10.1257/jep.26.4.57.

Li, H., Liu, Q., Fraumeni, B. and Zhang, X. (2014), Human capital estimates in China: New panel data 1985–2010, *China Economic Review* 30(September): 397–418. doi.org/10.1016/j.chieco.2014.07.006.

Lin, J.Y. (2013a), Demystifying the Chinese economy, *The Australian Economic Review* 46(3): 259–68. doi.org/10.1111/j.1467-8462.2013.12035.x.

Lin, J.Y. (2013b), From flying geese to leading dragons: New opportunities and strategies for structural transformation in developing countries, in J.E. Stiglitz, J.Y. Lin and E. Patel (eds), *The Industrial Policy Revolution II*, International Economic Association Series, 50–70, London: Palgrave Macmillan. doi.org/10.1057/9781137335234_3.

Lipton, M. (2007), Urban bias revisited, *The Journal of Development Studies* 20(3): 139–66. doi.org/10.1080/00220388408421910.

Liu, S. (2018), The structure of and changes to China's land system, in R. Garnaut, L. Song and F. Cai (eds), *China's 40 Years of Reform and Development: 1978–2018*, 427–54, Canberra: ANU Press. doi.org/10.22459/CYRD.07.2018.22.

McKay, H. and Song, L. (2010), China as a global manufacturing powerhouse: Strategic considerations and structural adjustment, *China & World Economy* 18(1)(February): 1–32. doi.org/10.1111/j.1749-124X.2010.01178.x.

Meinhardt, C. (2020), *China bets on 'new infrastructure' to pull the economy out of post-Covid doldrums*, Short Analysis, 4 June, Berlin: Mercator Institute for China Studies. Available from: merics.org/en/short-analysis/china-bets-new-infrastructure-pull-economy-out-post-covid-doldrums.

National Bureau of Statistics of China (NBS) (2021), *2020 Statistical Communiqué of the People's Republic of China on National Economic and Social Development*, [in Chinese], 28 February, Beijing: NBS. Available from: www.stats.gov.cn/tjsj/zxfb/202102/t2021 0227_1814154.html.

National Development and Reform Commission (NDRC) (2021), *The Fourteenth Five-Year Plan for the National Economic and Social Development of the People's Republic of China and the Outline of the Long-Term Goals for 2035*, Beijing: NDRC. Available from: www.ndrc.gov.cn/xxgk/zcfb/ghwb/202103/t20210323_1270124.html.

Pugh, C. (1996), 'Urban bias', the political economy of development and urban policies for developing countries, *Urban Studies* 33(7): 1045–60. doi.org/10.1080/00420989650011492.

Qin, Y. (2016), China's transport infrastructure investment: Past, present, and future, *Asian Economic Policy Review* 11(2): 199–217. doi.org/10.1111/aepr.12135.

Roberts, I., Saunders, T., Spence, G. and Cassidy, N. (2016), *China's Evolving Demand for Commodities*. Reserve Bank of Australia. Available from: www.rba.gov.au/publications/confs/2016/pdf/rba-conference-volume-2016-roberts-saunders-spence-cassidy.pdf.

Sheng, Y. and Song, L. (2019), Agricultural production and food consumption in China: A long-term projection, *China Economic Review* 53: 15–29. doi.org/10.1016/j.chieco.2018.08.006.

Song, L. and van Geenhuizen, M. (2014), Port infrastructure investment and regional economic growth in China: Panel evidence in port regions and provinces, *Transport Policy* 36(November): 173–83. doi.org/10.1016/j.tranpol.2014.08.003.

Song, L. and Zhou, Y. (2020), COVID-19 pandemic and its impact on the global economy: What does it take to turn crisis into opportunity?, *China & World Economy* 28(4): 1–25. doi.org/10.1111/cwe.12349.

Thirlwall, A.P. (2011), *Economics of Development*, New York: Palgrave Macmillan.

Thirlwall, A.P. (2015), A plain man's guide to Kaldor's growth laws, in *Essays on Keynesian and Kaldorian Economics*, Palgrave Studies in the History of Economic Thought Series, 326–38, London: Palgrave Macmillan. doi.org/10.1057/9781137409485_15.

United Nations Conference on Trade and Development (UNCTAD) (2021), *World Investment Report*, Geneva: UNCTAD. Available from: unctad.org/topic/investment/world-investment-report.

World Bank (2021), World bank country and lending groups, *Data*, Washington, DC: The World Bank. Available from: datahelpdesk.worldbank.org/knowledgebase/articles/906519-world-bank-country-and-lending-groups.

Xinhua (2021a), China's industrial robot output up 19.1 pct in 2020, *XinhuaNet*, 17 February. Available from: www.xinhuanet.com/english/2021-02/17/c_139747876.htm.

Xinhua (2021b), Huawei 5GtoB solution aims at 1,000 smart factories, *XinhuaNet*, 9 May. Available from: www.xinhuanet.com/english/2021-05/09/c_139934818.htm.

Yu, N., De Jong, M., Storm, S. and Mi, J. (2012), The growth impact of transport infrastructure investment: A regional analysis for China (1978–2008), *Policy and Society* 31(1): 25–38. doi.org/10.1016/j.polsoc.2012.01.004.

Yu, Y. (2018), A trade war that is unwarranted, *China & World Economy* 26(5): 38–61. doi.org/10.1111/cwe.12255.

Zhao, Z. (2011), China's demographic challenges from a global perspective, in J. Golley and L. Song (eds), *Rising China: Global Challenges and Opportunities*, 285–300, Canberra: ANU Press. doi.org/10.22459/RC.06.2011.16.

Zheng, X., Lu, Y., Yuan, J., Baninla, Y., Zhang, S., Stenseth, N.C., Hessen, D.O., Tian, H., Obersteiner, M. and Chen, D. (2020), Drivers of change in China's energy-related CO_2 emissions, *Proceedings of the National Academy of Sciences* 117(1): 29–36. doi.org/10.1073/pnas.1908513117.

Zhou, W., Gao, H. and Bai, X. (2019), Building a market economy through WTO-inspired reform of state-owned enterprises in China, *International & Comparative Law Quarterly* 68(4): 977–1022. doi.org/10.1017/S002058931900037X.

Zhou, Y. (2014), Role of institutional quality in determining the R&D investment of Chinese firms, *China & World Economy* 22(4): 60–82. doi.org/10.1111/j.1749-124X.2014.12075.x.

2

Tackling social challenges to avoid the middle-income trap

Cai Fang and Jia Peng

[T]hey have not any difficulties on the way up, because they fly, but they have many when they reach the summit.
— Niccolò Machiavelli, *The Prince*

Introduction

In 2018, the Chinese economy grew to equivalence to the economy of the euro area or two-thirds of the economy of the United States and accounted for 16 per cent of the global economy. With a growth rate of 6.1 per cent in 2019—higher than any other major economy—the Chinese economy further raised its importance in the world economy. At the same time, China's gross domestic product (GDP) per capita exceeded US$10,000—significantly above the average level of the upper middle-income countries.[1]

Many economists, think tanks and international institutions believe China's growth will continue to be robust in the near future. China is already in its transition to high-income status and seems certain to cross the threshold between middle-income and high-income countries in a few years. According to international experiences, this stage of development is critical to maintaining economic growth and social stability. In what follows, we summarise some aspects of those experiences.

---

1   Unless noted otherwise, this chapter uses the World Bank's criteria of 2010 US dollars to identify low-income countries (US$1,005 GNI per capita), lower middle-income countries (US$1,006–3,955), upper middle-income countries (US$3,956–12,235) and high-income countries (> US$12,235).

First, although the World Bank set a level of gross national income (GNI) per capita as the threshold for high-income countries (currently US$12,235), there has never been a guarantee that countries that fulfil the income criterion will maintain their high-income status; nor is the criterion a guarantee for sustained growth. Additional indicators are needed to determine whether a country can sustain its development. Indicators of social development are particularly important as they can embody the purpose and sustained sources of economic development.

Second, for most of the upper middle-income countries close to the high-income threshold, economic growth tends to slow, while there is divergence in growth performance among countries (Eichengreen et al. 2011, 2013). Countries that fail to properly tackle the slowdown—and, as a result, perform poorly in social development—often become stuck in the vicious cycle of growth stagnation and income gap widening, which economists call the 'middle-income trap'.[2]

Third, as the low-hanging fruits of growth drivers become scarce and opportunities to implement reform characterised by Pareto improvement diminish, countries must tackle the economic slowdown while also maintaining social mobility. Making a bigger pie and dividing it fairly require further reform by breaking up vested interests, tapping into new sources of growth through innovation and strengthening government redistribution.

Since China entered the group of upper middle-income countries (with per capita GDP exceeding US$4,000) in 2010, its demographic transition has shifted into a fundamentally different phase. The working-age population (aged 15 to 59) has been in rapid decline and the population dependency ratio has increased accordingly. As a result, labour shortages, slower human capital improvement, diminishing returns to capital investment and decelerated labour migration (which slows productivity increases) all lead to the weakening of potential growth capacity and a slowdown of actual growth.

The average annual growth rate of GDP fell significantly, from 10.1 per cent in the period 1980–2010 to 7.0 per cent in the period 2012–19. According to estimates of China's potential growth rate, its economy will continue to follow a downward trend until the growth rate regresses to the mean.[3]

---

2   Gill and Khara (2007) first use this concept for analysing challenges facing East Asian economies, whereas many researchers more often refer to Latin American countries as typical examples of it.

3   Pritchett and Summers (2014) predicted China's growth rate would regress to the mean (the average rate of the world economy) in 2015, which was proven wrong. As Cai and Lu (2013) estimate, as the deceleration of China's potential growth rate is moderate and gradual, the actual growth rate is expected to remain reasonably high compared with most other major economies for some time, regressing to the mean sometime close to 2050.

How the benefits of development are shared among the people lies in both the speed of making the pie and the mechanism of dividing it. With distribution patterns unchanged, slower growth of output tends to mitigate the level of sharing and to change the nature of sharing. In China, the narrowing trend of the income gap has retreated moderately since growth began to slow. The falling trend in the Gini coefficient of household income—from 0.491 in 2008 to 0.462 in 2015— has stalled since 2016. As for the distribution of household disposable income, its improvement was even more short-lived. The ratio of the top 20 per cent to the bottom 20 per cent in the quintile of urban household disposable income decreased from the high point of 5.77 in 2008 to 5.00 in 2012, and then increased to 5.90 in 2018. The same ratio for rural household income decreased from the high of 8.39 in 2011 to 7.41 in 2013 and then increased to 9.29 in 2018.

This chapter investigates global experiences based on cross-nation data to shed light on why economic growth slows and social development stagnates in the upper-middle-income stage. It particularly focuses on lessons that have implications for China as it transitions to high-income status.

Section two describes the changes in the economic growth rate and income distribution in relation to development stages based on cross-nation data. Section three explains why the economic slowdown tends to reduce social mobility in China. Section four explores institutional obstacles to social mobility in China's transition to high-income status. Section five concludes with a suggestion that, in response to the unique challenges facing China, redistribution policy should focus on equalising access to basic public services.

The economic slowdown and consequent worsening of distribution

Conventional theories of growth consider economic development as a homogeneous process—that is, nations expand their economy and increase per capita income by following a predetermined path without disturbance by changes in development stages. Under the neoclassical growth theory, the hypothesis of conditional convergence that correlates growth performance with initial per capita income expects countries with low incomes at the starting point to grow faster than those with higher initial incomes once they have the necessary endowments, institutions and infrastructure in place. The difference in growth rates between poorer and richer countries leads to a convergence among countries (see, for example, Barro and Sala-i-Martin 1995).

Those theories pay little attention to the differences in growth patterns between countries at different stages of development.[4] These differences, however, are what result in differentials in economic performance and related social development.

A simple observation of the relationship between initial income and subsequent growth performance suggests that, if there is any convergence, it closely relates to the stage of development. In Figure 2.1, we show the descriptive relationship between per capita GDP in 1990 and its growth rate in 1990–2018.

Figures 2.1a and 2.1b present scenarios for all 214 countries (and territories) with data availability and for 164 low and middle-income countries with per capita GDP lower than US$12,000, respectively. In both scenarios, there is little correlation between initial income and the growth rate—that is, no convergence is found.

Figure 2.1c presents the scenario for 116 middle-income countries with per capita GDP between US$1,000 and US$12,000. In this manifestation, there is an insignificant correlation between initial income and later growth, showing only a vague convergence. In the scenario expressed by Figure 2.1d, which includes 43 upper middle-income countries with per capita GDP between US$4,000 and US$12,000, the correlation between initial income and later growth and thus convergence is more apparent relative to the aforementioned scenarios.

These descriptive presentations of hypothetical convergence reveal the reality of developing countries in catching up to their more advanced counterparts in the period concerned.

Many low and lower middle-income countries have been stuck in a low-level equilibrium trap due to a lack of the necessary conditions for economic take-off, which is manifested in their cumulating around the threshold between lower middle-income and upper middle-income status. In such stages of development, countries vary significantly in terms of growth performance, with some being superstars in catching up and others trapped in stagnation.

Those low and middle-income countries that have successfully caught up with their high-income counterparts have by and large experienced the development of a dual economy and thus benefited from the demographic dividend. As can be predicted by the definition of convergence itself, the upper middle-income countries in such a state tend to see a moderate slowdown, because of a diminishing labour supply, high investment returns, resource reallocation efficiency and the advantages of technological backwardness.

---

4   Though empirical studies on 'convergence clubs' group together countries in different stages of development to see how they grow differentially, they do not particularly employ the perspective of development stages. For example, see Baumol (1986).

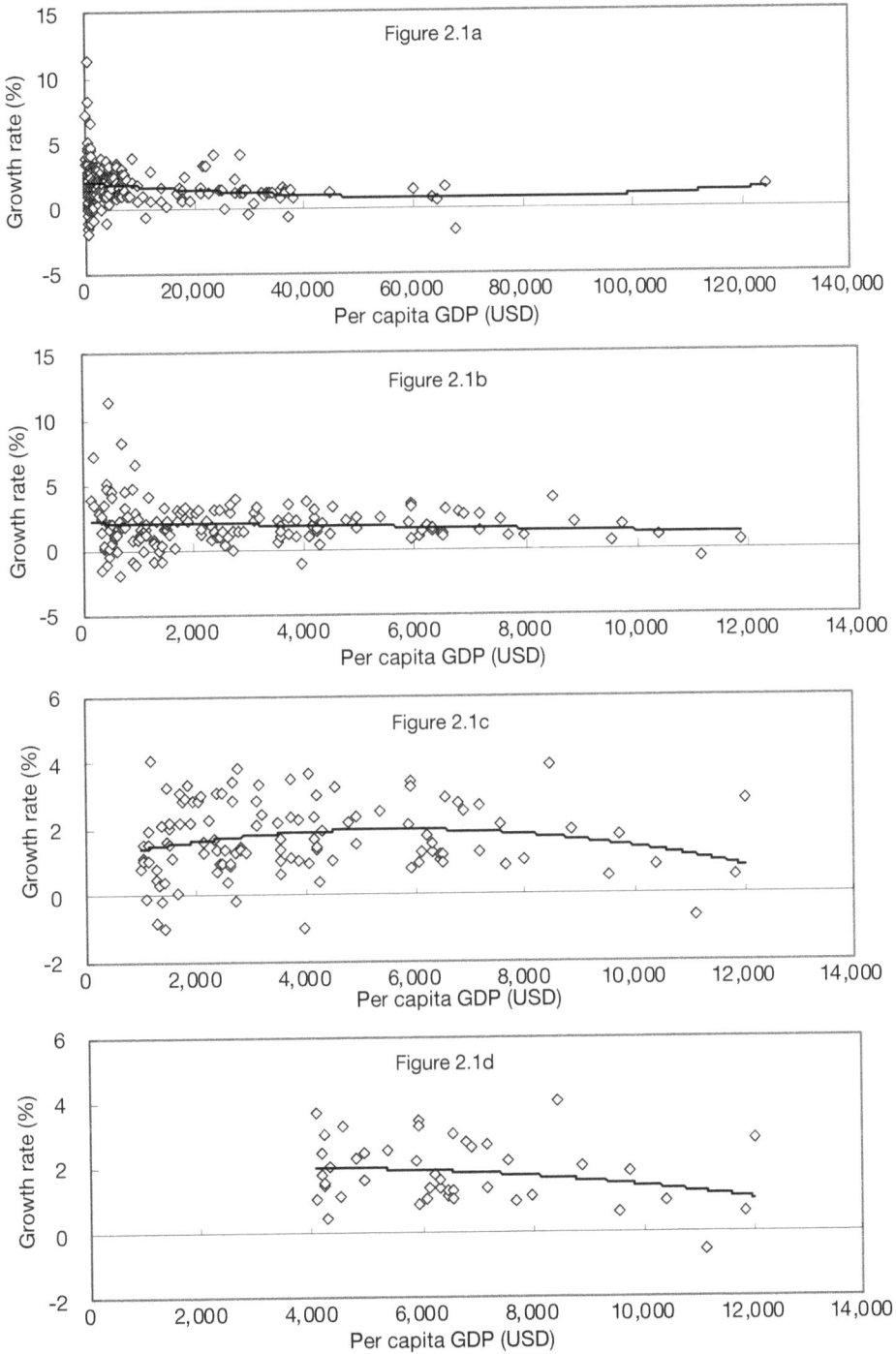

Figure 2.1 Stage of development versus economic growth

Source: World Bank (2021).

As is shown in Figures 2.1c and 2.1d, in the middle-income stage, and especially the upper middle-income stage, growth rates show a tendency for convergence among countries.

Those countries that experienced a slowdown in the later stage of transition to upper middle-income status—particularly near the high-income threshold—tended to diverge in growth performance depending on how successfully they tackled the growth slowdown. It is such a critical period that divides countries on to different tracks: moving up to high-income status or falling into the middle-income trap.

Let us turn to the nexus between income distribution and stages of development. By plotting data collected from the early industrialised countries, Kuznets (1955) found an inverted U-shaped curve for income inequality. That is, as per capita income increases, income inequality measured by, say, the Gini coefficient rises in the early stage of development and, after peaking—or reaching the Kuznets turning point—it begins to decline. Kuznets's observation has been widely criticised, in part because it is not confirmed by new evidence and in part probably because it has been cited to support various versions of 'trickledown economics'.

Again, we use World Bank data to see what the relationships between per capita GDP and the Gini coefficient look like in relation to stages of development. From Figure 2.2a, which plots 119 low and middle-income countries, one cannot find the pattern suggested by Kuznets where the Gini coefficient increases with increasing per capita GDP.

Figures 2.2b and 2.2c present income distribution in 94 middle-income countries and 40 upper middle-income countries, respectively, and both show little correlation between per capita GDP and the Gini coefficient. It is worth noting from these two figures that upper middle-income countries typically have high inequality.

Figure 2.2d depicts the pattern for all 153 countries with data availability. Since this scenario is formed after adding samples of high-income countries to the previous scenarios, the appearance of a Kuznets curve should be credited to high-income countries' pattern of income distribution.[5]

Some coarse findings are summarised here. First, the Kuznets curve does not exist—at least according to the data shown in Figure 2.2. Nor is there any empirical evidence to support an increasing Gini coefficient in step with per capita income in the early stage and a mechanical Kuznets turning point.

---

5   The diverging trends in income distribution among countries, especially among upper middle-income countries, deserve to be noted. That is, with the increase in per capita income, income distribution has been improved in some countries, while it has deteriorated in others.

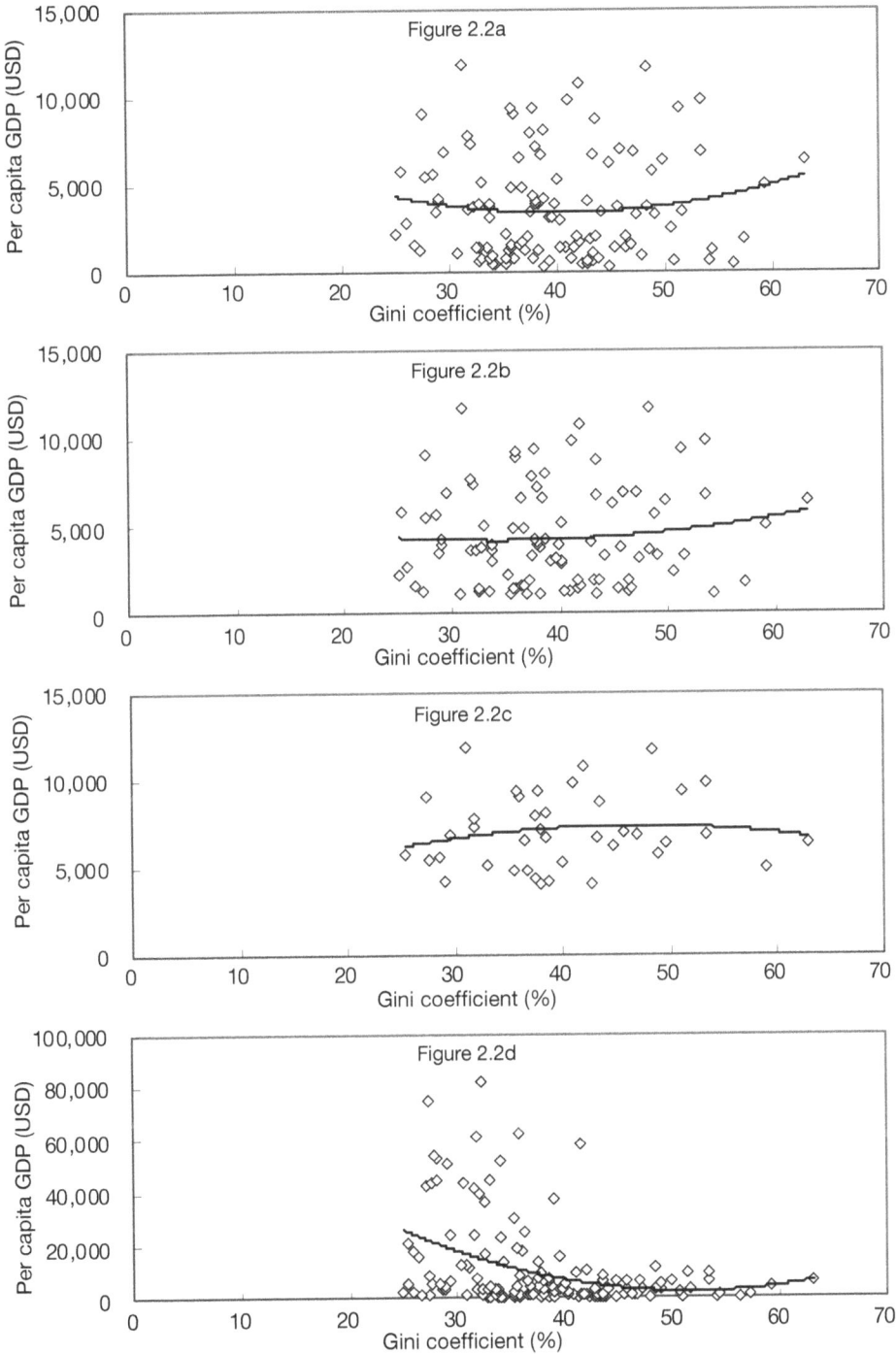

Figure 2.2 Income distribution and stages of development

Source: World Bank (2021).

Second, although there is great variation in the income inequality index among countries in all stages of development, there appears to be a certain nexus between the Gini coefficient and per capita GDP, especially when looking at the upper middle-income and high-income countries. That adds to the evidence that upper middle-income countries are subject to the middle-income trap, which usually manifests in an economic slowdown and a widening of the income gap.

Third, the smaller Gini coefficients—namely, equitable income distribution—shown in high-income countries are actually the results after adjustment for taxes and transfers. Together with the second finding, it can be said that redistribution policies become increasingly important when countries enter the upper middle-income stage and move to the high-income stage.

The same factors that cause a growth slowdown in the upper middle-income countries weaken the function of the labour market in reducing inequality and social mobility (primary distribution). In this stage of development, as redistribution policies are not yet well prepared, countries are apt to be troubled by worsening income distribution.

Admittedly, redistribution and related policy measures do not necessarily result in a narrowing of the income gap. In reality, there are many cases where redistribution policies either remain little more than window dressing due to slower growth or actually increase inequality as a result of the stronger bargaining power of vested interest groups. Still, such phenomena imply that this is a critical stage at which to introduce redistribution policies and choose an effective way of implementing them. What these findings imply for China in promoting social mobility in its transition to high-income status will be discussed in what follows.

Changes in social mobility as China moves to higher-income status

What we conclude so far is that the stage of development is helpful for understanding economic growth and social development and for interpreting countries' success or failure in these processes. In moving closer to high-income status, China has witnessed not only an economic slowdown but also weakening social mobility.

The fruits of rapid growth of the Chinese economy during the reform period from the late 1970s have been widely shared among Chinese people, mainly through labour market mechanisms. The nature and mechanism of sharing have been closely related to China's specific development stage and the unique growth pattern the Chinese economy adopted in the period—until both changed.

From the 1980s to the 2010s, China had a favourable opportunity window with regards to population, in which the working-age population increased and the population dependency ratio declined—both rapidly. Relevant reforms that eliminated institutional obstacles to labour migration have transferred surplus labourers in agriculture and redundant workers in urban enterprises to employment in newly emerged sectors, which has simultaneously enhanced the incomes of rural and urban households and reallocated resources in the economy as a whole.

Through participation in the global economy, China's abundant labour force has translated into comparative and competitive advantages for manufacturing commodities. Capitalising on its comparative advantage in labour-intensive manufacturing in global industrial chains, China exchanges its abundant labour factor for capital factors, with which the developed countries are abundantly endowed.[6] By and large, such a trading pattern tends to increase returns on labour in China and, therefore, Chinese workers have shared the benefits of reform, opening up and the resulting growth.

Specifically, in the period when there was a massive surplus of labourers in agriculture and redundant workers in urban enterprises, which curbed the increase in wages, total income and the share within it of the wage earnings of rural and urban households increased through fuller participation in wage employment. As the economy passed the Lewis turning point,[7] total income and its share of rural and urban household wages increased more depending on wage rate inflation, as employees gained stronger bargaining power in the labour market.

Therefore, for most of the past four decades, China's development process has been characterised by the synchronisation of economic growth, employment expansion and income increases. In the period 1978–2019, the annual growth rate of commodity imports and exports was 18.4 per cent in nominal terms, and the annual growth rates in real terms were 9.4 per cent for GDP, 4.0 per cent for employment in secondary and tertiary sectors and 8.4 per cent for per capita disposable income.

As the demographic window closed after the three decades from 1980 to 2010, the Chinese economy has no longer been characterised by an unlimited supply of labour. This is manifest in the slowdown in labour migration, which has resulted in slowing growth of urban employment, a weakening comparative advantage in manufacturing and declining shares of Chinese commodities trading with developed countries.

---

6   From the 1980s to the 2000s, the share of China's commodities exports to developed countries remained above 75 per cent, while the share of China's commodities imports from developed countries was also high. Both shares have since been in a declining trend.

7   Cai (2016) suggests 2004 can be viewed as the Lewis turning point in which a labour shortage occurred in China's coastal areas and was afterwards widespread throughout the country.

It can be expected that, along with these changes in the economic domain, improvements in income distribution will tend to decelerate and, most importantly, social mobility will weaken. We can observe social mobility and its trend from both horizontal and vertical perspectives. In general, through labour migration—namely, horizontal mobility—individuals and families can realise their desired vertical mobility by changing their occupation and income status across time, cohorts and generations. So, social mobility is not only about reallocation of labour and population; most importantly, it is also about patterns of social stratification, a sense of happiness, consensus on ideas of social justice and thus social cohesion. In what follows, we discuss the trends of social mobility in China via some revealed indicators.

Since the reforms initiated in the late 1970s, China has witnessed surplus labourers transferring from agriculture and migrating from rural to urban sectors, which has led to substantial changes in sectoral structures and regional patterns of development. In the period 1978–2018, the share of agricultural labour in total labour declined from 70.5 per cent to 26.1 per cent, while the proportion of the permanent urban population in the total increased from 17.9 per cent to 59.6 per cent.

As the result of the demographic transition and labour reallocation, however, labour migration has decelerated in recent years (see Cai et al. 2016), as is shown in Figure 2.3. This diminishing trend in labour mobility between rural and urban areas and across regions and sectors tends to drag down social mobility, which is manifested as changes in occupation, income status and social identity.

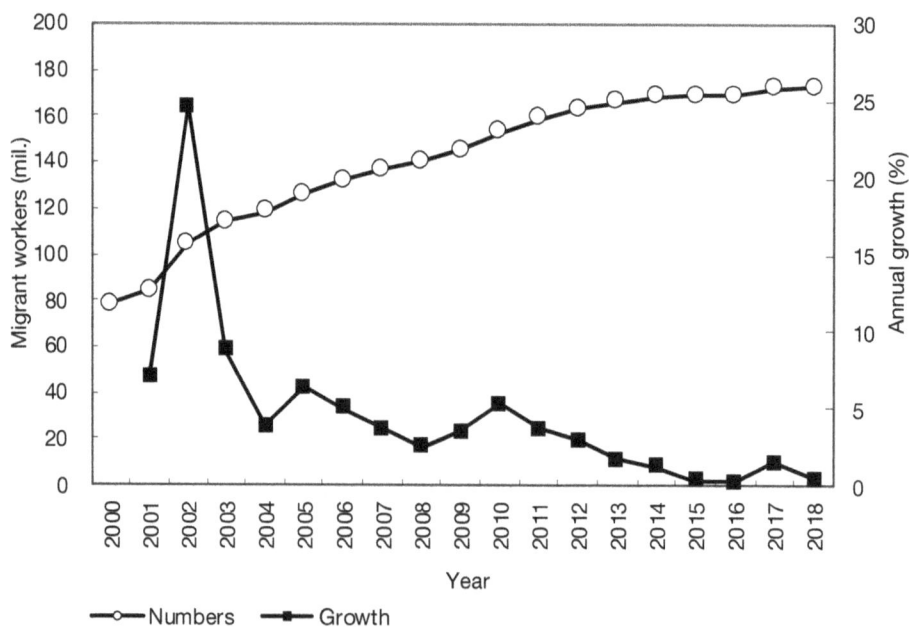

Figure 2.3 Trends in labour migration
Sources: Early data are from estimates in Cai (2016: 30); updated data are from NBS (2019).

Theoretically, in a stage of development characterised by rapid economic growth, marked changes in sectoral structure, dramatic expansions in education and massive labour mobility across regions and sectors, a country's occupational structure tends to rapidly upgrade towards a more human capital–intensive pattern, which promotes overall upward mobility across society. Meanwhile, while society creates more opportunities for people to climb the occupational and income ladders, it does so without the expense of others moving downward. Greater upward mobility and less downward mobility mean that, not only is economic development shared, but also social mobility experiences a Pareto improvement.

There are two critical factors in elevating the occupational structure: the upgrading of the sectoral structure as a demand-side factor and improvements in the education of the working-age population as a supply-side factor. Both have seen substantial changes in the past decades in China, forming the unique pattern of social mobility and its change.

Based on data from the fifth and sixth national population censuses (in 2000 and 2010, respectively),[8] we calculate two indicators to see such changes. The first is years of schooling by age. According to each age's school completion rate, we assign zero for no schooling, completion of primary school is six years, nine years for junior high school, 12 years for senior high school, 15 years for junior college, 16 years for university and 19.3 years for graduate school (weighted average of master's and PhD students). The second indicator is the proportion of technical personnel and office staff among workers,[9] which is supposed to show the state of occupational upgrading.

Plotting the indicators in Figure 2.4, one can find two features concerning educational attainment and occupational upgrading in relation to time and age. First, both human capital and the job mobility of employees improved significantly in the period 2000–10, which shows mutual promotion among economic growth, structural change and education expansion.[10] Second, from comparisons at specific points across ages, the average education and occupational upgrading in 2000 and 2010 decreases as age increases. This implies that, while human capital plays a positive role in promoting job mobility, population ageing tends to weaken the human capital endowment and job mobility.

---

8   Please refer to the website of the National Bureau of Statistics of China (data.stats.gov.cn) for more details of the fifth and sixth national population censuses.

9   One can consider it a proxy of the proportion of 'white-collar workers', though we omit those who are identified as cadres because that categorisation does not distinguish management personnel from administrative and government cadres.

10   Compared with the developed countries, the uniqueness of the Chinese case is the rapid development of both its economy and its education system. In the United Kingdom, for example, the role of education in occupational change is not decisive. See Goldthorpe (2016).

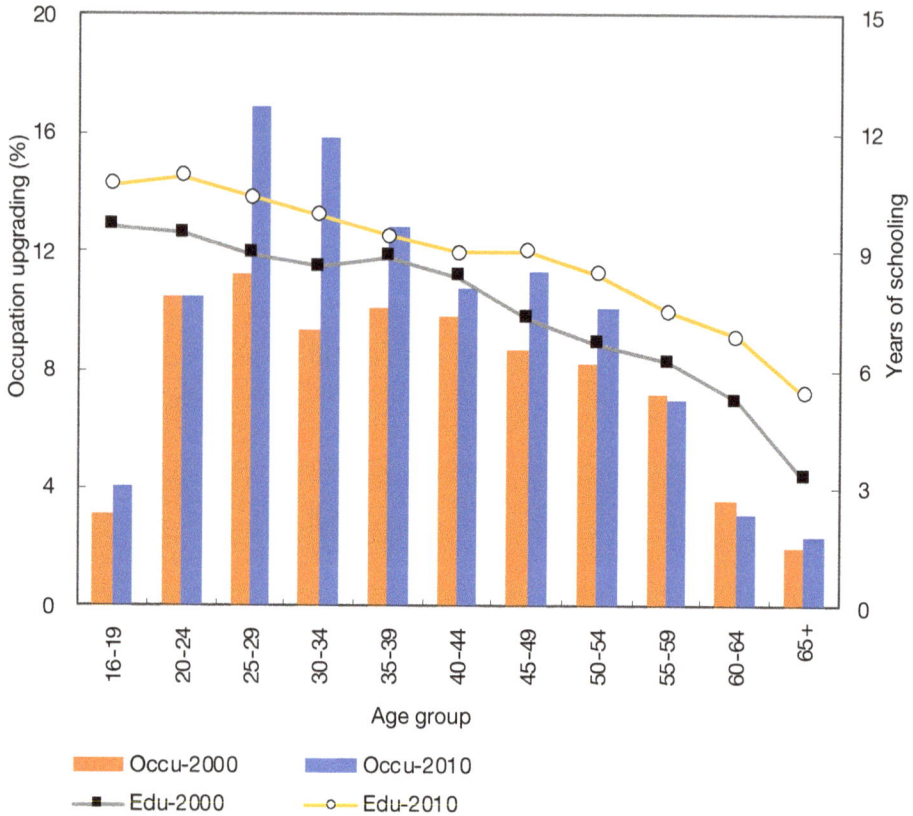

Figure 2.4 Educational attainment and occupational upgrading by age
Source: NBS website: www.stats.gov.cn/.

Further examination shows that the average proportion of technical personnel and office staff in the population aged 16 and older increased from 12.5 per cent in 2002–06 to 18.9 per cent in 2012–17. As those factors that promote occupational upgrading alter, however, one can expect a decelerating trend in job mobility.

Almost all changes accompanied by the disappearance of the demographic dividend—such as slowing human capital improvement, the shrinking share of manufacturing in the economy, contracting employment in the secondary sector and the dominance of the service sector in absorbing employment[11]—tend to drag down occupational upgrading and thus mitigate social mobility.

---

11 Unlike employment transfer from agricultural to non-agricultural sectors, which is of productivity-promotion type, the employment transfer from secondary to tertiary sectors has led to a decline in labour productivity of the overall economy. For example, in 2018, the employment share of primary, secondary and tertiary sectors was 26.1%, 27.6% and 46.3%, respectively, whereas their labour productivity (value added per labour) was 32,000 yuan, 171,000 yuan and 136,000 yuan, respectively.

Trends for social mobility, therefore, can move in different directions depending on the country's stage of development. First, with rapid economic growth and structural change, social mobility is more likely to be a type of positive-sum game, or Pareto improvement. It is mainly through this type of social mobility that Chinese residents have been sharing the fruits of economic development over the past decades. Second, in a state of relatively static economic growth and structural change, opportunities for occupational upgrading become scarcer, and some people's upward mobility may be accompanied by others' downward movement. This is also a possible scenario for a slower-growing China.

The scenario in which social mobility takes the form of a zero-sum game may accordingly produce an adverse effect. That is, as all individuals and families strive for the top, those already at the top and trying to maintain their status unavoidably clash with those on the bottom and trying to break the existing pattern of social stratification. Such conflicts in turn make social mobility less of a win-win situation, reducing the sense of happiness at the individual level and of cohesion at the societal level.

The massive expansion of the working-age population, rapid economic growth and a rapidly changing sectoral structure are all phenomena of a particular stage of development, whereas social mobility should occur at any stage of development. Therefore, the way to promote social mobility should be changing over time.

It is widely believed that growth is the ultimate way to eliminate growing pains. However, it is pointless to suggest that the only thing one should do to address the unfairness in dividing the pie is to make a bigger pie. The causes of social immobility and income inequality are rooted in institutions. Therefore, promoting social mobility and reducing income inequality require social and economic reforms. In what follows, we will discuss how China can enhance social mobility and improve income distribution by removing various institutional obstacles.

What institutional barriers deter China's social mobility?

Social immobility not only widens the income gap, it also extends it to future generations, causing solidification of social divisions. As labour market mechanisms increasingly become inadequate to tackle immobility and inequality, the government should step in and implement redistribution policies that include not only progressive taxation, income transfers and public services provision, but also a much broader range of policies that promote social mobility.

In China today, the differentiated access to basic public services between rural and urban areas, across regions and among groups of residents serves as a major institutional barrier, stymieing social mobility—and the household registration (*hukou*) system legitimises such gaps.

The initial purpose of the *hukou* system—established as part of the planning system—was to deter people's migration between rural and urban areas and across regions through strict population registration and segregated, exclusive provision of public services. After its formation in 1958, and except for limited occasions such as university enrolment, military conscription and planned recruitment, there was hardly any migration between regions, and especially between rural and urban areas in the 1960s and 1970s. This blocking of occupational change and the consequent income gap between rural and urban sectors in the pre-reform period made China the least mobile society in the world.

Since the mid-1980s, labour migration between rural and urban areas and between regions has been expanded. However, although the original intention of the *hukou* system has changed, its function of separating the provision of basic public services remains unchanged. The longstanding dual structure of society resulting from this segregation creates a special group of people—namely, migrant workers—who face not only tangible obstacles to becoming legitimate residents of the cities, but also intangible barriers to climbing the social status ladder.

In 2018, there were 172.7 million migrant workers living in places other than the townships in which their *hukou* was registered. As entitlements to public services in urban areas are largely determined by people's *hukou* status, migrant workers (78.2 per cent of whom are in cities) are not treated equally in terms of access to social protection. Based on China Urban Labour Survey (CULS) data,[12] we found significant gaps in workplace treatment and public service provision between migrant and local workers, with only minimal improvement during the period 2010–16 (Table 2.1).

First, migrant workers' wages are still systemically lower than their local counterparts. In 2016, the hourly wage of migrant workers was 73 per cent of that of local workers. Despite migrant workers' efforts to increase their monthly earnings through overtime—for example, their working hours are 26 per cent higher than those of local workers—that does not eliminate the wage gap. Based on data from

---

12 The fourth round of the CULS was conducted by the Institute of Population and Labour Economics at the Chinese Academy of Social Sciences in 2016. It sampled 15,448 individuals from 6,478 households in 260 communities in Shanghai, Fuzhou, Wuhan, Shenyang, Xi'an and Guangzhou. Of the total sample, 9,753 individuals from 3,897 households were local and 5,695 individuals from 2,581 households were migrants. For details, see: iple.cssn.cn.

an early round of the CULS, Wang (2005) found that *hukou* status could explain 43 per cent of the wage difference between the two groups. That is, after controlling for education and other individual characteristics, the wage gap remains.

Second, migrant workers' participation in social insurance programs is significantly low. For example, the percentage of migrant workers participating compared with their local counterparts is 40 per cent for basic pension insurance, 44 per cent for unemployment insurance and 45 per cent for basic medical insurance.

Table 2.1 Differential treatment in the urban labour market

	2010		2016	
	Migrants	**Locals**	**Migrants**	**Locals**
Work and pay				
Weekly working hours	57.00	43.70	55.20	43.90
Monthly wage (RMB)	2,158.00	2,368.00	4,839.00	5,206.00
Hourly wage (RMB)	9.80	13.50	24.10	33.00
Coverage rate (%)				
Pension insurance	26.40	77.90	32.60	80.80
Unemployment insurance	10.40	51.80	31.60	71.10
Medical insurance	26.30	74.10	37.50	82.60
Other (%)				
Children's attendance at local school*	—	—	67.00	100.00
Receiving minimum living guarantee	—	4.20	0.70	1.90

* 'Children's attendance at local school' includes only those at senior high school or lower; as the questionnaire does not ask the location of the school, we presume it is a local school in the surveyed cities.
— No data available.

Because of migrant workers' insecure employment, employers are unwilling to contribute social insurance for migrant workers, migrant workers themselves are not willing to participate in either employee-based or resident-based social insurance programs and many migrants find work through labour-dispatch agencies, which provides both the agencies and the employers with an excuse to exclude workers from social insurance coverage.

Finally, migrant workers also lack equal access to other public services in the cities where they live and work. For example, the proportion of migrants receiving a minimum living guarantee is 35 per cent of that of locals, and only 67 per cent of migrant children attend local schools. According to the National Bureau of Statistics (NBS 2019), the proportion of migrant children attending local public and private schools (with government financial support) is 82.2 per cent and 11.6 per cent, respectively, at the primary level, and 84.1 per cent and 10 per cent at the secondary level. As for migrants' housing, 19 per cent were purchased, 61.3 per cent were rented, 12.9 per cent were provided by employers and only 2.9 per cent were provided through a local government subsidy.

Conclusion and policy suggestions

In the upper middle-income stage of development, even though an economic slowdown naturally occurs, relatively moderate but more sustainable growth can be realised if the growth pattern can be transformed to fit the new stage. Similarly, nurturing labour market competition and implementing more redistribution policies can maintain social mobility and thus the sharing of the fruits of development.

What challenges China today is that the existing institutional barriers stymie social mobility in general and the *hukou* system, in particular, prevents labourers from fully integrating into cities. There is a paradox to removing those barriers—that is, on the one hand, it is the central government's responsibility to initiate the necessary reforms and, on the other, central and local governments are the ones who must practically implement existing policies. In what follows, we suggest some policy proposals to solve that dilemma.

The first is to separate public service provision from *hukou* by introducing more inclusive, universal social protection programs. At present, the provision of basic social insurance, guaranteed minimum living standards, compulsory education and subsidised housing is the responsibility of local governments. That local governments provide basic public services in accordance with de facto residence status (living in cities for six months or longer) rather than de jure residence status (having local *hukou*) can essentially break the barriers to social mobility.

A second proposal is to strengthen the central government's responsibility for bearing the costs of reform of the *hukou* system so as to incentivise both levels of government in pushing reform forwards. At present, there is a lack of incentive for local government in providing equal public services to migrants and in carrying out the *hukou* system reform aimed at legitimising migrants' residence status.

According to Lu and Cai (2014), the *hukou* system reform can increase the potential growth rate through raising labour supply, creating resource reallocation efficiency and expanding consumption, which increase revenues for both central and local governments. Those reform dividends, however, cannot be exclusively obtained by specific localities while local governments bear almost all the reform-related costs such as the expense of incorporating migrants into full coverage of local public services.

Given the *hukou* system reform has positive externalities to China's economic and social development, the central government taking major responsibility for financing the reform is not only the key to breaking the deadlock, but also in line with policymaking and institutional logic.

A third proposal is to transform local governments' role from promoting GDP growth to improving social development by getting the focus right on the public finance system. In an era of population ageing, individual cities can undoubtedly benefit from attracting incoming, often more productive, residents as long as the central government pays the initial costs.

Further reforms should focus on properly defining the function and boundaries of public finance, reasonably dividing revenues and expenditures between central and local governments and granting municipal governments the power, responsibility and autonomy to provide public services. This way, local governments will have appropriate motivation to compete for migrant workers and their families by providing better public services.

The link between local public service provision and labour migration and social mobility can be understood in the theoretical framework coined by Tiebout (1956) and McGuire (1974). These authors model two corresponding behaviours—that is, local governments or communities intentionally attract or expel residents by altering the type and magnitude of public goods provision, on the one hand, and potential migrants choose where they want to reside in accordance with their preference for public goods, on the other. Social mobility—horizontal and vertical—is obviously in the utility function of both behaviours.

References

Barro, R. and Sala-i-Martin, X. (1995), *Economic Growth*, New York: McGraw-Hill.

Baumol, W.J., (1986), Productivity growth, convergence, and welfare: What the long-run data show, *The American Economic Review* 76(5): 1072–85.

Cai, F. (2016), *China's Economic Growth Prospects: From Demographic Dividend to Reform Dividend*, Cheltenham, UK: Edward Elgar.

Cai, F. and Lu, Y. (2013), The end of China's demographic dividend: The perspective of potential GDP growth, in R. Garnaut, F. Cai and L. Song (eds), *China: A New Model for Growth and Development*, 55–74, Canberra: ANU Press. doi.org/10.22459/CNMGD. 07.2013.04.

Cai, F., Guo, Z. and Wang, M. (2016), New urbanisation as a driver of China's growth, in L. Song, R. Garnaut, F. Cai and L. Johnston (eds), *China's New Sources of Economic Growth. Volume 1: Reform, Resources, and Climate Change*, 43–64, Canberra: ANU Press. doi.org/10.22459/CNSEG.07.2016.03.

Eichengreen, B., Park, D. and Shin, K. (2011), *When Fast Growing Economies Slow Down: International Evidence and Implications for China*, NBER Working Paper No. 16919, Cambridge, MA: National Bureau of Economic Research. doi.org/10.3386/w16919.

Eichengreen, B., Park, D. and Shin, K. (2013), *Growth Slowdowns Redux: New Evidence on the Middle-Income Trap*, NBER Working Paper No. 18673, Cambridge, MA: National Bureau of Economic Research. doi.org/10.3386/w18673.

Gill, I. and Khara, H. (2007), *An East Asia Renaissance: Ideas for Economic Growth*, Washington, DC: The World Bank Group. doi.org/10.1596/978-0-8213-6747-6.

Goldthorpe, J.H. (2016), Social class mobility in modern Britain: Changing structure, constant process, *Journal of the British Academy* 4: 89–111. doi.org/10.5871/jba/004.089.

Kuznets, S. (1955), Economic growth and income inequality, *American Economic Review* 5: 1–28.

Lu, Y. and Cai, F. (2014), China's shift from the demographic dividend to the reform dividend, in R. Garnaut, F. Cai and L. Song (eds), *Deepening Reform for China's Long-Term Growth and Development*, 27–50, Canberra: ANU Press. doi.org/10.22459/DRCLTGD.07.2014.02.

McGuire, M. (1974), Group segregation and optimal jurisdictions, *Journal of Political Economy* 82(1): 112–32. doi.org/10.1086/260173.

National Bureau of Statistics of China (NBS) (2019), *2018 Migrant Workers Monitoring Survey Report*, Beijing: NBS. Available from: www.stats.gov.cn/tjsj/zxfb/201904/t20190429_1662268.html.

Pritchett, L. and Summers, L.H. (2014), *Asiaphoria Meets Regression to the Mean*, NBER Working Paper No. 20573, Cambridge, MA: National Bureau of Economic Research. doi.org/10.3386/w20573.

Tiebout, C.M.A. (1956), A pure theory of local expenditures, *Journal of Political Economy* 64(5): 416–24. doi.org/10.1086/257839.

Wang, M. (2005), Employment opportunities and wage gaps in the urban labour market, *Social Sciences in China* (5): 36–46.

Wolf, M. (2019), Hypocrisy and confusion distort the debate on social mobility, *The Financial Times*, 3 May.

World Bank (2021), *World Development Indicators*, Washington, DC: The World Bank Group. Available from: datatopics.worldbank.org/world-development-indicators/.

3

China's agricultural trade: A global comparative advantage perspective

Rao Sihang, Liu Xingshuo and Sheng Yu

Introduction

The past two decades have witnessed rapid growth in agricultural production and consumption as well as a growing gap between food demand and supply in China. This makes the country one of the leading food importers on the global agricultural market. Between 1978 and 2018, China's agricultural output (in terms of real value-added measure) grew at the rate of 4.7 per cent per annum—far more than the population growth rate (1.0 per cent per annum)—helping to stabilise domestic food consumption prices (Huang and Rozelle 2018; NBS 2019). However, ongoing economic and population growth since then have driven food demand to outpace food supply, thus putting great pressure on domestic agricultural production, which was already constrained by the limited supply of land and water resources. To resolve the emerging conflict between domestic food demand and supply, imports of agricultural products from the international market have been increasing over time.

The increased food imports by China has aroused growing concerns over whether China's demand for food will impact global food security in the future. For instance, China's total food imports in 2018 accounted for less than 2 per cent of its food consumption, but this already represented more than 8 per cent of global tradable agricultural products. This made China one of the largest importers of agricultural products in the world by 2018—second only to the European Union (WTO 2019). Meanwhile, forecasts suggest China's food self-sufficiency ratio will decline from 98 per cent in 2020 to 93 per cent in 2035, even if agricultural total factor productivity (TFP)—an indicator of technological progress—is able to grow at a rate of 2 per cent per annum (CAE 2020). This implies that the volume of agricultural products sourced by China from the international market will more than double by 2035. Should global food production and trade face more uncertainties caused by the outbreak of natural disasters, the impacts of climate change or deteriorating international relations, China's food demand would compete with demands from other developing countries, imposing greater pressures on the global food supply.

However, the above concerns could be redundant if global agricultural resources were properly exploited based on dynamic comparative advantage. There are more than 3.5 billion hectares of land suitable for agriculture throughout the world, but only around 1.5 billion hectares are being used effectively (FAO 2020). The majority of the spare arable land is in places such as the pan-Amazon region and major agricultural countries in Eastern Europe and Africa, and yields below the world average. If trade and investment relationships could be rearranged between China and the rest of the world based on their comparative competitiveness, the global food supply would significantly increase. For instance, the increased agricultural trade between China and African countries in recent years has provided economic incentives for both parties to increase their investment in agricultural production and facilitate the adoption of advanced agricultural technologies (Sheng et al. 2020). In this sense, rearranging agricultural trade between China and her trading partners could present a win-win strategy for China as well as for the world.

To demonstrate this point, this chapter utilises global agricultural trade data organised by commodity (obtained from FAOSTAT database) to systematically analyse agricultural trade between China and the rest of the world and its underlying determinants for the period 1978–2018. We first investigate China's agricultural trade patterns and characteristics, before going on to estimate the revealed comparative advantage (RCA) and relative trade advantage (RTA) indices for major agricultural commodities, which are categorised into 10 types of crops and seven types of livestock products. Then, we compare and analyse the complementarity between China and the rest of the world for each category of commodity, with the aim of sorting out the potential patterns of agricultural trade. Lastly, we discuss how agricultural trade between China and the rest of the world could be rearranged to enable better allocation of global resources based on countries' comparative advantage and competitiveness.

The results show that the existing pattern of agricultural trade between China and the rest of the world does not fully reflect these countries' dynamic comparative advantages. In particular, North America's comparative advantage in agricultural commodities has been declining over time compared with the rest of the world, although it currently accounts for a large proportion of China's imports. This, combined with the intensified trade friction between China and the United States, limits the potential for bilateral agricultural trade. With further increases in domestic demand, China is expected to diversify its agricultural imports by turning to potential markets in the developing world—that is, Eastern Europe, South America and Africa. Countries in these regions have different advantages in different agricultural products, which may enable them to become alternative and reliable agricultural trading partners for China in the near future.

The rest of the chapter is organised as follows. Section two discusses the pattern of China's agricultural trade and its characteristics over the past 40 years. Section three provides a measure of the RCA index, the RTA index and overall bilateral complementarity (OBC). Section four analyses the comparative and competitive advantages of China's major agricultural products over the past 40 years compared with the rest of the world. Section five examines the complementarity by commodity between China's agricultural products and those of the world's major agricultural countries, thus identifying several potential future trade partners, while section six concludes.

China's agricultural trade from 1978 to 2018

China's agricultural trade pattern

China's agricultural trade started to increase in 1978 and has long been used as an important means to balance domestic agricultural production and consumption. Figure 3.1 depicts the changes in China's total agricultural imports, exports and net trade at current prices for the past 40 years. From 1978 to 2018, China's agricultural trade increased from US$5.45 billion to US$179.4 billion, with an average annual growth rate of 9.1 per cent, which was about twice the growth of output value (5.3 per cent per annum) for the same period (Huang and Rozelle 2018). Underlying the aggregated agricultural trade, agricultural imports increased from US$3.1 billion in 1978 to US$123.3 billion in 2018, with an average growth rate of 9.6 per cent per annum, exceeding that of agricultural exports (8.2 per cent per annum) over the same period (agricultural exports increased from US$2.4 billion in 1978 to US$56.1 billion in 2018).

Agricultural imports have grown more quickly than exports, especially in recent years, showing China's growing dependence on the international market to feed its own population. While China's agricultural trade remained in surplus from 1984 to 2002, its trade deficit in agricultural commodities, which began in 2003, has been growing over the past two decades. By 2018, China's agricultural trade deficit reached US$67.2 billion—45 times its agricultural trade deficit in 2003 (of US$1.5 billion). In addition to the increased net food demand caused by rapid population and economic growth, the open-to-trade policy and the decline of China's relative comparative advantage after its accession to the World Trade Organization (WTO) are also considered important drivers of the growing agricultural trade deficit (Huang and Rozelle 2018).

This rapid growth in net imports of agricultural products also led to China's improved status in global agricultural trade. Figure 3.2 shows the trend in China's share of total global agricultural exports and imports between 1978 and 2018. From 1978 to 2000, China's share increased with some fluctuation, with the average share of imports remaining close to that of exports. However, from 2000, China's share of total global agricultural imports increased sharply, from 2 per cent to 8 per cent, before gradually levelling off in recent years. This is in contrast with a more modest rise in its share of total global exports (from 3 per cent to about 4 per cent). Consequently, China had become the world's second-largest food importer by 2018 (WTO 2019).

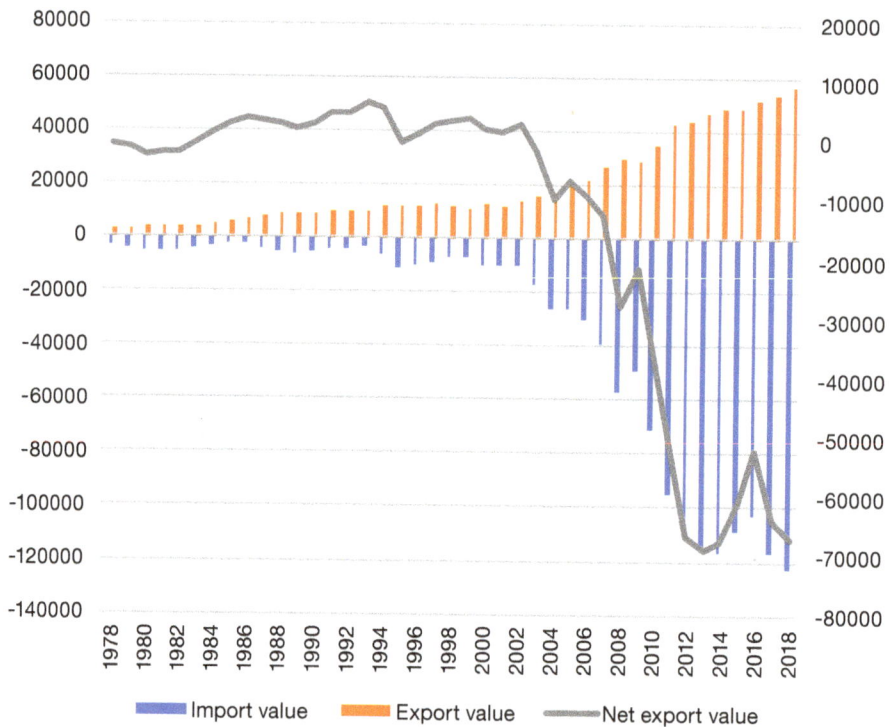

Figure 3.1 China's agricultural trade, 1978–2018 (millions of US$)
Source: FAOSTAT database.

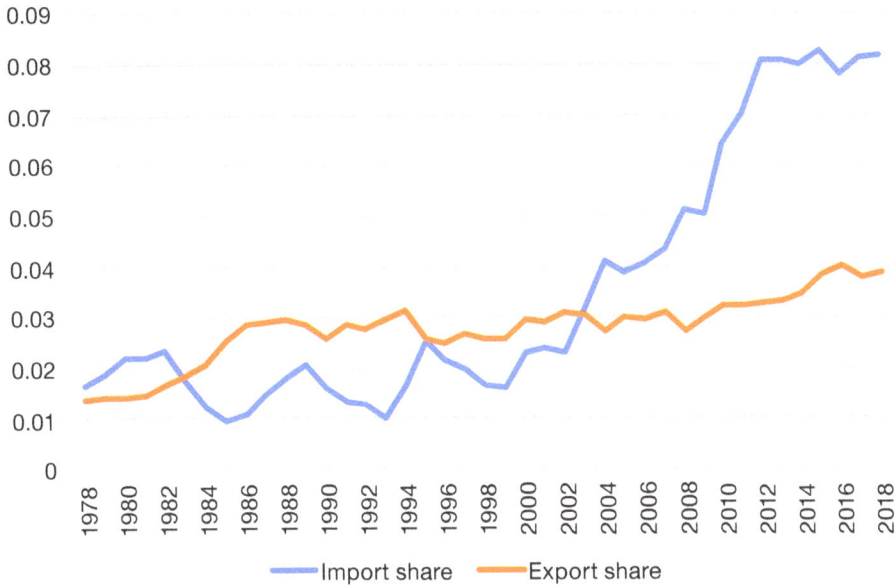

Figure 3.2 China's share of global agricultural exports and imports, 1978–2018 (per cent)

Source: FAOSTAT database.

The increasing agricultural trade deficit triggered China to intensify support for domestic production and enact trade protection policies. Since the late 2000s, the average levels of producer support ratios and trade protectionism have been increasing in China, contrary to the earlier trend in the 2000s immediately before its WTO accession, as well as the trends in many developed and developing countries. Both Organisation for Economic Co-operation and Development (OECD) countries and non-OECD countries have significantly reduced their levels of producer support and agricultural protection over the recent decade and have gradually shifted their policies towards promoting marketisation and improving the competitiveness of their agricultural products. As is shown in Figures 3.3a and 3.3b, the average ratio of the producer support estimate (PSE) to agricultural output value among OECD countries has declined—attributable to the efforts of their governments to adjust the structure of domestic production and improve trade competitiveness. The increase in domestic support for agricultural production and trade protection in China has, to some extent, biased resource reallocation domestically, and could negatively affect efforts to improve agricultural comparative advantage and competitiveness.

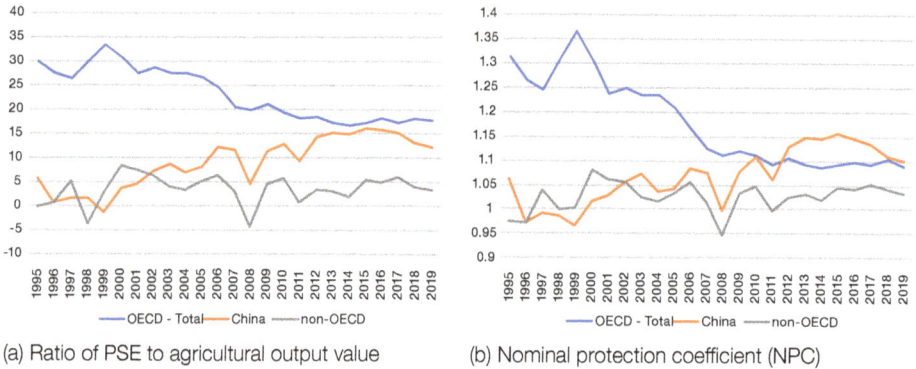

(a) Ratio of PSE to agricultural output value

(b) Nominal protection coefficient (NPC)

Figure 3.3 Production support and trade protection in China, OECD countries and non-OECD countries, 1995–2015

Source: OECD PSE database.

In sum, China's net imports of agricultural products have been rapidly increasing over the past two decades to supplement the shortfall in domestic agricultural production. In addition to the increased food demand caused by rapid population and economic growth, changes in the relative productivity and competitiveness of agricultural production and intensified trade protectionism could also be important drivers of China's agricultural trade deficit.

Changes in agricultural trade patterns by commodity and by region

In addition to the characteristics at the aggregate level, agricultural trade in China possesses some distinct features according to commodity and region. We attempt to summarise some of these characteristics from two perspectives.

First, the commodity structure of agricultural trade has changed substantially over the past 40 years. Figure 3.4 depicts the changes in the commodity structure of China's agricultural trade between 1978 and 2018. It is apparent that the increase in China's agricultural trade is concentrated in several types of commodities. For crop products, the growth comes mainly from China's increased exports of fruits and vegetables, while the rapid growth in total crop imports is caused mainly by the expansion of oil crop imports, including oilseeds and soybeans. For livestock products, exports of poultry meat have been growing rapidly since 2000, but China has become more dependent on the international market for the supply of dairy and other meat products, such as beef and mutton.

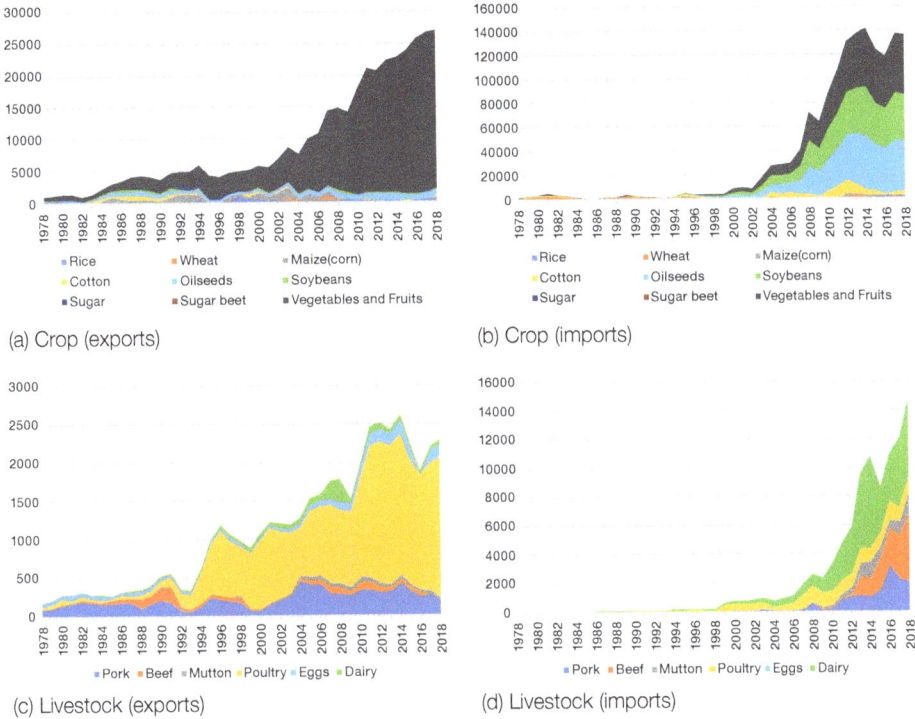

(a) Crop (exports)

(b) Crop (imports)

(c) Livestock (exports)

(d) Livestock (imports)

Figure 3.4 Changes in the structure of China's agricultural trade, 1978–2018

Source: FAOSTAT database.

However, a closer look at the commodity-level trade data shows that almost all products were in deficit in recent years—even those that registered a strong export increase such as vegetables and fruits. Figure 3.5 shows the data by commodity for China's exports and imports of major crops and livestock products. On the one hand, China was a net exporter of several crop products before the twenty-first century, but it has lost its comparative advantage and come to increasingly rely on the international market over the past 20 years. On the other hand, for livestock products, China remained almost entirely self-sufficient over the first 30 years of the reform and opening-up period, before showing a growing dependence on international trade in the past 10 years. With further population and economic growth, it is foreseeable that Chinese domestic demand for pork, beef, lamb and dairy products will continue to grow in the future. By 2018, major agricultural products—with the exception of sugar beet, poultry and eggs—were all in trade deficit, and this trend is predicted to continue to increase. The rapid growth of imports and trade dependence not only reflects the widening gap between domestic production and demand, but also indicates that agricultural production is gradually losing its comparative advantage in China.

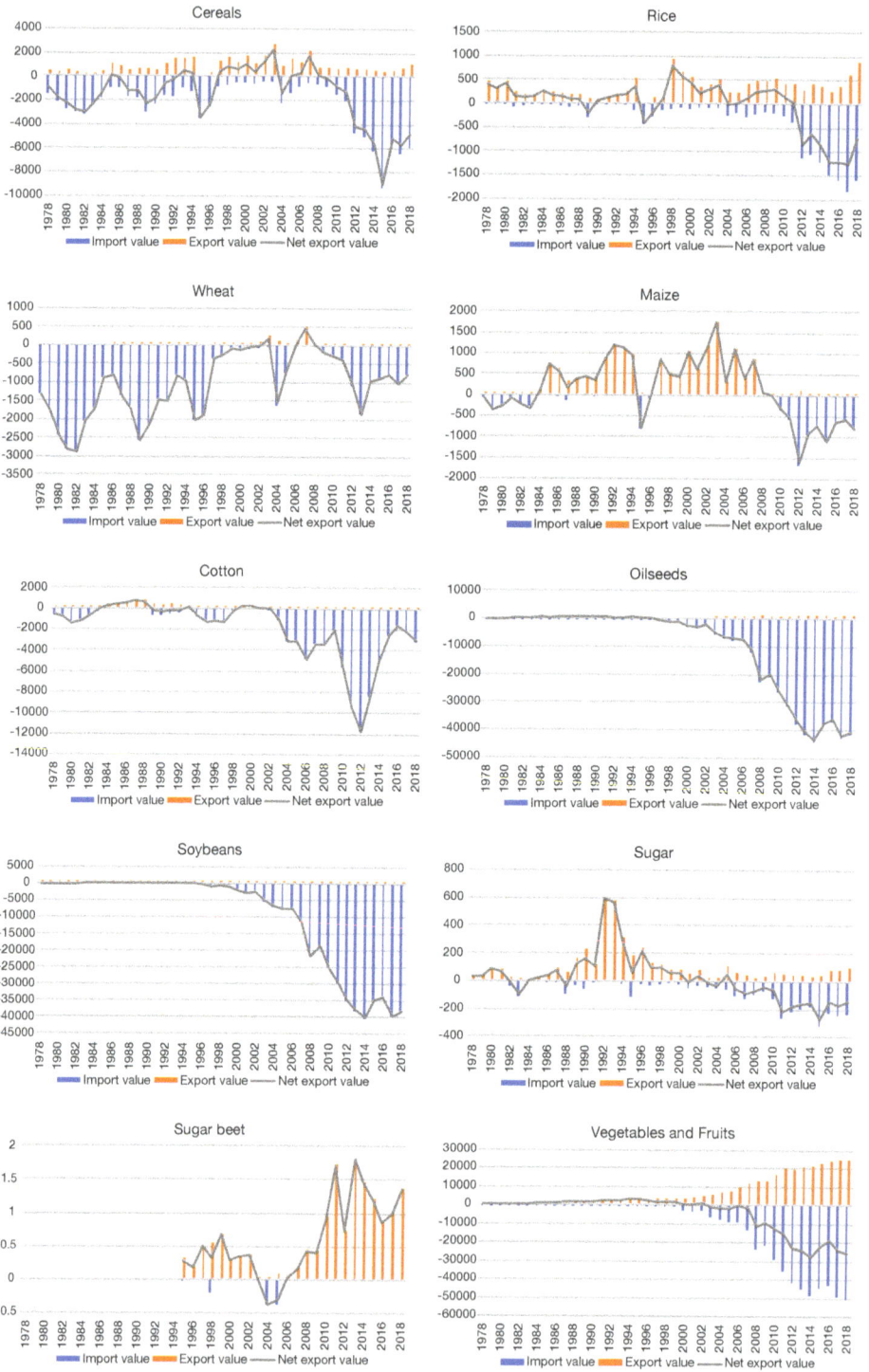

Figure 3.5(a) Crops

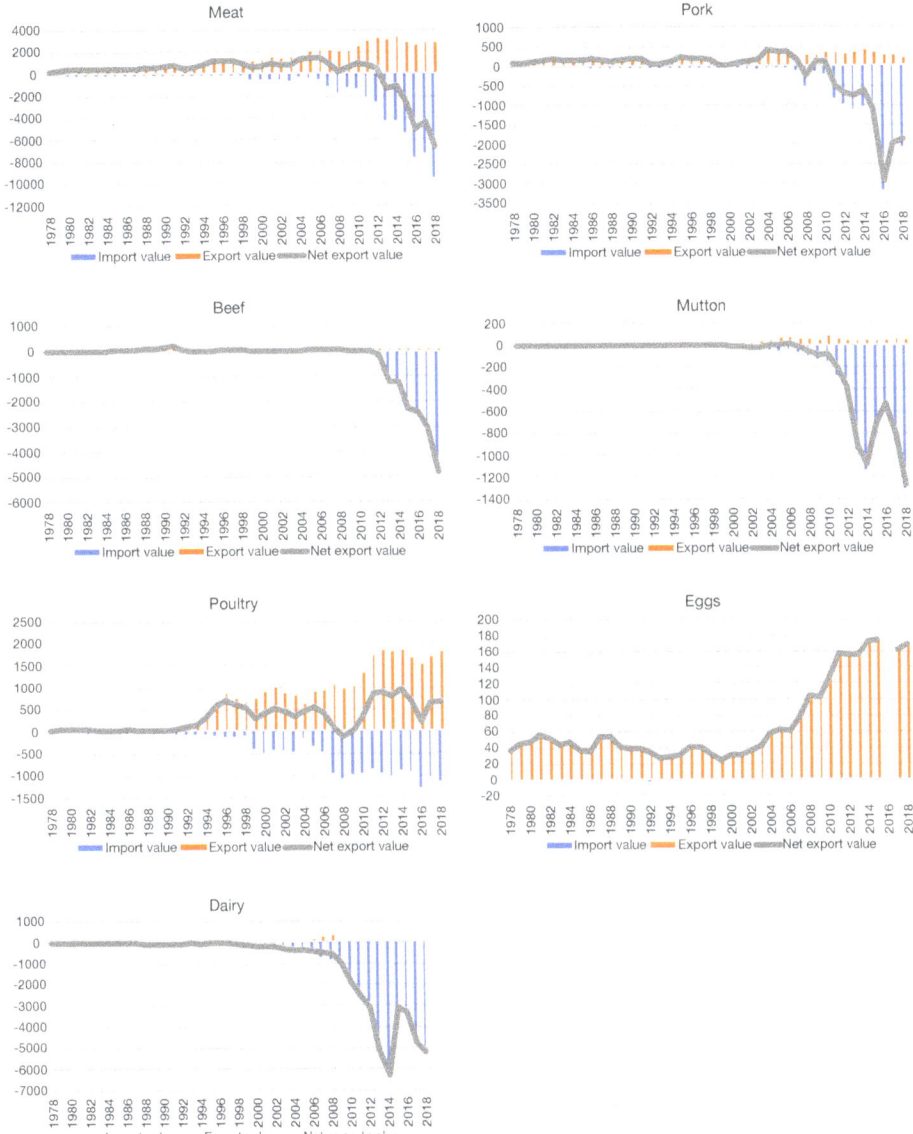

Figure 3.5(b) Livestock products

Figure 3.5 Value of China's imports and exports of major agricultural products, 1978–2018

Source: FAOSTAT database.

Second, the regional distribution of China's agricultural trade has diversified over recent years, but it remains unbalanced (Figure 3.6). China's agricultural exports were once concentrated in Asia, but exports to other continents have continued to increase over recent years. For instance, in 2018, more than 60 per cent of China's agricultural exports were concentrated in Asia, especially in Japan and South Korea, while its exports to non-Asian countries except the United States, although still relatively small, have displayed an increasing trend since 2010. In contrast, China's agricultural imports once originated primarily from developed countries; however, sources for imports have shown an inclination towards land-rich developing countries in recent years. For instance, previously more than half of China's agricultural imports originated from developed countries including the United States, Canada, Australia and New Zealand, but Brazil has grown to become the largest source of China's agricultural imports in recent years. Figure 3.7 reports China's imports of soybeans and beef in thousand metric tonnes by region including countries like Australia, the United States, Brazil and Argentina. Given that China has a growing demand for land-intensive products, it will show an increasing inclination towards land-rich developing countries in the future.

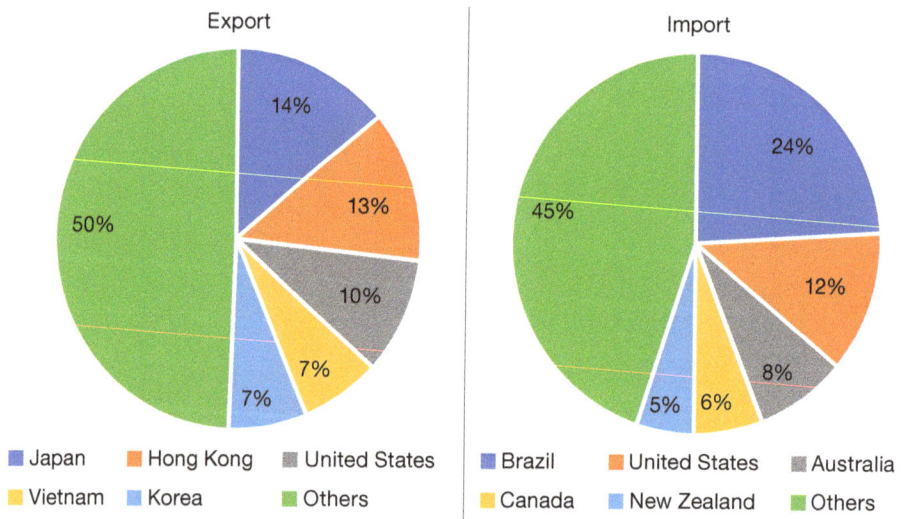

Figure 3.6 Regional distribution of China's agricultural exports and imports, 2018

Source: MoFCOM (various years).

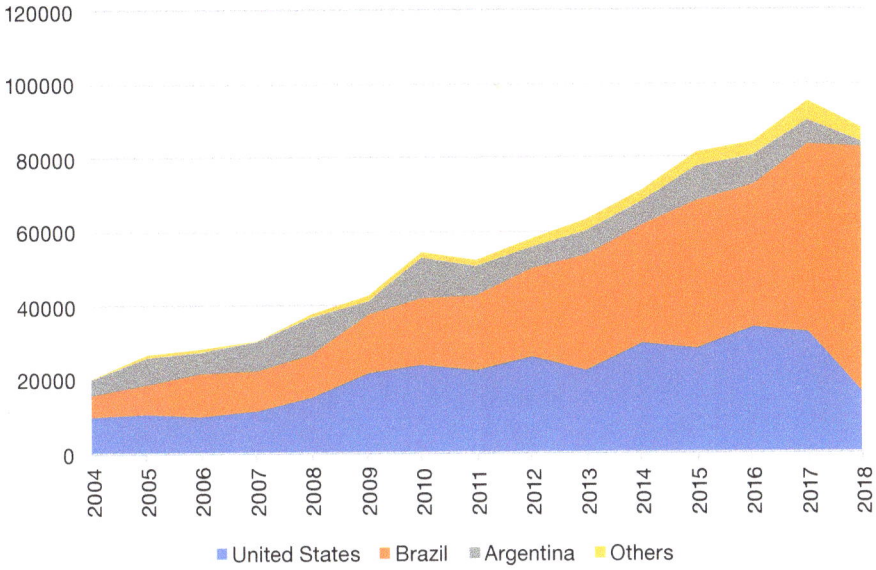

Figure 3.7(a) Soybeans

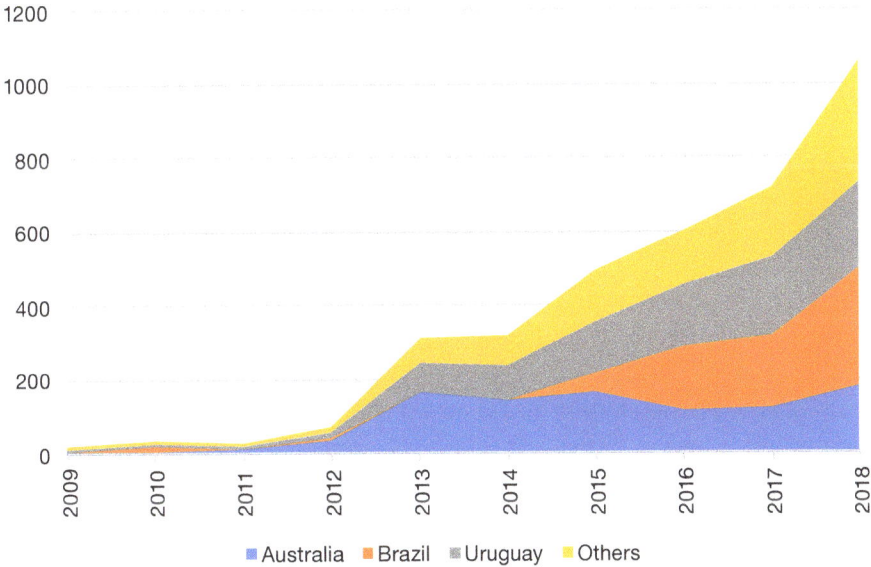

Figure 3.7(b) Beef and beef by-products

Figure 3.7 China's imports of soybeans and beef, by region (thousand metric tonnes)

Source: MoFCOM (various years).

In sum, China has significantly increased its agricultural imports over the past 20 years, partly because of its constrained resource endowments, increased production costs and the rapid growth of domestic demand. Such trends will continue to increase in the foreseeable future as population and income levels continue to grow. To meet China's growing demand while ensuring global food security, it is important to know what China will import and from where these increased imports should come. This will therefore require an in-depth analysis of the production and trade comparative and competitive advantages of each major agricultural product in China (which will determine the trade) compared with the rest of the world.

Methodology

According to international trade theory, comparative advantage is the fundamental determinant of agricultural trade patterns throughout the world. As one of the world's largest producers and consumers of agricultural products, China should rearrange its agricultural trade to reflect its comparative advantages compared with the rest of the world, as global agricultural production and consumption change over time. To predict China's future agricultural trade, it is essential to use standard approaches to measure and analyse the changes in the comparative advantage and international competitiveness of China's major agricultural products.

The RCA and RTA indices

In the literature, the most commonly used measures of a country's trade competitiveness are the trade competitiveness index, world market share (WMS), the RCA index and the RTA index. Although different indices have different advantages, their results are generally mutually consistent when providing a measure of revealed comparative and competitive advantages at the commodity level. Based on both the availability of data and project length, we chose to use the RCA index and the RTA index in this study.

Most previous studies have focused on the competitiveness of either a single agricultural product or agricultural products as a whole, while neglecting competitiveness analysis according to product between major agricultural countries. In this study, we propose to use the RCA and RTA indices to measure and compare the changing comparative and competitive advantages for 17 major agricultural products in China and its major trading partners. Detailed information on these 16 agricultural products/product groups are presented in Appendix Table 3.1.

A standard RCA index takes the form of Equation 3.1, and the corresponding relation between the RCA index and the level of trade comparative advantage is given in Table 3.1.

Equation 3.1

$$RCA_{ij} = \frac{X_{ij} / X_{it}}{X_{jw} / X_{wt}}$$

In Equation 3.1, X_{ij} is the export value of agricultural product j in country i; X_{it} is the total value of agricultural exports from country i; X_{wj} is the export value of agricultural product j in world trade; and X_{wt} is the total value of global agricultural exports.

Table 3.1 RCA and the corresponding level of trade comparative advantage

RCA	Level of trade comparative advantage
RCA > 2.5	Extremely strong
1.25 ≤ RCA ≤ 2.5	Relatively strong
0.8 ≤ RCA < 1.25	Medium
RCA < 0.8	Relatively weak

While the RCA index provides a good measure of comparative advantage for a country based on its exports, the structure of its import demand should also be included. To deal with this problem, the RTA index is also introduced. Unlike the RCA index, the RTA index fully represents comparative advantage based on the use of all resources. In practice, a standard RTA index is defined as in Equation 3.2.

Equation 3.2

$$RTA_{ij} = \frac{X_{ij} / X_{io}}{X_{wj} / X_{wo}} - \frac{M_{ij} / M_{io}}{M_{wj} / M_{wo}}$$

In Equation 3.2, X_{ij} (M_{ij}) is the export (import) value of agricultural product j in country i; X_{io} (M_{io}) is the total export (import) value of all other agricultural products except j in country i; X_{wj} (M_{wj}) is the export (import) value of agricultural product j in world trade; and X_{wo} (M_{wo}) is the total export (import) value of all other agricultural products except j in world trade. A positive RTA indicates that agricultural product j of country i has a comparative advantage over other countries, while a negative RTA indicates no comparative advantage.

The overall bilateral complementarity index

An analysis of the comparative advantage of China's agricultural trade over the past 40 years can indicate which products China will import. However, it will not tell us from where the newly created agricultural trade will come. In particular, if the current trading partner cannot fully meet China's growing demand, it will be important to know whether there will be alternative trading partners that could help to fill the gap.

In theory, the relationship and cooperation potential between two countries (or regions) in the trade of a certain product can be measured by constructing a bilateral trade index. One of the most commonly used measures is overall bilateral complementarity (OBC), which is mainly used to analyse the competitive or complementary relationship between two countries (or regions) in the trade of a certain commodity. OBC is defined as Equation 3.3.

Equation 3.3

$$OBC_{ij}^p = -\frac{Cov(RTA_{ip}, RTA_{jp})}{\sqrt{Var(RTA_{ip}) \times Var(RTA_{jp})}}$$

In Equation 3.3, RTA_{ip} and RTA_{jp} represent the RTA indices of product p in country (or region) i and j, respectively. A positive OBC index indicates that the covariance between the RTA indices of two countries (or regions), i and j, in the trade of product p is negative, and that these two countries (or regions) are complementary in the trade of product p, with one country at a comparative advantage and the other at a comparative disadvantage. On the other hand, a negative OBC means that the covariance of RTA indices is positive, which indicates that these two countries (or regions) are in a competitive situation in which both have a comparative advantage in the international trade of product p. It should be noted that, if one country's comparative disadvantage is worsening while the other is losing its comparative advantage, although the signs of the two countries' RTA indices are not the same (that is, the former is negative, while the latter is positive), the two countries are on the same trend—that is, the covariance is positive. In this case, although the OBC is negative, the two countries are not in a competitive situation, as one of them does not have a comparative advantage and the other is losing its competitiveness.

Unlike the RCA and RTA indices, which only calculate the trade advantage at a certain point, the OBC reflects the trade of two countries or regions over time. Although the changes in comparative advantage over a certain period can be represented by the RCA and RTA indices and their changes, the OBC can reflect the bilateral trade relations and cooperation potential between two countries or regions in a better and more intuitive way.

Estimation strategy

Based on the proposed approaches, our estimation process consists of three steps. First, we used the RCA and RTA indices to measure the changes in the comparative and competitive advantages of crops and livestock products at the aggregate level and by commodity in China for the past four decades. Second, we identified the major producers of each agricultural product in the world, using the criteria that their share of global production should total more than 1 per cent, before calculating their RTA and RCA indices for the past 20 years (1998–2018). By comparing the RTA and RCA indices in China with the indices of the selected countries, we determined China's comparative advantage in international trade. Third, to identify China's potential trade partners, we selected several countries and regions with comparative advantage in different agricultural products and used the OBC to check their complementarity with China.

The comparative and competitive advantages of China's agricultural trade and changes over time

Changes in comparative and competitive advantages in China's agricultural trade

Using the data on the imports and exports of major crops and livestock products in China over the period 1978–2018, we calculate the RCA and RTA indices for 17 types of agricultural commodities and analyse the comparative and competitive advantages of each commodity and their changes over the past 40 years. The estimated RCA and RTA indices for the crops and livestock products at the aggregate level and by commodity are shown in Figures 3.8 and 3.9, respectively.

China had a comparative advantage in producing major crops during the early reform period, but this gradually declined after the mid-2000s. As is shown in Figure 3.8a, the RCA indices for rice, corn and cotton used to be above 2.5 over a certain period before 1991, suggesting there was a strong revealed comparative advantage for the production of these three products. For other crop products such as oilseeds, soybeans, sugar/sugar beet, vegetables and fruits, the average RCA indices were also above 1.25, which implies they held a relative comparative advantage. However, the comparative advantages of major crops have gradually declined since the late 2000s. As shown in Figure 3.8a, the average RCA indices of nine out of 10 commodity groups (with the exception of vegetables and fruits) are significantly below 0.8, which suggests the comparative advantage for most crops—in particular, land-intensive products—has been disappearing.

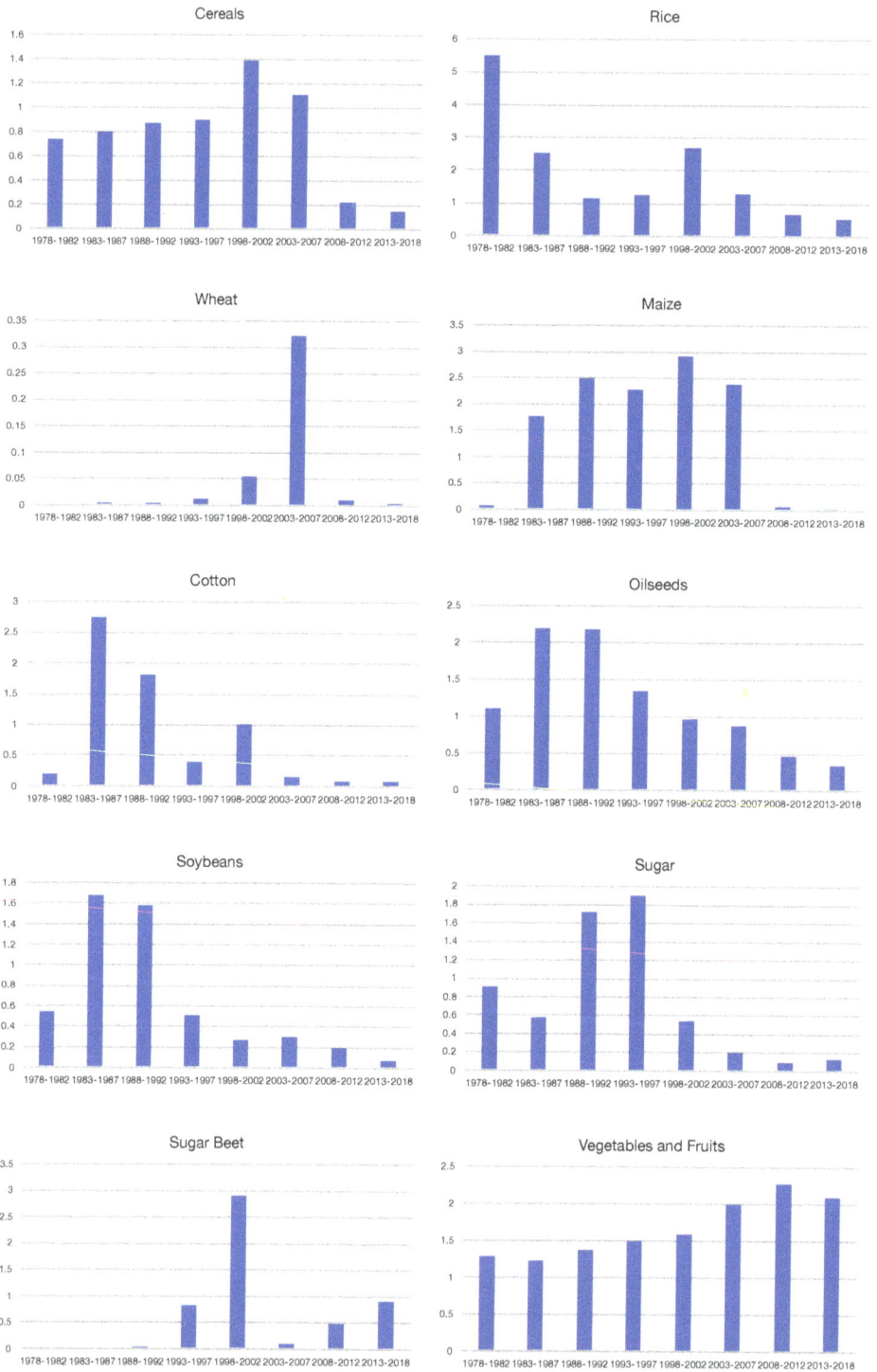

Figure 3.8(a) Crops

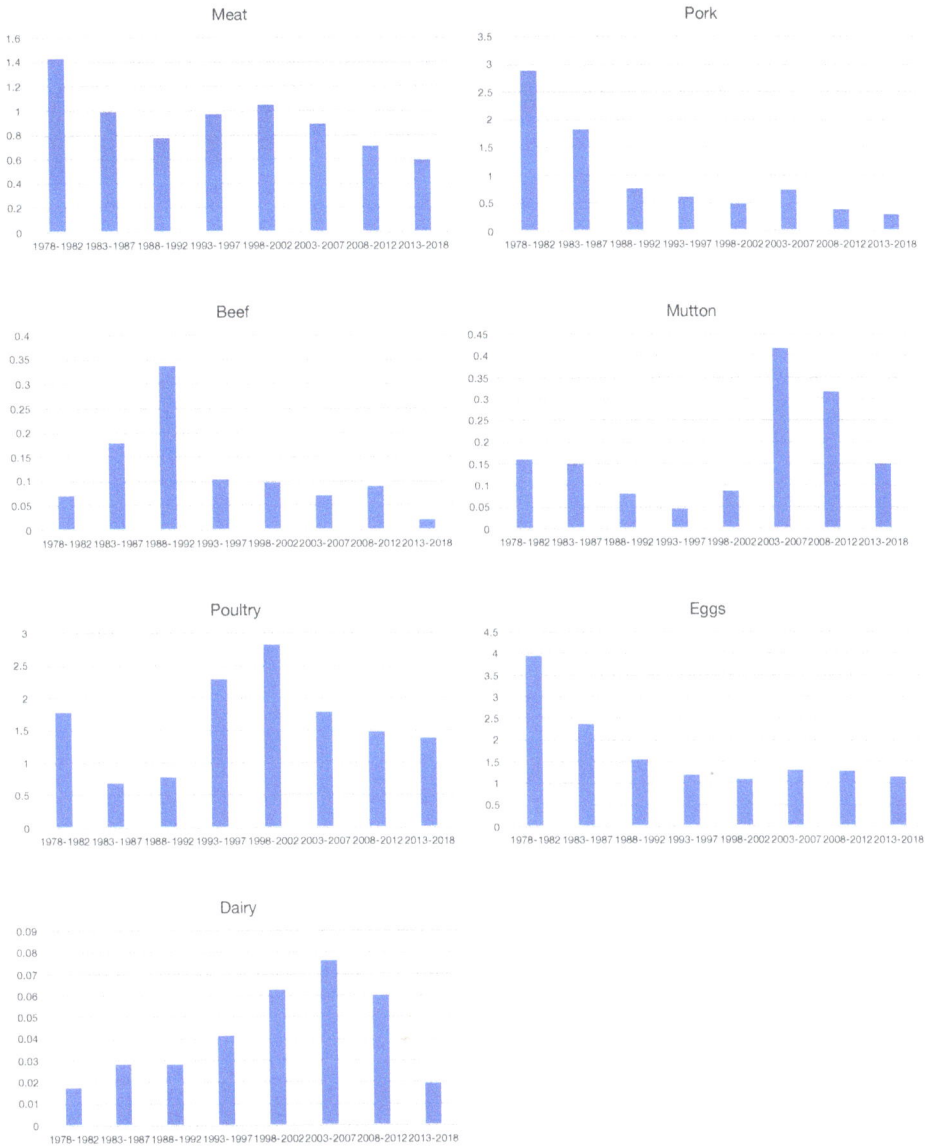

Figure 3.8(b) Livestock products

Figure 3.8 The RCA index of major agricultural products in China, 1978–2018

Source: Authors' estimates by using FAOSTAT database.

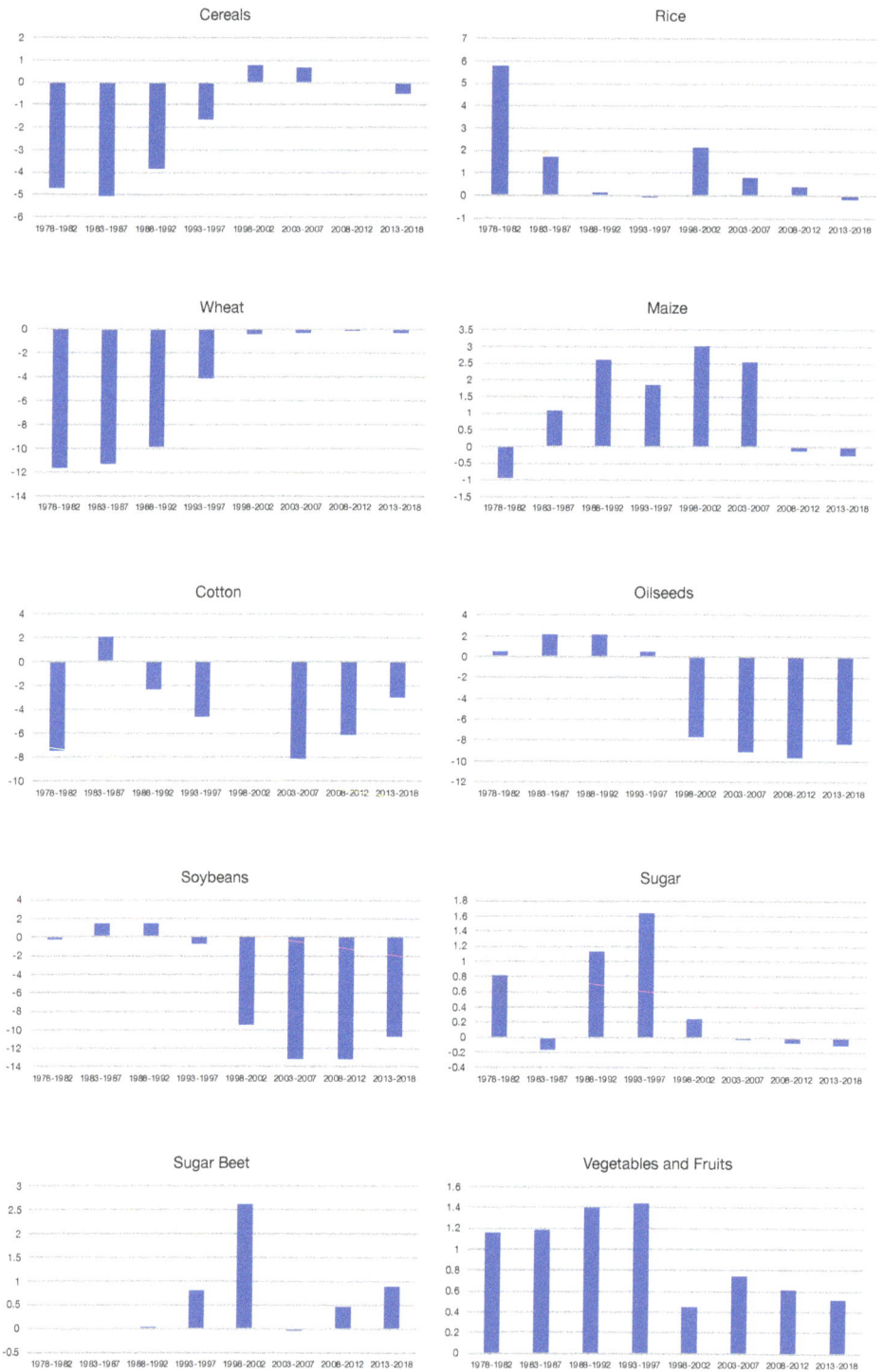

Figure 3.9(a) Crops

Meat

Pork

Beef

Mutton

Poultry

Eggs

Dairy

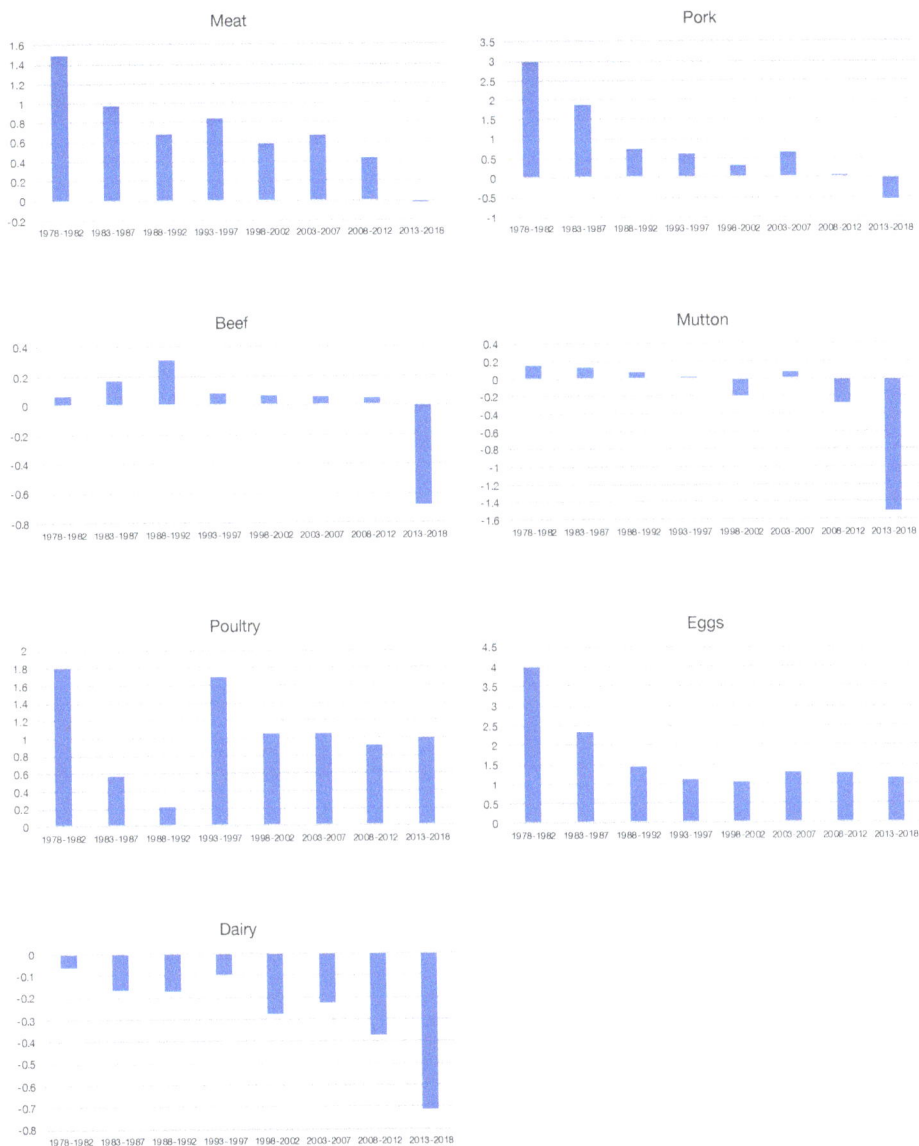

Figure 3.9(b) Livestock products

Figure 3.9 RTA indices of China's major agricultural products, 1978–2018

Source: Authors' estimates by using FAOSTAT database.

A similar trend change has also been seen in livestock products. As shown in Figure 3.8b, China once had a strong comparative advantage in the production of pork and eggs (the RCA indices used to be more than 2.5), a moderate comparative advantage in poultry meat (the RCA indices were between 1.25 and 2.5) but no advantage in beef, lamb and dairy (the RCA index was below 1). However, the comparative advantage of the majority of livestock products has been in decline over the past 10 years. Apart from poultry and eggs, whose RCA indices are still above 1, the RCA indices of other livestock products are significantly below 1.

Figure 3.9 further shows the change in the competitive advantage for China's major agricultural products between 1978 and 2018 using the RTA index. Consistent with the comparative advantage analysis, we show that China used to have a competitive advantage in trade for almost all agricultural products except wheat, cotton and dairy. However, the competitive advantages of major agricultural products have gradually declined over time. In the past 10 years, China has had only a relatively modest competitive advantage in the trade of sugar beet, fruits, vegetables, poultry and eggs, the production of which has been rapidly scaled up and industrialised.

In sum, China had comparative and competitive advantages in many crop and livestock products during the early reform era, going back to the 1980s and the 1990s. However, its comparative and competitive advantages for most agricultural products in the global market have gradually declined over time. For the moment, except for sugar beet, vegetables, fruits, poultry and eggs, for most agricultural products (in particular, land and resource-intensive products such as coarse grains and oilseeds), China has almost no comparative or competitive advantage compared with the rest of the world. This, to some extent, reflects the fact that the growth of domestic agricultural output (due either to the limited improvement in production efficiency or constrained resource supply) has not been able to meet the growth in domestic demand caused by rapid population and economic growth. Thus, imports of these agricultural products are being used to fill the gap between production and consumption.

Comparing the comparative and competitive advantages of major agricultural products across countries

How are the comparative and competitive advantages of major agricultural products changing in the rest of the world? Are they also falling over time? To answer this question, we further calculate the RCA and RTA indices for major crops and livestock products at the aggregate level and by commodity in their major producing regions. The purpose of this is to understand which countries or regions have the potential to supply the international market with each commodity.

Cereal crops

Although China's wheat production never held a comparative or competitive advantage during the past four decades, rice and corn production did once possess a comparative and competitive advantage, before being gradually lost over the past decade. To understand how the world market has changed over time, we measured the comparative and competitive advantages of cereal crops in their major producing countries throughout the world. Figure 3.10 presents the changes in the RCA and RTA indices for other major producing countries and regions from 1998 to 2018, compared with China.

The RCA and RTA indices for rice in China are at a lower level relative to other major producing countries, and have been declining over recent years, indicating that rice production in China is losing its comparative and competitive advantages. Since the domestic demand for rice has decreased and shifted towards high-value/high-quality products, such a change in the comparative advantage is more likely to be caused by production-side factors. There are two possible reasons: one is related to increasing production costs, given the dominance of smallholder farms in the industry and the rise of labour and land costs in recent years. The other is the lack of technological innovation in the rice-processing industry. There are few large domestic processing enterprises in China. Indeed, 95 per cent of processors are small or medium-sized, and they are suffering from the impact of massive imports of cheap rice from neighbouring countries.

In contrast to the changing trend in China, the comparative and competitive advantages of rice production are rising or have continued to be maintained at a relatively high level in some other developing countries in South and Southeast Asia, including Myanmar, Cambodia, Thailand, Vietnam, India and Pakistan. Most of these countries have a tropical or subtropical monsoon climate and conditions amenable to intensive rice cultivation, as well as low economic development and an abundant supply of cheap labour. The comparison of the RCA and RTA indices of China with those of rice-producing countries/regions shows that South and Southeast Asia—especially Cambodia and Pakistan—may possess great potential to provide additional supplies of rice to the international market in the near future.

Although wheat production is gradually increasing in China, it remains an industry at a competitive disadvantage compared with the rest of the world. Throughout the past two decades, net wheat imports remain at a high level. While the wheat price on the international market has been falling due to the recent increase in supply, China's domestic wheat price has continued to increase due to increasing production costs. This has exacerbated China's comparative and competitive disadvantages in the international wheat market.

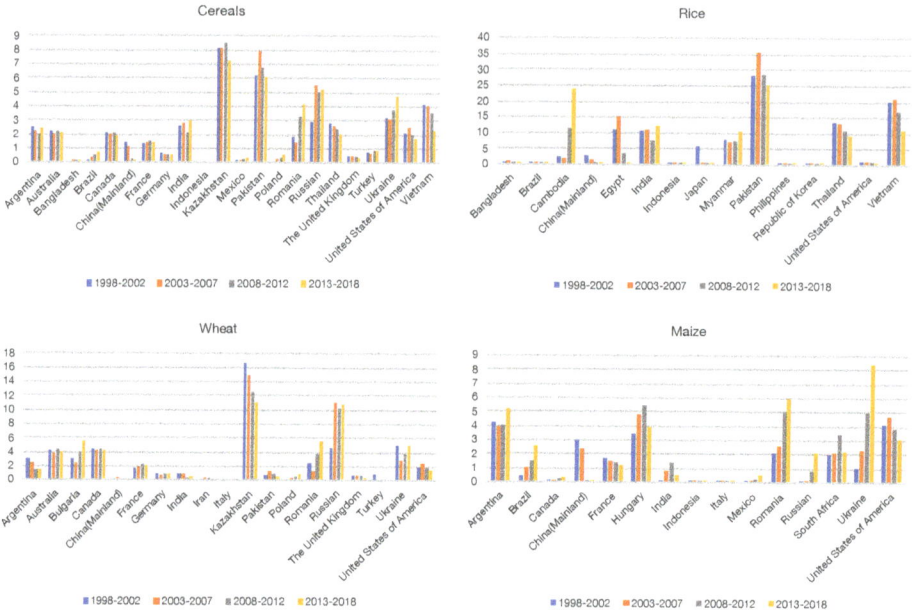

Figure 3.10(a) RCA index

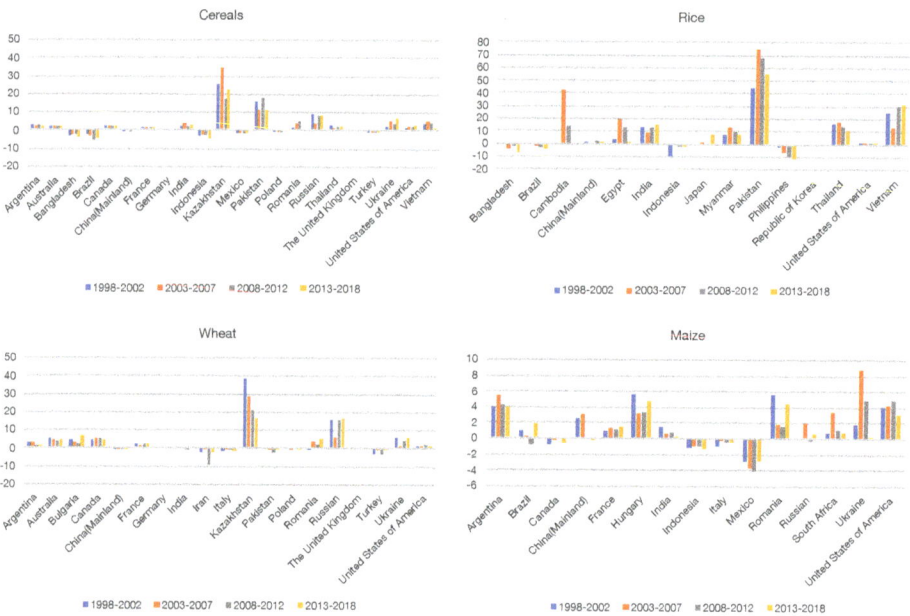

Figure 3.10(b) RTA index

Figure 3.10 RCA and RTA indices of cereal crops for China and other major producers, 1998–2018

Source: Authors' estimates by using FAOSTAT database.

In addition to China, for the moment, Central Asia, North America, Eastern Europe and Australia are the world's four-largest wheat producing/exporting regions. Among these regions, the RCA and RTA indices of Kazakhstan and Russia are significantly higher than those of the other major producers. With greater potential for productivity improvement and the development of spare land, the comparative and competitive advantages of wheat production for those countries/regions will continue to increase, and they are expected to provide a greater supply of wheat to the international market.

As one of the most important feed crops, corn has surpassed rice to become the largest cereal crop in China, yet its comparative advantage has diminished in recent years. With increasing domestic demand and declining comparative and competitive advantages, China is expected to increase its imports of corn in the near future due to the rapid expansion of its livestock industry (and its use of corn for feed). Based on our estimates of the RCA and RTA indices, South Africa, North America, South America and Eastern Europe now possess strong market competitiveness in corn production, and South America and Eastern Europe have displayed significant growth in their advantages in recent years. In particular, Ukraine, Romania, Brazil and Argentina have relatively large advantages in corn trade, which have been on the rise in the past 20 years. Therefore, these countries and regions should have great potential to increase corn supply to the international market in the future.

Economic crops

In contrast to cereal crops, economic crops have a relatively higher market value since they have a wider range of industrial usages. From the early 1980s, marketisation reform gradually changed the enterprise structure of agricultural production in rural China, and the proportion of economic crops in total crop output significantly increased. However, similar to cereal crops, many economic crops are losing their comparative and competitive advantages in the international market.

Figure 3.11 presents the changes for China in the RCA and RTA indices of six types of economic crop, compared with the major producing countries in the rest of the world, between 1978 and 2018.

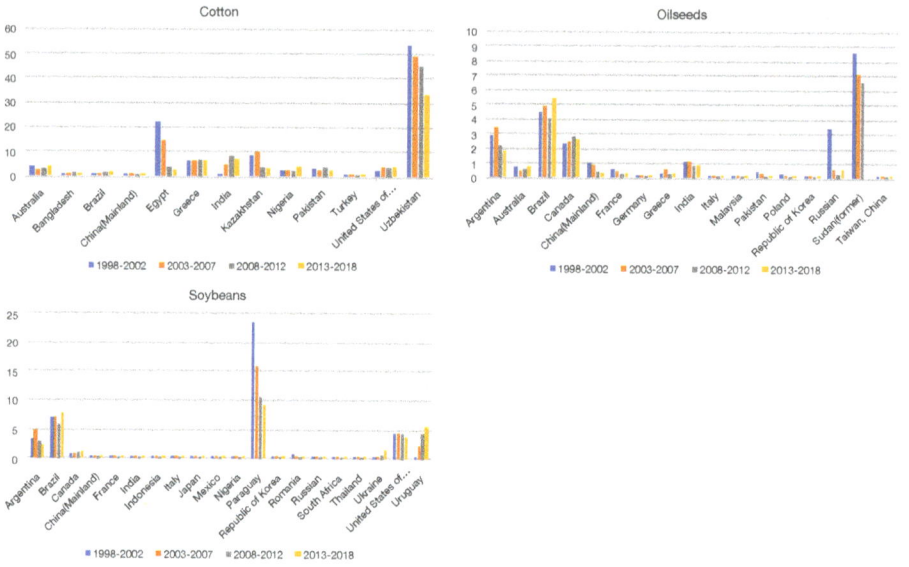

Figure 3.11(a) RCA I

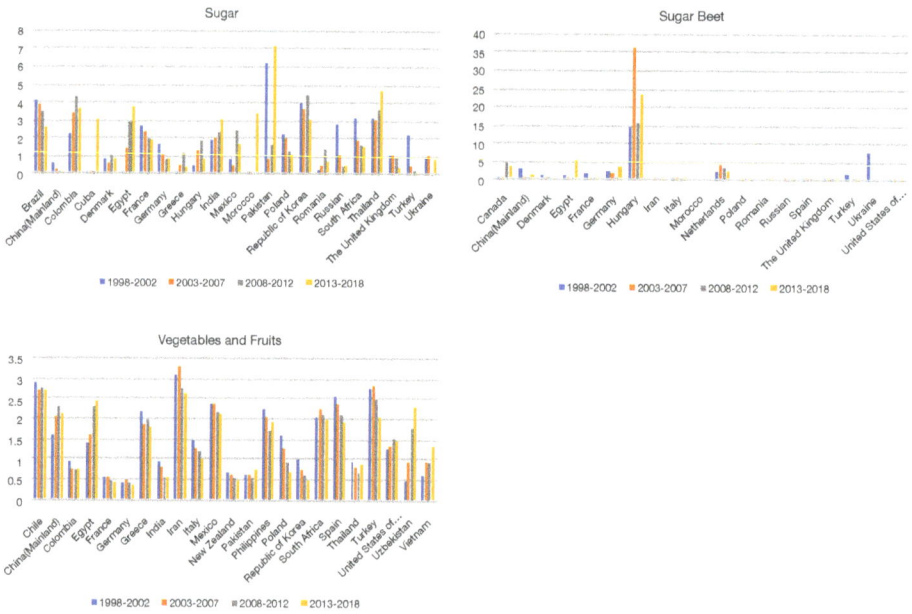

Figure 3.11(b) RCA II

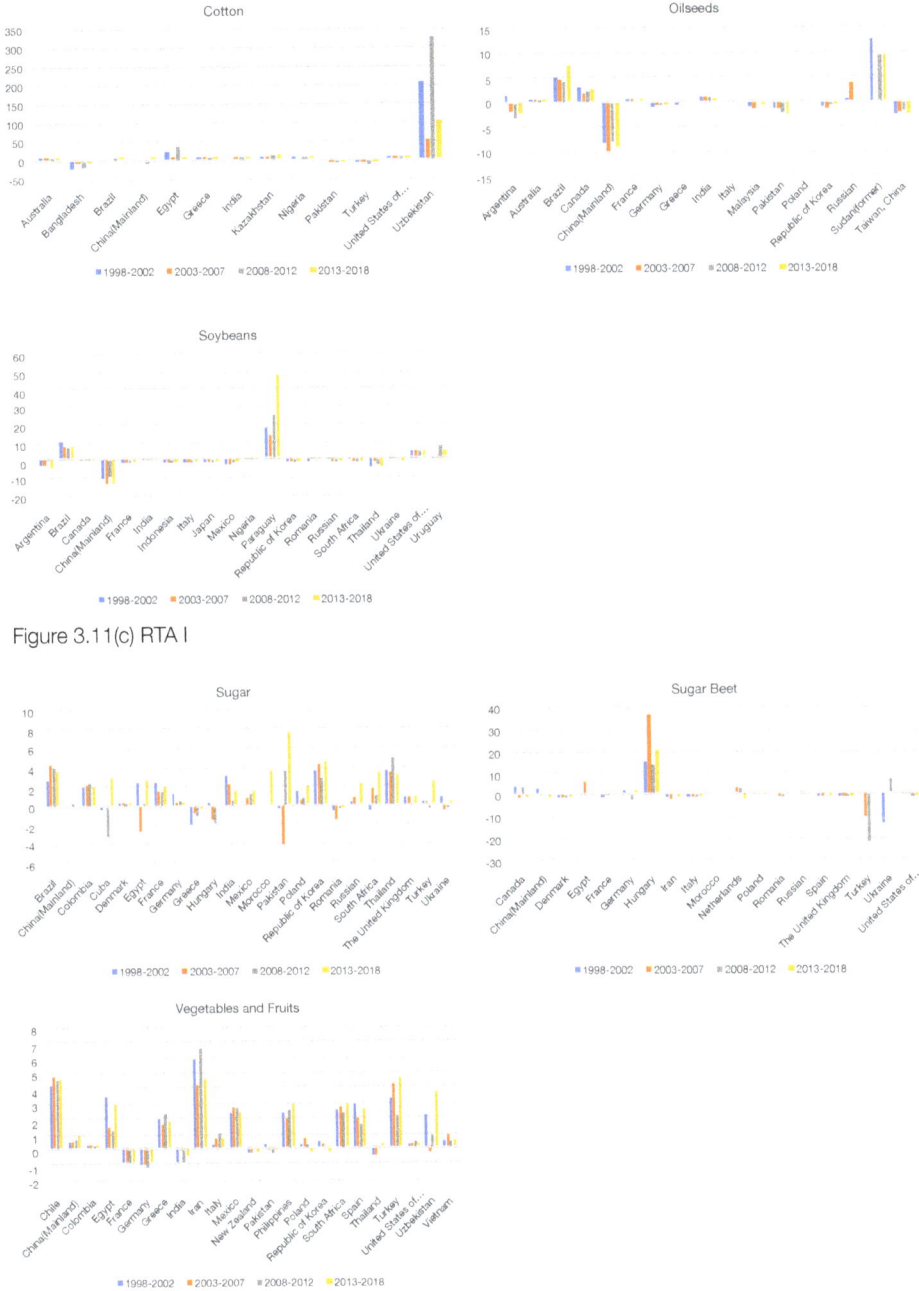

Figure 3.11(c) RTA I

Figure 3.11(d) RTA II

Figure 3.11 RCA and RTA indices of economic crops for China and other major producers, 1998–2018

Source: Authors' estimates by using FAOSTAT database.

Although China used to be one of the largest cotton producers in the world, it has lost its comparative advantage in recent decades compared with other major producing countries. In the 1980s and the 1990s, China's demand for cotton increased along with the development of its domestic textile industry, providing strong incentives for farmers to produce cotton. However, this trend has changed since 2000. Our measures of the RCA and RTA indices show that China used to have a comparative advantage in cotton production in the past but has shifted to increasing imports gradually. As potential suppliers to China, Uzbekistan has a far greater comparative advantage, while Kazakhstan, India and Egypt are also important cotton producers. With the development of China's Belt and Road Initiative, there exists great potential for future cooperation between China and these countries in the cotton trade.[1]

Oilseeds and soybeans are not only important oil crops, but also can be processed to make feedstuff. The production of these two crops in China is falling far short of the increasing domestic demand, causing a heavy reliance on the international market to make up for the shortfall. As an example, soybean production in China has continued to decline in recent years, with more than 80 per cent of domestic demand being met by the international market (mainly imports from North America). Throughout the world, South and North America still dominate the production and supply of these two crops. In particular, Brazil, Argentina, Paraguay, Uruguay, the United States and Canada have significant comparative and competitive advantages in the international market. Since China–US trade frictions have increased uncertainties around future economic cooperation, more attention is being placed on diversifying the import markets in South America to cultivate more stable and reliable supplies of oil crops.

Sugar production in China has never had any comparative advantages compared with other major global producers, especially as the planting area for sugar crops in China has continued to decline due to rising production costs and declining international prices over recent years. In contrast, many developing countries— including Pakistan, Egypt, Thailand and Cuba—have increased their comparative advantage in sugar production over the past decade. Given their price advantage in the international market, there will be a continuing increase in the sugar supply from these countries.

---

1   It is noteworthy that, although China's cotton market has been faced with short supply, cotton imports have dropped significantly in recent years. This is partly because the domestic textile industry has shifted in recent years to Southeast Asian countries in response to increased labour and material costs. If this trend continues, China's trade dependence on cotton imports will decline in the future.

Vegetables and fruits are among the few agricultural products in China that still hold a moderate comparative advantage, even though their trade has been in deficit for the past decade. Over the past 40 years, driven by increasing per capita incomes, vegetables and fruits have become indispensable products in the national diet. Meanwhile, China's total and per capita outputs of fruits and vegetables have been growing rapidly, with total imports and exports also expanding. The production of vegetables and fruits is evenly distributed throughout the world, while the diversity of fruits and vegetables in each country due to differences in climate and environment is an important factor contributing to the active international trade in these products. With the uptick in domestic consumption and the enhancement of national awareness about nutrition and health, demand for vegetables and fruits in China will inevitably continue to expand, meaning foreign imports will also continue to increase and diversify.

Livestock products

Figure 3.12 depicts the changes in the comparative and competitive advantages of livestock products in China and the world's major producers between 1998 and 2018. At the aggregate level, the comparative and competitive advantages of livestock products have declined in China for the past two decades, but the country maintains a comparative advantage for some products, such as poultry and eggs.

Pork is the most important livestock product in China, accounting for around 60 per cent of total meat consumption, yet it has become a disadvantaged industry in recent years compared with other producing countries. Although domestic total and per capita pork production have been growing, there is still a widening gap between domestic production and demand due to the increase in domestic consumption and the impact of factors such as breeding costs and food safety. Consequently, Chinese pork imports have increased since 2010. In the rest of the world, pork production is concentrated mainly in the Americas, including Brazil, Chile, Mexico, the United States and Canada, and Europe, in Denmark, Germany, the Netherlands, Poland and Spain. Among these regions, the comparative and competitive advantages of Latin American countries have increased rapidly, alongside Western and Eastern Europe's traditional hold on relatively high comparative and competitive advantages in this industry.

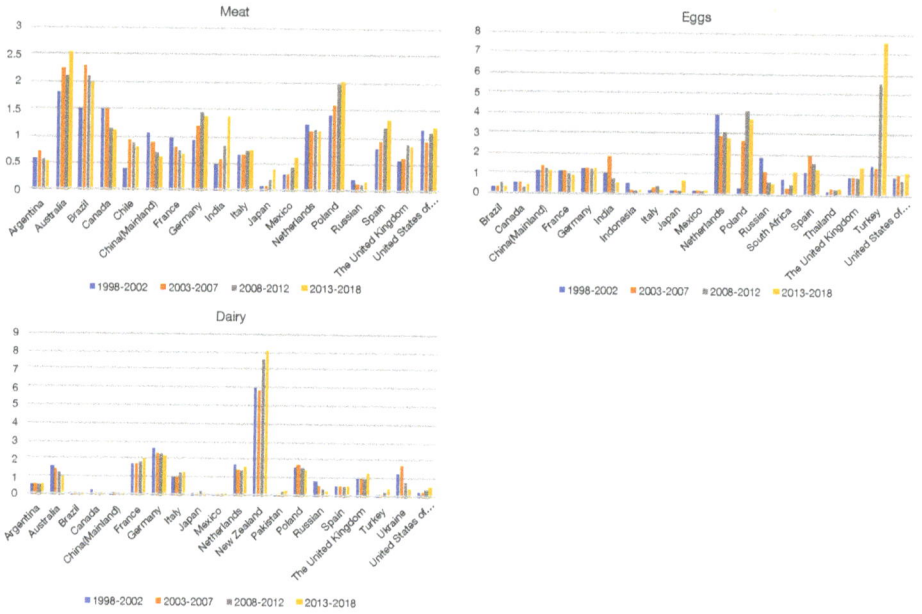

Figure 3.12(a) RCA I

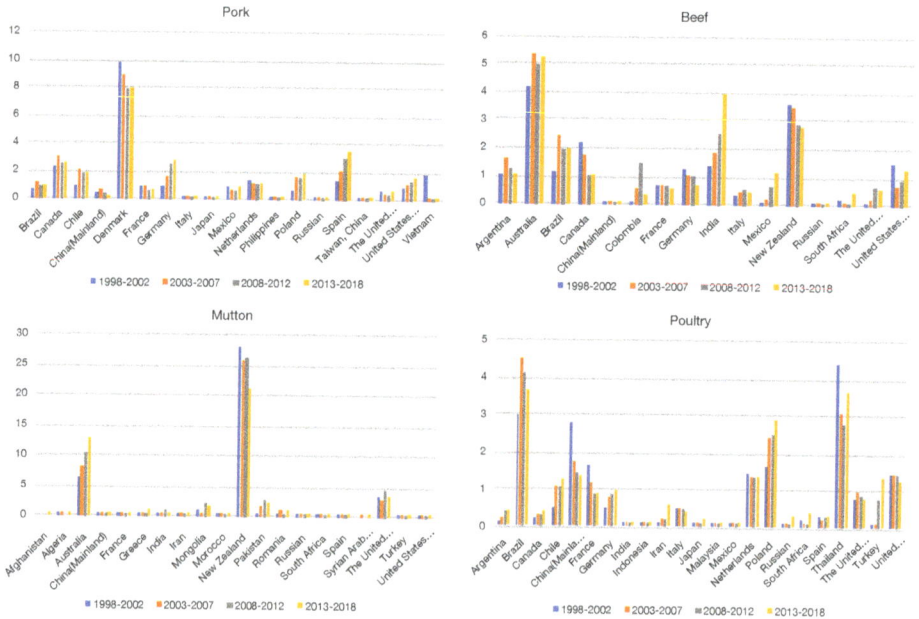

Figure 3.12(b) RCA II

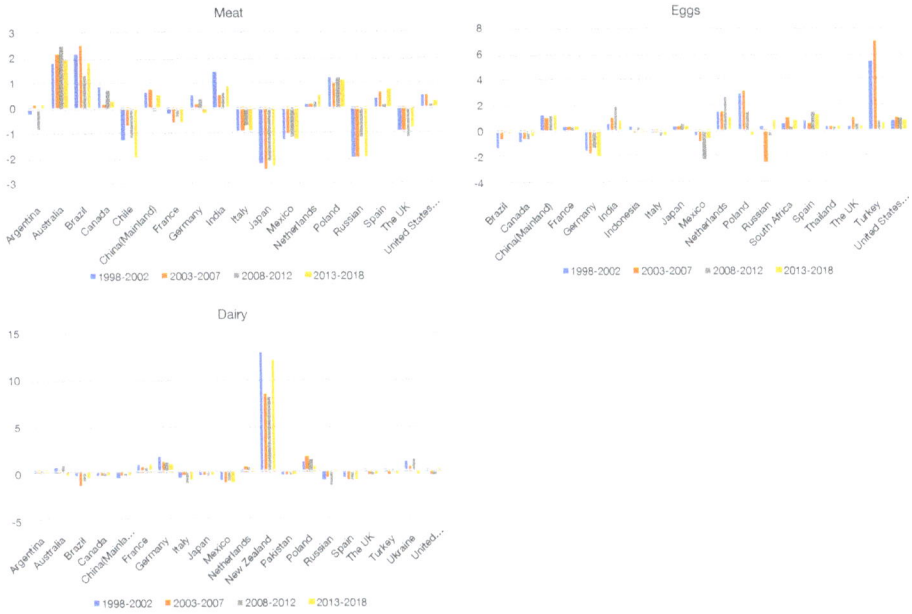

Figure 3.12(c) RTA I

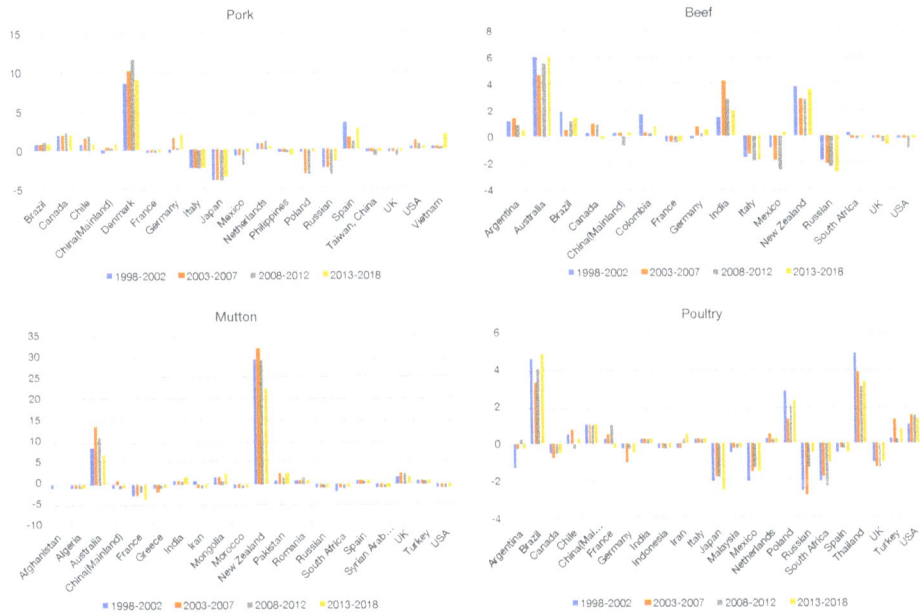

Figure 3.12(d) RTA II

Figure 3.12 RCA and RTA indices of livestock products for China and other major producers, 1998–2018

Source: Authors' estimates by using FAOSTAT database.

Similar to pork, the production of beef and lamb in China has no comparative or competitive advantage compared with the rest of the world. Since 2010, China's beef and lamb imports have entered a stage of explosive growth in recent years. Because of constrained domestic production due to high land prices and farming costs, the increased demand for beef and lamb in China is expected to depend on the international market for supply. The major beef producers in the world are Australasia, South Asia, South America and Europe, among which Australia, New Zealand, India, Brazil and Argentina have a relatively large comparative advantage. For the moment, in China's imported beef market, the medium and high-end products come mainly from Australia and New Zealand, while the medium and low-end products are supplied mainly by South America. Constrained by the farming conditions and production technologies in different countries, this pattern is not expected to change much in the near future. As for lamb, China's total imports grew rapidly from 2000. Globally, Australia, New Zealand and the United Kingdom have a strong comparative advantage in trade among the world's major producers, making them suitable lamb suppliers for the international market in the future.

In China's national dietary structure, poultry meat is second only to pork among major meat products and there is a high degree of substitution between the two. Among major livestock products, poultry and eggs are the only ones for which China still possesses some comparative and competitive advantages and also maintains a trade surplus. Although the comparative advantage of poultry and eggs in China has also declined over the past two decades, that advantage is still greater than for most of the world's major producers. Apart from China, other net exporters of poultry and eggs to the international market include Brazil, Thailand, Poland and the Netherlands for poultry, and Turkey and European countries such as Poland and the Netherlands for egg products.

China's dairy production has been at a disadvantage in international trade, and this continues to worsen. China lags far behind the major producers in terms of both quantity and quality. With the growth of domestic demand for dairy products, the deficit has begun to accumulate, and China's domestic market has become more and more dependent on international imports. For the moment, the main suppliers of dairy products are Australia, New Zealand and several European countries, including France, Germany, Italy, Poland and the United Kingdom, all of which have regional advantages and high technological supports; therefore, these countries and regions will remain major sources of China's dairy imports in the future.

In sum, the comparative and competitive advantages of most agricultural products in China have been in decline for the past 20 years compared with the rest of the world. As well as the United States and European countries, many developing countries in Asia, Africa and Latin America have been able to gradually increase their comparative and competitive advantages in the production of particular agricultural products. This will increase the potential supply of agricultural products to the international market and offer alternative regions for China to source its future demand.

China's potential trading partners: Complementarity analysis

As China's population and per capita income continue to grow, the coming decade will witness further increases in domestic food demand. In addition to increasing domestic agricultural productivity, it is inevitable that China will source more of its domestic supply from the international market. As has been illustrated in the previous sections, both China and the rest of the world will stand to benefit from the expansion of China's agricultural trade if these increases are based on the respective countries' comparative advantage and competitiveness. Thus, in this section, we first provide a forecast of food demand by commodity in the near future, and then use the OBC index to list potential source countries.

China's future net demand for agricultural products

While the comparative advantage of major agricultural products in China has declined over the past 20 years, it is still important for China to maintain a relatively high level of self-sufficiency in its food supply. There is a belief that, given China's huge population and continuing growth trends, it will be hard for the world to meet such a dramatic increase in China's demand for food imports. As previously noted, China currently imports less than 2 per cent of its total food, which accounts for more than 8 per cent of global tradable food.

Based on forecasts made by the China Center for Agricultural Policy (CCAP), China will continue to maintain a high food self-sufficiency ratio over the next decade or two through improvements in agricultural productivity. However, with China's population continuing to grow until 2035, its food self-sufficiency ratio may drop from 98 per cent in 2020 to 92–95 per cent in 2035. This implies that more than twice the current domestic food demand will need to be sourced from the international market in the next two decades.

Table 3.2 compares the self-sufficiency ratio of major agricultural products for 2025, 2035 and 2050. Although production of and demand for the main cereal crops will be roughly balanced domestically, there will be a widening gap between domestic demand and supply of most economic crops and livestock products. This, to some extent, reflects the shift in domestic food consumption towards high-value and high-quality products driven by increasing per capita income. In addition, this will be a good way for China to improve the efficiency of resource reallocation by importing more agricultural products in which it has relatively low comparative and competitive advantages.

Table 3.2 Self-sufficiency ratio of China's major agricultural products in 2025, 2035 and 2050

Commodities	Self-sufficiency ratio (%)		
	In 2025	In 2035	In 2050
Rice	98	98	98
Wheat	98	98	98
Maize (corn)	92	82	81
Cotton	74	67	55
Oilseed	87	87	90
Sugar	58	40	22
Vegetables	100	100	100
Fruits	100	100	100
Pork	99	98	98
Beef	85	77	65
Lamb	91	85	75
Poultry	100	99	98
Eggs	100	100	100
Dairy	72	68	60

Source: CCAP forecast based on the ChinaAgro Model.

Based on our estimates of the RCA and RTA indices, China's major cereal crops, including rice, wheat and corn, are gradually losing their comparative advantage. However, the self-sufficiency ratios of rice and wheat are predicted to remain above 98 per cent, as they are top priorities for national development.[2] This implies that domestic food grain production will be able to roughly meet domestic consumption demand, despite the shortage of land resources and rising production costs. In contrast, there will be increasing demand for feed grain (in particular, corn), which will need to be sourced from elsewhere as the demand for livestock products increases over time. Given that US–China trade frictions have cast doubts on the future stability of international cooperation, it is clear that China will seek to broaden its import channels to ensure diversified sources of future imports.

Compared with cereal grains, economic crops including cotton, oilseed and sugar have more comparative disadvantages. By 2025, about 13 per cent of oilseed, 26 per cent of cotton and 42 per cent of sugar demand for the domestic market had to be met through imports. Along with the decrease in the self-sufficiency ratios for these agricultural products over the coming decade or two, their imports will increase substantially due to their relatively lower comparative advantage in China compared

---

2   The issue of grain supply is a fundamental and critical issue affecting the national economy and people's livelihood. Since the 18th National Congress of the Communist Party of China (CPC), China has established a national grain security strategy of 'giving priority to China, relying on domestic resources, ensuring production capacity, with moderate imports and technological supports.'

with other crop products in China and the rest of the world. This does not include soybeans, of which more than 90 per cent are already coming from the international market. Nowadays, most of these products are imported from new continental countries, such as North and South America and Australia. Yet, the question remains whether these regions and countries will continue to increase their supply.

As for livestock products, China's total imports have soared since 2010, caused largely by increased domestic production costs. With the exception of poultry and eggs, the production of most livestock products in China is still based on the household production system and/or small-scale businesses, which are sensitive to land resources, labour prices and feed costs. As a consequence, domestic livestock production in China is at a price disadvantage and has lost its competitiveness. By 2020, 9 per cent of beef, 10 per cent of lamb and 25 per cent of dairy products were coming from the international market, though pork production roughly met domestic demand. With increased consumption demand and competition from the rest of the world, a greater proportion of feed grain, as well as beef and lamb, is expected to come from imports, even if self-sufficiency in pork is maintained.

Predictions of China's future agricultural trading partners

Given its forecast future food demand structure, China will need to increase its imports of high-value and land- and water-intensive agricultural products to free up more resources for the production of agricultural products for which China possesses a relative comparative advantage. This arrangement can only be achieved when other countries are able to supply enough to meet China's demand. China's existing trading partners are more or less constrained by their potential supply capacity (because of limitations in their natural endowment supplies or difficulties in the bilateral relationship). Thus, it is necessary for China to identify new trading partners, according to their potential (rather than real) complementarity in agricultural production with China.[3]

In this sense, we are most interested in analysing the trade potential between China and land-abundant developing countries. This is because these countries have great potential to increase agricultural output due to the availability of spare land and other agricultural resources, although they are yet to use them effectively due to a lack of economic investment and technological support. Therefore, if the comparative advantage of these countries in agricultural products complements China's future imports, the potential of increased agricultural exports to China will bring economic incentives to scale up and industrialise their agricultural production, thus increasing global agricultural output and contributing to global food security.

---

3   The potential complementarity between two countries was interpreted based on their OBC coefficient as well as their RTA changing trends.

Figure 3.13(a) shows the complementarity between China and major producing countries and regions for the three major cereal crops. As for the maize market, the OBC index for corn between South America, Eastern Europe and China was enhanced between 2012 and 2018, as their comparative advantage in corn production increased. In particular, Argentina and Russia have shown great potential for providing additional supplies of maize to China, beyond China's existing trading partners.

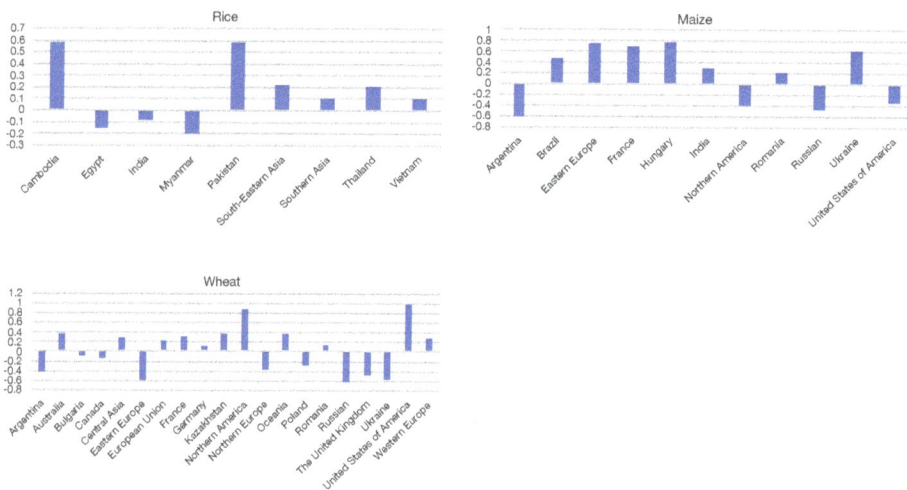

Figure 3.13(a) Cereal crops

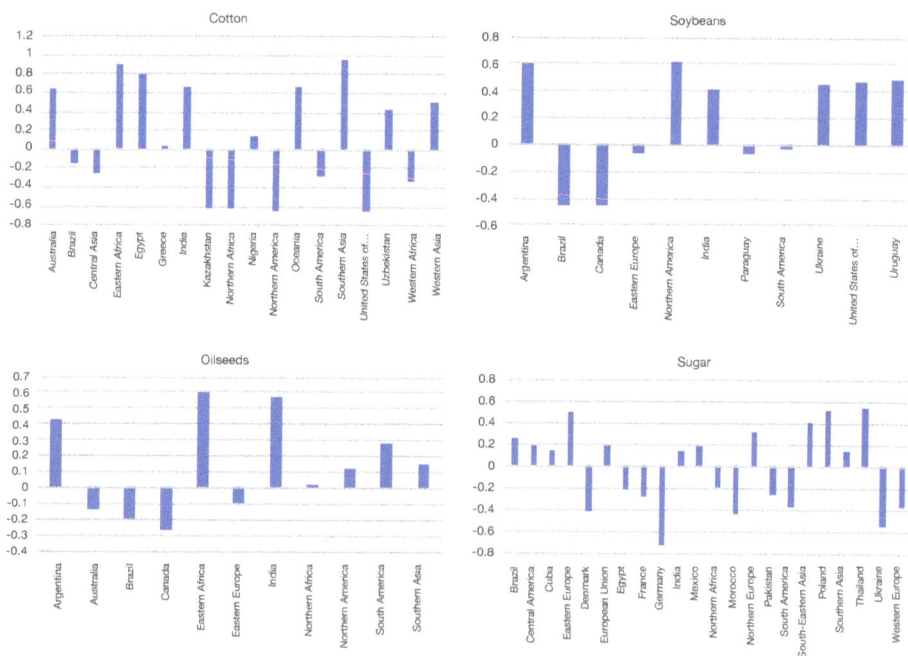

Figure 3.13(b) Economic crops

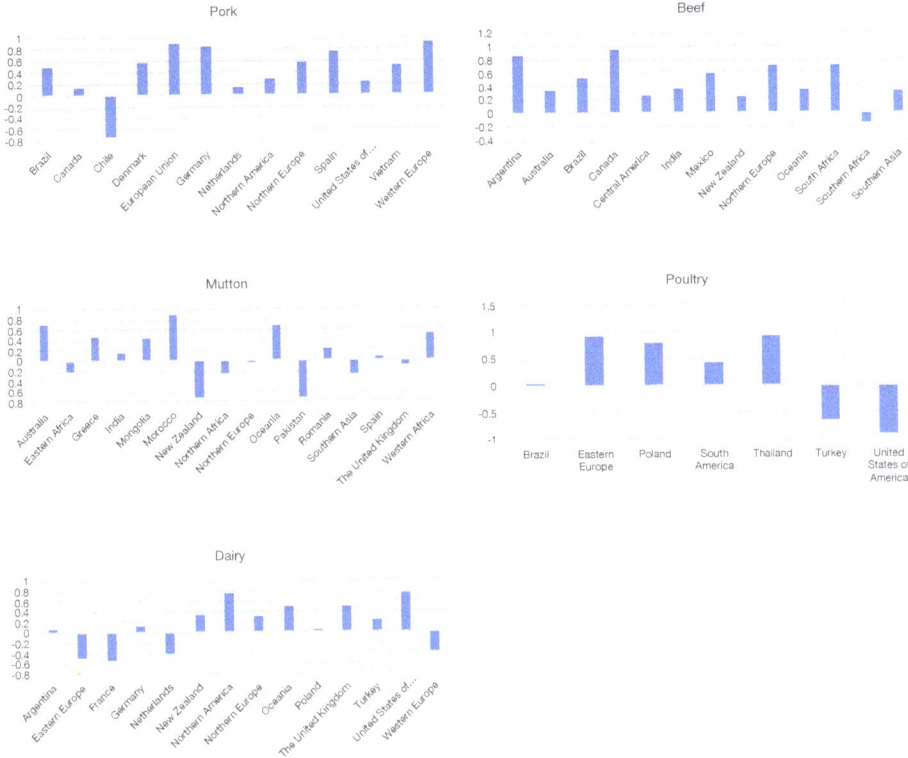

Figure 3.13(c) Livestock products

Figure 3.13 OBC coefficients for agricultural commodities between China and the world's major producers, 2012–18

Source: Authors' estimates by using FAOSTAT database.

Compared with food crops, the self-sufficiency rate for economic crops in China is much lower. Imports of cotton, oilseeds and sugar crops have been rising sharply over the past decade, due to high domestic production costs and international competition. In the foreseeable future, trade dependence on these three products will continue to rise.

Figure 3.13(b) shows the complementarity for economic crops between China and other trade-advantaged countries and regions for the period 2012–18. First, among the world's major cotton exporters, the comparative advantages of South America, North America and Central Asia in the cotton trade have increased significantly. In particular, developing countries such as Brazil and Kazakhstan are alternatives for China's cotton product imports. Second, for soybeans, the OBC coefficient between China and South America is positive. This suggests the comparative advantage of oil crops in South America may have more complementarity in agricultural trade with China. Third, sugar imports for China, which are influenced heavily by domestic policies, have increased with some cyclical fluctuation over time. Among major exporters, Thailand shows high complementarity with China. Thus, if the sugar trade is dominated by market behaviour in the future, Thailand could be a promising alternative to Cuba.

As for trade in livestock products, China's imports (in particular, of beef, lamb and dairy products) currently come primarily from Australia, Europe and North America. However, our estimates of the OBC coefficients for these three products show that some developing countries in South Asia, North America, South America and Europe also have strong capacity to supply those products (Figure 3.13[c]). In particular, as the comparative advantage of the United States has decreased in recent years, the comparative advantage of countries in South Asia, South America, Africa and Australia has been increasing. Therefore, these countries could become new sources for China of livestock products, especially given the current trade tensions between China and the United States. Specifically, while medium-range to high-end meat and dairy products will come mainly from traditional trading partners including developed countries like Australia, New Zealand, the United Kingdom and Germany, developing countries in South Asia, South America and Africa, including India, Brazil and Argentina, will be able to supply China with low-end to medium-range products. With growing export advantages, these countries will be suitable future sources of livestock imports for China.

Conclusions

Using global commodity-level agricultural trade data for the period 1978–2018, this chapter systematically examines the comparative and competitive advantages of crop and livestock products at the aggregate level and by commodity in China and changes over time. In addition, we investigate the potential production complementarities that exist between China and its potential suppliers of each product. The results indicate that the comparative and competitive advantages of major agricultural products in China have declined rapidly in recent years, making China (with its increasing demand) an important food importer on the international market. In addition to relying on existing trading partners, China needs to explore the potential supply of particular agricultural products from developing countries with increased comparative advantages. Based on relative comparative advantages, this newly created agricultural trade will help not only to improve the welfare of China and its trading partners, but also to ensure global food security by boosting global food production.

At the commodity level, we show that many developing and developed countries have high levels of complementarity with China in the bilateral trade of feed grains, oil crops and other agricultural products, including developing countries in Eastern Europe, South America and Africa. These countries have different advantages in agricultural production, holding the potential to become alternative and reliable agricultural trading partners for China in the future. Properly increasing China's agricultural trade with the rest of the world, based on comparative advantage and competitiveness, will not only help to alleviate domestic pressure on relatively scarce agricultural and ecological resources, but also provide the world with economic incentives to increase its agricultural production, and thus contribute to global food security.

Appendix Table 3.1 Trade and production data of agricultural commodities

Commodities	Code	
	Trade data	Production data
Cereals	1944	1717
Rice	1946	27
Wheat	15	15
Maize (corn)	56	56
Cotton	767	1753
Oilseeds	1899	339
Soybeans	236	236
Sugar	164	/
Sugarcane	/	156
Sugar beet	157	157
Vegetables	1889	1735
Fruits		1738
Meat	2077	1770
Pork	2027	1055
Beef	1924	867
Lamb	1925	1012
Poultry	2074	1808
Eggs	1942	1783
Dairy	2030	1780
Total agricultural products	1882	/

/ = no data about certain commodities in original database

Source: FAOSTAT database.

References

China Centre for Agricultural Policy (CCAP) (2019), *Global and China's Agricultural Development Toward 2050*, [In Chinese], Beijing: CCAP.

Chinese Academy of Engineering (CAE) (2020), *China Agriculture Development Strategy in 2050*, [In Chinese], Beijing: Chinese Academy of Engineering Press.

Food and Agriculture Organization of the United Nations (FAO) (2020), Agricultural land area: World, 1961–2018, *FAOSTAT: Land use*, [Dataset], Rome: FAO. Available from: www.fao.org/faostat/en/#data/RL/visualize.

Huang, J. and Rozelle, S. (2018), China's 40 years of agricultural development and reform, in R. Garnaut, L. Song and F. Cai (eds), *China's 40 Years of Reform and Development: 1978–2018*, 487–506, Canberra: ANU Press. doi.org/10.22459/CYRD.07.2018.24.

Meat & Livestock Australia (MLA) (2020), *Market Information: China beef imports— Monthly trade summary*, Sydney: MLA. Available from: www.mla.com.au/globalassets/ mla-corporate/prices--markets/documents/os-markets/steiner-reports-and-other-insights/china-beef-imports---global-summary---july-2020.pdf.

Ministry of Commerce (MoFCOM) (various years), *Monthly Brief Statistics on China's Agricultural Imports and Exports*, [In Chinese], Beijing: MofCOM. Available from: wms. mofcom.gov.cn/article/ztxx/ncpmy/ncpydtj/200603/20060301783733.shtml.

National Bureau of Statistics (NBS) (2019), *China Statistical Yearbook*, Beijing: China Statistics Press.

Sheng, Y., Shan, Y. and Huang, J.K. (2020), *Analyzing the determinants underlying exports of major agricultural commodities from African countries to China*, CCAP Working Paper & Bill and Melinda Gates Foundation Report, Beijing and Washington, DC.

UN Comtrade (2014–17), *UN Comtrade Database*, [Online]. Available from: comtrade. un.org/.

World Trade Organization (WTO) (2019), *World Trade Statistical Review 2019*, Washington, DC: WTO. Available from: www.wto.org/english/res_e/statis_e/wts2019_e/wts2019 chapter08_e.pdf.

4

China's urbanisation in the new technological revolution

Wang Wei, Deng Yusong, Shao Ting, Wang Ruimin,
Niu Sanyuan and Liu Xin

By the end of 2019, China's urbanisation rate had reached 60.6 per cent, indicating its entrance into the mid-to-late stage of urbanisation. Facing the future, China must grasp the vast opportunities to promote urbanisation along a healthy trajectory, clarifying its driving mechanisms, studying new trends and characteristics and properly responding to existing risks and challenges.

The process of China's urbanisation

China's urbanisation development model is endogenous to its economic development path and the transformations of its industrial structure. Under the strategy of giving priority to the development of heavy industry during the planned-economy period, China's urbanisation experienced a rapid process of industrialisation, resulting in a large number of industrial cities. Nevertheless, urbanisation at this stage was constrained by some institutional mechanisms, preventing it from enjoying the benefits from the global third technological revolution after World War II. Since the period of reform and opening up and with the establishment and improvement of the socialist market economy with Chinese characteristics, the economy has been integrated into the global economic system and has developed rapidly. Cities in China have come to make full use of the diffusion and spillover effects of foreign advanced technologies to transform and upgrade their industrial structure.

The tortuous development stage of urbanisation, 1949–1978

When the People's Republic was founded in 1949, China's urban population was 57.65 million, accounting for 10.6 per cent of the country's total population. From 1949 to 1957, due to the strategy of prioritising the development of heavy industry, many cities were built and expanded around 694 key industrial projects. In 1958, the Great Leap Forward campaign triggered the migration of large numbers of rural people to China's cities. During the Cultural Revolution, China's economic and social development were severely disrupted and the urbanisation process was reversed (Figure 4.1). At this stage, the process of urbanisation mainly revolved around the geographic distribution of major industries, especially the location of key national defence projects. Population size and industrial structure were subject to strict controls by the central planning system. Cities were regarded mainly as administrative centres, and their importance for economic growth and social governance was neglected.

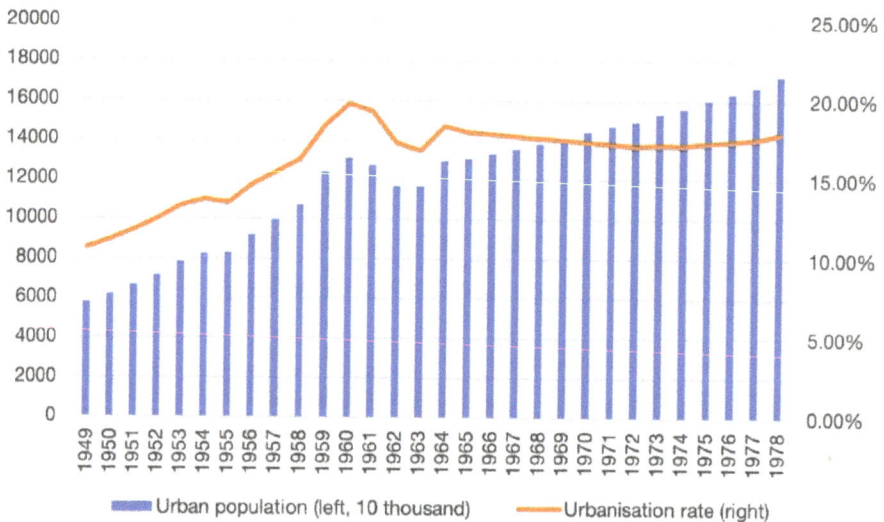

Figure 4.1 Changes in China's urbanisation rate, 1949–1978
Source: National Bureau of Statistics.

The smooth start of urbanisation, 1978–2000

From 1978 to 1984, China adopted a new development mode of 'strictly controlling the expansion of large cities, encouraging the growth of small cities and developing rural towns' (State Infrastruction Commission of the People's Republic of China 1980). The growth of township enterprises promoted urbanisation by encouraging peasants to leave their farms and work in factories in towns. In 1984, the reform of China's urban economic system was initiated. Many villages were transformed into towns, and large segments of the rural population moved into small towns. After Deng Xiaoping's 'Southern Tour' in 1992 and the socialist market economy reforms in 1994, China began to implement urban-driven regional development and a 'coastal city first' development strategy. From 1990 to 2000, the number of cities rose from 467 to 663, the urban population increased from 300 million to 460 million and the urbanisation rate increased from 26.4 per cent to 36.2 per cent (Figure 4.2). At this stage, advanced economies in the world had successively entered the era of comprehensive informatisation, and China also seized the huge industrial development potential brought about by this revolution in information technology. Using its advantages in low labour and land costs in coastal areas, China took the lead to develop related industries, and the electronic information industry quickly became important in many coastal cities.

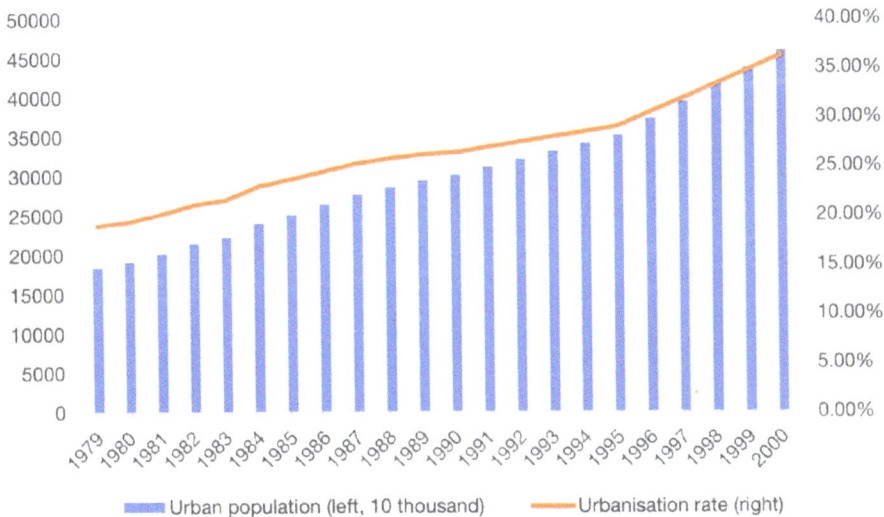

Figure 4.2 Changes in China's urbanisation rate, 1978–2000
Source: National Bureau of Statistics.

The rapid development stage of urbanisation, 2000–2011

After China joined the World Trade Organization (WTO) in 2001, it rapidly developed into an important global manufacturing base, accelerating its urbanisation process. Between 2000 and 2011, China's urbanisation rate increased from 30.89 per cent to 51.27 per cent—the fastest period of urbanisation witnessed during the 40 years of reform and opening up (Figure 4.3). Referring to the urbanisation model, the Twelfth Five-Year Plan in 2011 proposed that China 'rely on large cities and focus on small and medium-sized cities to gradually form urban clusters with large radiation effects'. With the deep integration of China's industrial development into the international division of labour and participation in global market competition, the focus of industrial policy shifted to comprehensively supporting technology and product upgrades in capital-intensive industries, nurturing technology-intensive industries and continuing to expand the scope of opening up. The proportion of tertiary industries steadily increased from 39.8 per cent to 45.5 per cent, surpassing secondary industries for the first time (Figure 4.4). The process of urbanisation and the upgrading of the industrial structure progressed synchronously, and the quality of urbanisation gradually improved.

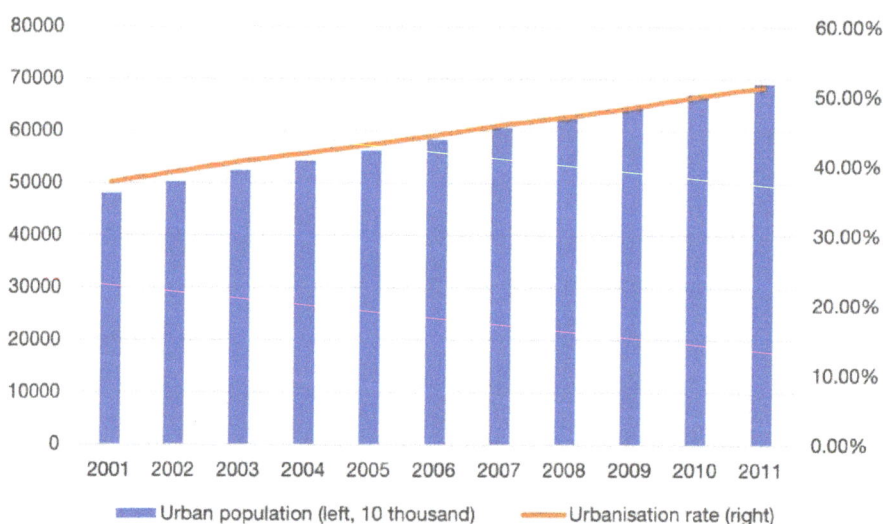

Figure 4.3 Changes in China's urbanisation rate, 2001–2011
Source: National Bureau of Statistics.

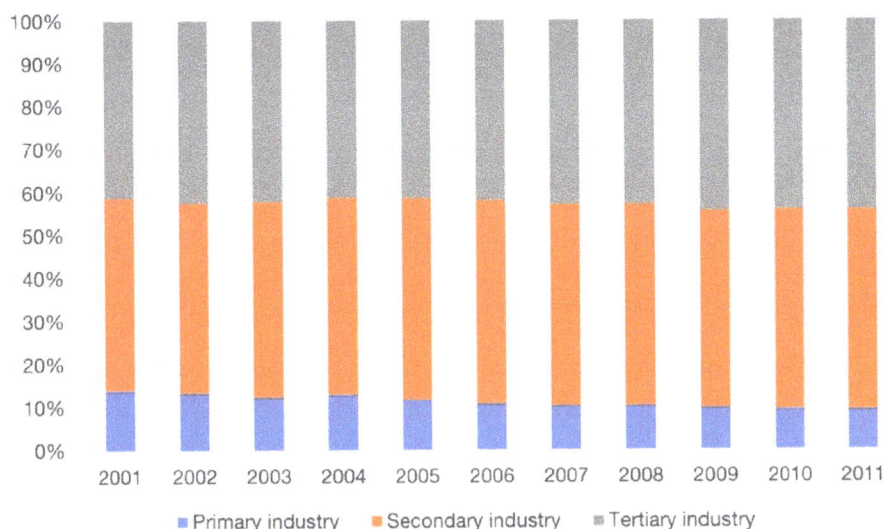

Figure 4.4 Changes in China's industrial structure, 2001–2011
Source: National Bureau of Statistics.

New urbanisation development stage, from 2012

Since the Eighteenth National Congress of the Chinese Communist Party, China's economic and social development have entered a new era. The Central Urbanisation Work Conference held on 12 December 2013 proposed following the new urbanisation path characterised by intensive, intelligent, green and low-carbon development. Significant breakthroughs have been made in the construction of pilot free-trade zones and the opening up of inland border areas. A number of central inland regional cities—such as Chongqing, Chengdu, Wuhan and Zhengzhou—have entered a period of rapid growth. In 2013, China proposed the Belt and Road Initiative to further expand its economic axis and development corridors and become a new driving force for urbanisation. In 2016, the Thirteenth Five-Year Plan proposed 'taking urban agglomerations as the main form' of urbanisation and accelerating their construction and development. China's urbanisation rate increased from 52.6 per cent in 2012 to 60.6 per cent in 2019 (Figure 4.5). A new round of global technological change has been accelerating, and a series of new technologies, industries and models has emerged in China. The proportion of tertiary industries rose from 45.5 per cent to 53.9 per cent, showing that China's urbanisation has entered a new pattern dominated by service industry development (Figure 4.6).

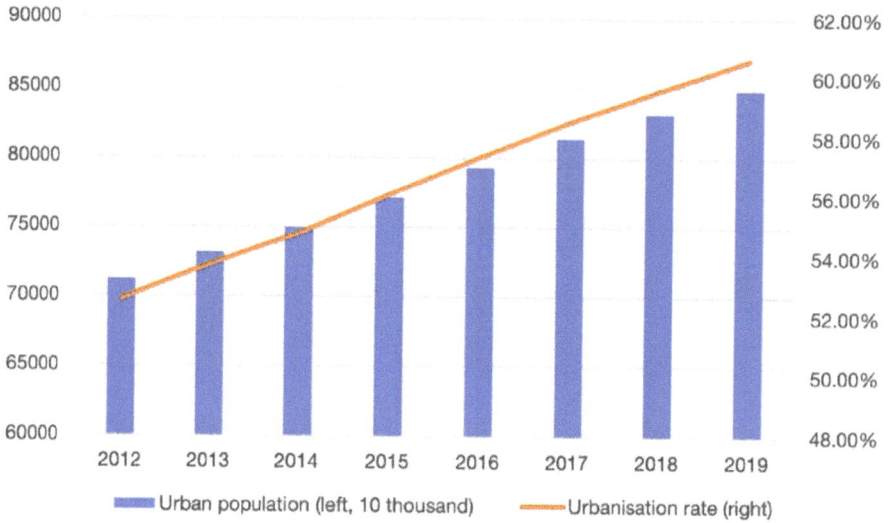

Figure 4.5 Changes in China's urbanisation rate, 2012–2019

Source: National Bureau of Statistics.

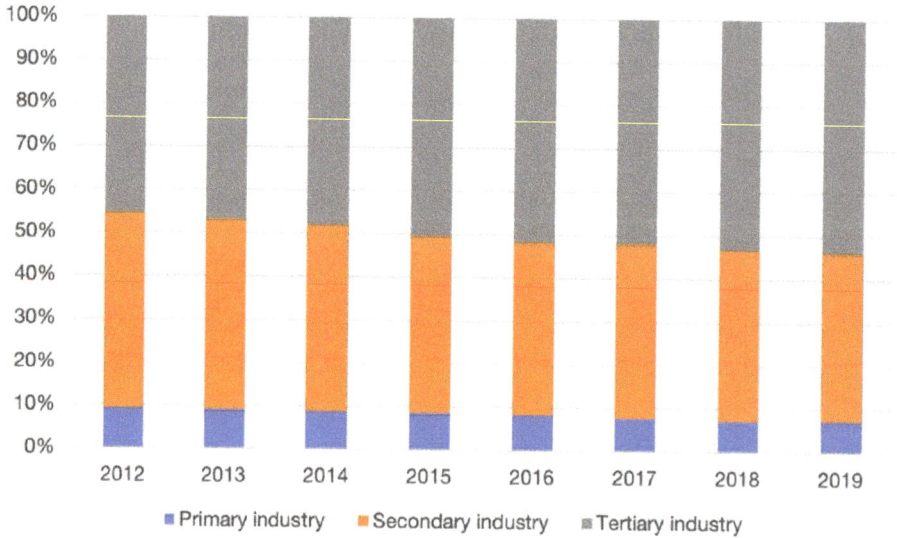

Figure 4.6 Changes in China's industrial structure, 2012–2019

Source: National Bureau of Statistics.

China's urbanisation achievements

The urbanisation level is steadily increasing

During the 40 years of reform and opening up, China's urbanisation level increased rapidly. From 1978 to 2019, the urbanisation rate increased from 17.9 per cent to 60.6 per cent, and the total urban population reached 848 million (Figure 4.7). The urban area of Chinese cities increased from 178,100 sq km in 2008 to 208,900 sq km in 2018, while the built-up area increased from 30,400 sq km in 2004 to 58,500 sq km in 2018 (Figure 4.8).

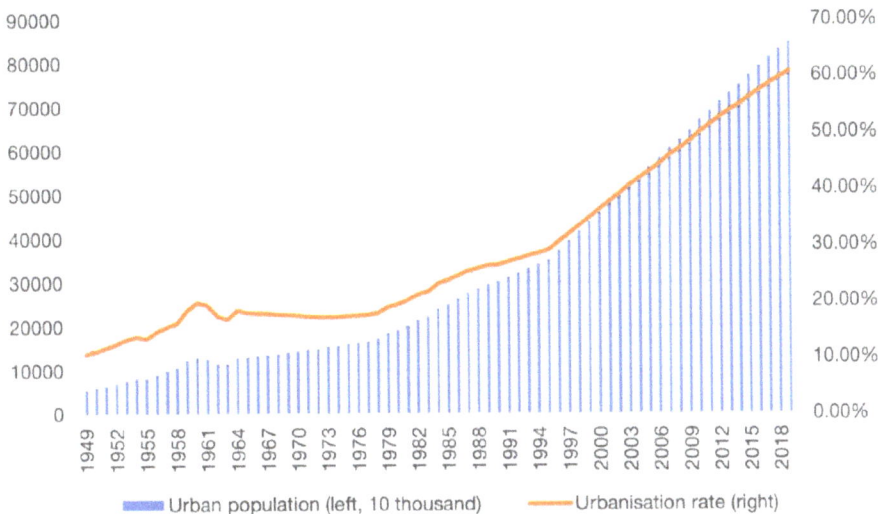

Figure 4.7 Urban population and urbanisation rate in China, 1949–2018

Source: National Bureau of Statistics.

Continuous optimisation of urban patterns

The number and scale of Chinese cities have expanded rapidly. At the end of 2017, there were 14 cities with a registered household population of more than 5 million, 16 cities with a population of 3–5 million and 219 cities with a population of 0.5–3 million (Figure 4.9). The urbanisation pattern has been continuously optimised and the construction of the three major urban agglomerations—Beijing–Tianjin–Hebei, the Yangtze River Delta and the Pearl River Delta—has accelerated. The '19 + 2'[1] urban agglomeration pattern was formed and has developed steadily.

---

1   The '19 + 2' urban agglomerations are: Beijing–Tianjin–Hebei, Yangtze River Delta, Pearl River Delta, Shandong Peninsula, West of the Taiwan Strait, Harbin–Changchun, Southeastern Liaoning, Central China, Middle of the Yangtze River, Chengdu–Chongqing, Guanzhong Plain, Beibu Gulf, Middle Shanxi, Hohhot–Baotou–Erdos–Yuzhong, Middle Guizhou, Middle Yunnan, Lanzhou–Xining, Ningxia, North Mount Tianshan, as well as Lhasa and Kashgar.

In 2016, the abovementioned three most influential urban agglomerations were home to 18 per cent of the population on 2.8 per cent of the country's land area, and produced 36 per cent of national gross domestic product (GDP).

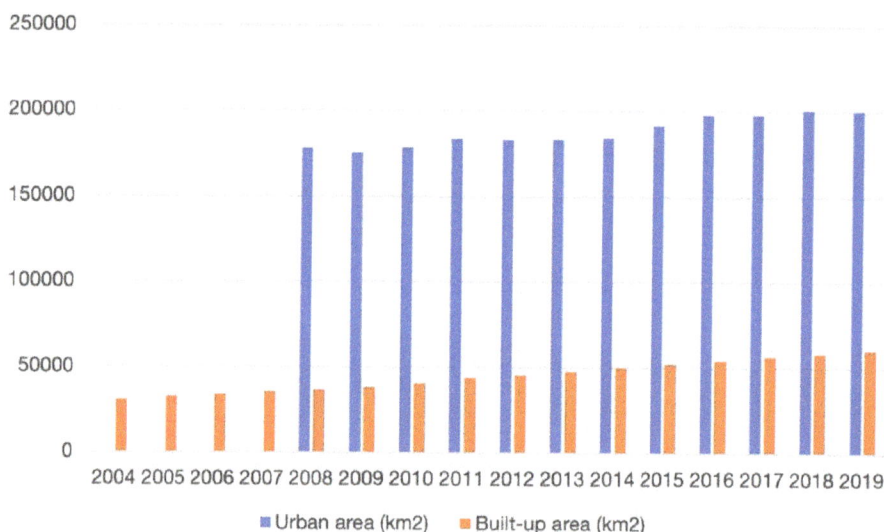

Figure 4.8 Urban and built-up areas in China, 2004–2019
Source: National Bureau of Statistics.

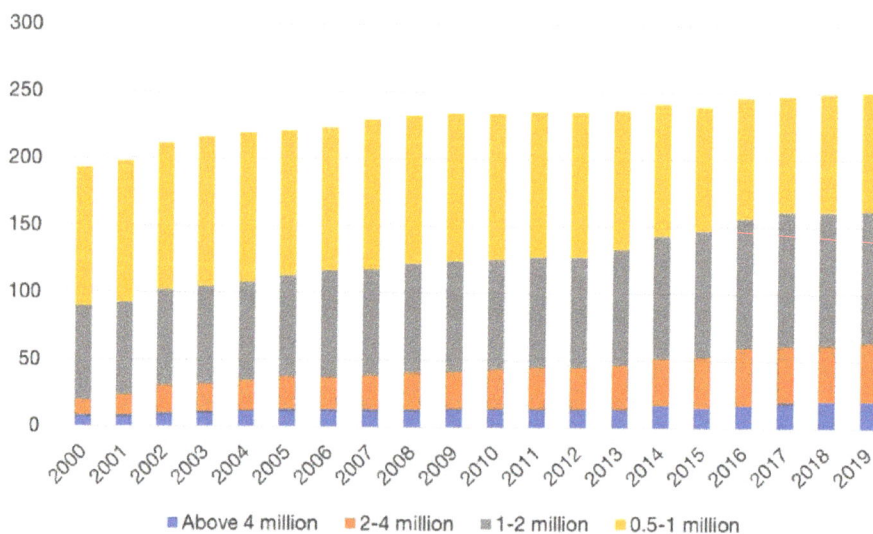

Figure 4.9 Number of China's prefecture-level cities, 2000–2019
Source: National Bureau of Statistics.

The comprehensive competitiveness of China's cities has increased significantly

After 70 years of urbanisation, China's urban economy has continued to expand. The urban industrial structure has been continuously optimised, while overall competitiveness has increased significantly. In the *Global Urban Competitiveness Report* for 2019–20, jointly released by the Chinese Academy of Social Sciences and the United Nations Human Settlement Program (CASS and UN-Habitat 2019), 103 of the 291 cities in China ranked higher than previously for competitiveness. Among them, Shenzhen, Shanghai, Hong Kong, Beijing and Guangzhou entered the world's top-20 competitive cities.

The appearance of cities and residents' lives have improved rapidly

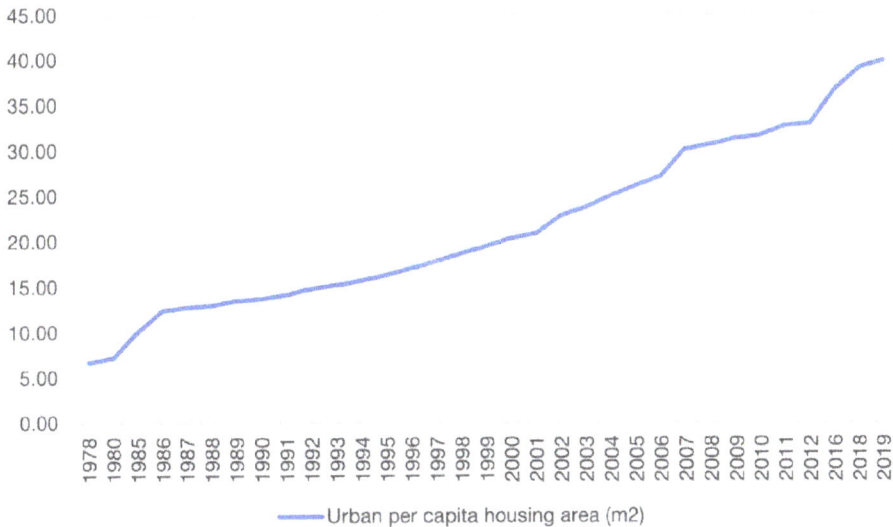

Figure 4.10 Changes in China's urban per capita housing area, 1978–2019
Source: National Bureau of Statistics.

With the advancement of urbanisation, shortages of public services and infrastructure such as urban water, power and gas supplies, drainage, sewerage and garbage disposal have been greatly alleviated, and residents' travel and living conditions have been greatly improved. In 2017, the area of country's urban road network reached 7.89 billion m². By the end of 2018, 35 cities had established rail transit networks, operating 185 lines, with a total length of 5,761.4 km. At the end of 2017, the urban water supply penetration rate was 98.3 per cent, the gas penetration rate was 96.3 per cent, the sewage treatment rate reached 95.5 per cent, the domestic garbage treatment rate reached 99.0 per cent and the treatment rate of sewage was 97.7 per cent. In 2018, China's urban average per capita housing area reached 39 square metres, on top of a 3.7-fold increase between 1949 and 1978 (Figure 4.10).

Continuous improvements in urban public services and governance systems

Today, China has essentially established a sustainable social insurance system with wide coverage and basic guarantees. Health and other urban public services have been continuously improved, while the process of guaranteeing more equal access to basic public services has been steadily advancing. The number of urban residents participating in pension insurance increased from 57.1 million in 1989 to 435 million in 2019, and the number of people participating in basic medical insurance likewise increased, from 42.9 million in 2007 to more than 1 billion in 2019 (Figure 4.11). Many cities in China are in the process of establishing cross-department, cross-industry and cross-regional-government information-sharing and business collaboration, accelerating the modernisation of urban governance.

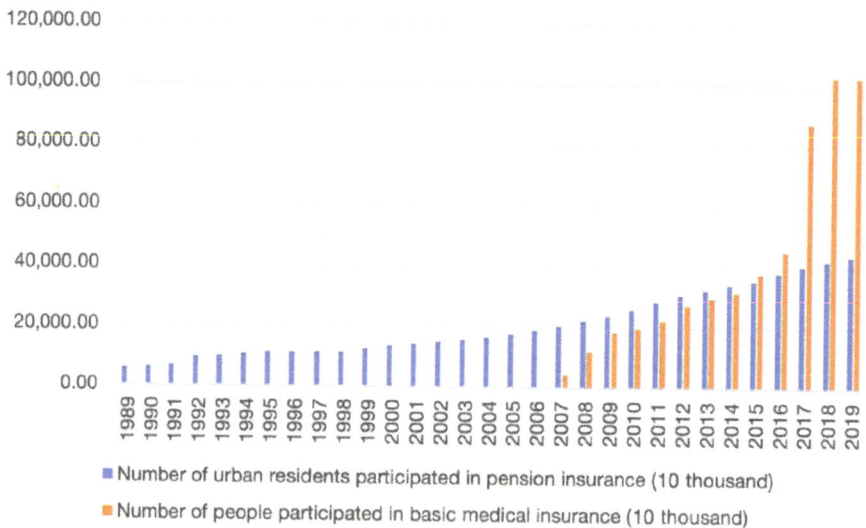

■ Number of urban residents participated in pension insurance (10 thousand)

■ Number of people participated in basic medical insurance (10 thousand)

Figure 4.11 The number of Chinese urban residents participating in pension insurance and basic medical insurance, 1989–2019

Source: National Bureau of Statistics.

The new industrial structure is dominated by the service industry

With reference to the changes in the industrial structure of developed economies at different stages of development, the value added of tertiary industry in the United States, the United Kingdom and France has come to account for more than 70 per cent of their respective GDP. On the other hand, advanced manufacturing in Germany and Japan developed well, and their proportion of secondary industry is significantly higher than that of other advanced economies. In 2019, the service industry accounted for 53.9 per cent of GDP in China, indicating it is the primary leader of the country's urbanisation. It is expected that the value added of China's tertiary industry in 2020, 2035 and 2050 will increase to 55.3 per cent, 63 per cent and 70 per cent of GDP, respectively. Overall, the process of urbanisation from 2020 to 2050 will see China's industrial structure undergo major adjustments and transformations. The potential for tertiary industry development is still large, while primary and secondary industries will continue their downward trend. A new type of industrial structure characterised by producer services and the integration of primary, secondary and tertiary industries will be gradually stabilised.

The impact of the new technological revolution on China's urbanisation

The new technological revolution and high-quality development of China's economy are highly intertwined and can provide major opportunities for ongoing urbanisation. This will not only effect the degree and speed of urbanisation, accelerating the development of metropolitan areas and urban agglomerations, but it will also improve levels of urban governance, gradually narrowing the gap both between regions and between urban and rural areas, while simultaneously promoting high-quality development.

Providing impetus for high-quality urbanisation

The main mechanism by which the new technological revolution will impact the high-quality development of cities will be the development of new production factors and industries, as well as the promotion of high-tech industries and productive services. Judged according to the current fields of application, digital technologies typified by big data, cloud computing, artificial intelligence and so on have already been put into large-scale commercial use. Additionally, smart manufacturing, new-energy vehicles, smart cities and mobile phone technology have rapidly multiplied and become new economic engines. The use of modern logistics and information and other technologies can further reduce the cost of urban–rural exchanges and promote the transfer of technology to the countryside, thereby improving agricultural productivity and efficiency, which is conducive to the continued transfer of rural surplus labour to the city.

Shenzhen is a typical example of high-quality urbanisation driven by the technological revolution. In 2019, Shenzhen was awarded approximately 12,000 patents from the Patent Cooperation Treaty (PCT)—the highest ranking in China. According to the *Report on High-Quality Development of Chinese Cities in 2020*, published by the 21st Century Economic Research Institute (2020), Shenzhen also ranks as the top city for high-quality development in China. Shenzhen has provided strong financial support for technological innovation, successfully aggregating technological industries and related employment. Another example is the Yangtze River Economic Belt urban agglomeration. An empirical study by Yang and Yang (2019) used indicators such as economic vitality, innovation efficiency, green development, people's quality of life and social harmony to show how the level of high-quality development in the Yangtze River Economic Belt has improved significantly. In terms of driving factors, technological innovation can significantly improve the level of a city's high-quality development, and it has a significantly higher promotional effect than other factors. Moreover, there is also an overlay effect for the urban clusters in the lower reaches of the Yangtze River where development quality is already high.

Promoting low-carbon, green and sustainable urban development modes

The new technological revolution is leading the low-carbon and green development of Chinese cities through industrial restructuring, which enhances the position of Chinese cities in the global value chain and industrial division of labour. Information technology and manufacturing are deeply integrated. Big data are generated through intelligent manufacturing. By changing the relative combination of production factors, the global industrial chain and division of labour will also be shifted. Second, the new technological revolution improves labour productivity and energy factor inputs. Reductions in carbon emissions in a single city are achieved without simply transferring high-emission industries to other cities, but by improving labour productivity and energy factor inputs through technological progress. Third, the new technological revolution changes the original production mode, which was extensive in scale but lacking in customisability. Intelligent, incremental manufacturing and other technologies can help realise customisation by incorporating user needs into production. Finally, the concept of green transportation will reshape citizens' behaviour. New transportation modes such as electric vehicles, the Internet of Vehicles and share-bicycles significantly lower the carbon emissions from urban transportation systems.

Empirical studies show that, during China's rapid urbanisation, industrial upgrading and rising incomes contributed to lower energy intensity in all regions (World Bank 2007). The China National Petroleum Corporation (CNPC 2017) estimated that non–fossil fuels will account for 35 per cent of primary energy generation in China by 2050, and carbon emission intensity will fall to 18 per cent of 2010 levels. Innovation in energy technology will see the levelised cost of electricity (LCOE) of photovoltaic power and wind power drop by 71 per cent and 58 per cent, respectively (Chen 2018). For example, the Xiong'an New Area has created a zero-carbon smart green-energy system and recently achieved 'carbon neutrality'. This was realised by taking advantage of its own geothermal energy and fully adopting technology systems such as multiple energy coordination, source–network–load–storage coordination, as well as centralised and distributed coordination via the energy internet. It is expected that zero carbon emissions can be achieved in the Xiong'an New Area through full reliance on renewable energies after 2040 (Guo and Gao 2018). New-energy electric vehicles (EVs) are the main breakthrough for China's automobile industry to overtake. Since 2014, the EV industry in China has reached sales of more than 1 million, ranking it first in the world (Chen 2009; Zhou 2018). According to Zheng et al. (2019), from 2011 to 2017, the top-five provinces for EV sales had reduced their carbon emissions by 612,000 tonnes (combined total).

Promoting the industrial and population capacities of cities

Most of the new types of businesses represented by the digital economy are located in large cities. They have become places of high efficiency, high concentrations of job opportunities, platform economies and innovative enterprises—all of which bring challenges to the capacities of cities. The new technological revolution has brought about continued improvements in metropolitan transportation systems: first, by replacing traditional radial modes of expansion of central and peripheral areas of a city. Interconnection and interoperability help to accelerate the co-urbanisation of metropolitan areas. Second, traffic congestion in large cities is eased, significantly increasing their population carrying capacity, thus making better use of the scale and density effects of population agglomeration. Third, the complementary effects of the functional division and spatial allocation of labour and other resources within the city are maximised, promoting the coordinated development of industry (Liu 2001).

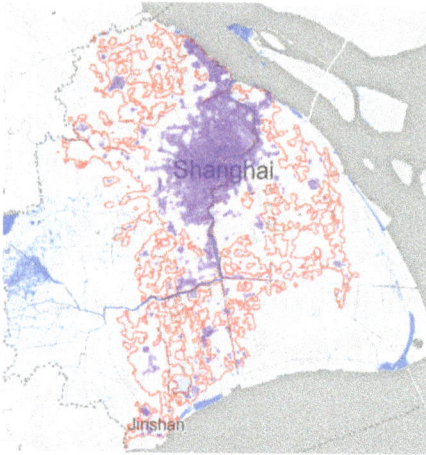

Figure 4.12(a) The spatial expansion of Shanghai City, 1991

Source: School of Transportation Engineering, Tongji University.

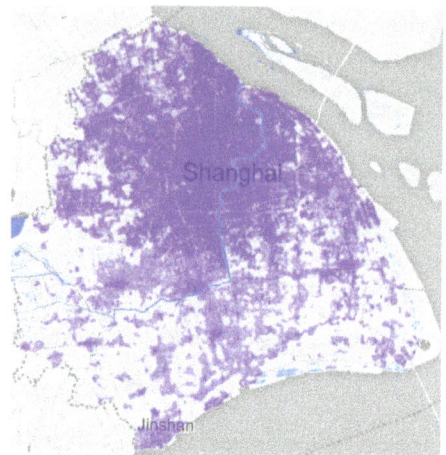

Figure 4.12(c) The spatial expansion of Shanghai City, 2015

Source: School of Transportation Engineering, Tongji University.

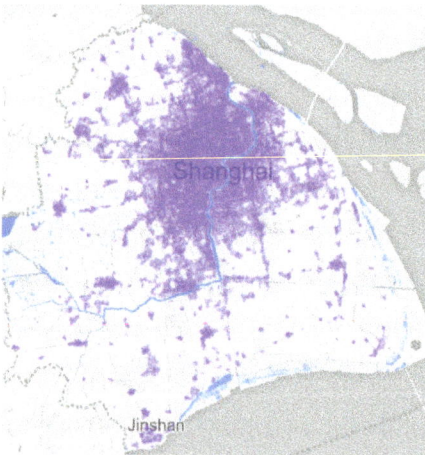

Figure 4.12(b) The spatial expansion of Shanghai City, 2000

Source: School of Transportation Engineering, Tongji University.

Taking Shanghai as an example, from 1990 to 2015, the amount of urban construction land increased by more than 1,500 sq km, and more than RMB1 trillion was invested in the construction of a comprehensive transportation system including hubs, highways, expressways and rail transit, to meet the transportation demands of expanding production activities (Figure 4.12). Urban residents' average daily travel increased from 4.5 km in 1995 to 6.9 km in 2014—a rise of more than 50 per cent (School of Transportation Engineering 2019). This increase indicates that residents have accessed more employment opportunities and more public services over a larger area. For example, Deng (2015) indicated that the Guangzhou–Zhuhai intercity rail improved the spatial agglomeration rate of primary and secondary industries by 20 per cent because they were particularly reliant on physical transportation. The increase in the population density of cities is as high as 2,246 people per sq km. It can be seen that intercity rail transit plays a very important role in promoting the overall development of urban agglomerations.

Improving the capacity of urban governance

Since the beginning of the reform and opening-up period, China's urban governance has undergone a transition from governments having overall control of the allocation of resources, through the planned economy to the application of institutional innovation and advanced technologies. The widespread application of digital and smart technologies in cities has promoted changes in urban management and improved the supply and efficiency of public services.

Let us take Hebi City, Henan Province, as an example. As a prefecture-level city in central China, Hebi is socioeconomically small compared with developed cities in the Yangtze and Pearl river deltas, and it lags on various economic indicators. However, with the local government's emphasis on the modernisation of urban governance and the construction of 'smart Hebi' and other digital government projects, the city's telecommunications business has grown rapidly and stimulated the development of thriving tertiary industries. The public's satisfaction with their participation in governance, levels of online services, emergency response times and public safety has reached above 88 per cent (Niu 2017). In addition, urban governance models such as 'grid management' have been successfully explored in many parts of China. As of 2012, more than 90 cities had adopted or were in the process of implementing grid management.

Resolving inequalities in the process of urbanisation

According to the 'China Comprehensive Social Survey 2008 to 2015', China's inequality of opportunity index fell from 0.254 in 2008 to 0.176 in 2015 (Li 2019: Figure 4.13). However, from a global perspective, the impact of China's inequality of opportunity on income inequality is still relatively high, and the rural inequality of opportunity index (0.1738 in 2015) remained higher than that of urban areas (0.0805 in 2015). There are obvious differences in environmental factors (gender, place of birth, social status of father, and so on) between urban and rural areas that result in inequality of opportunity. The inequality of opportunity caused by unequal access to education has decreased significantly in rural areas, but it is still higher than in urban areas.

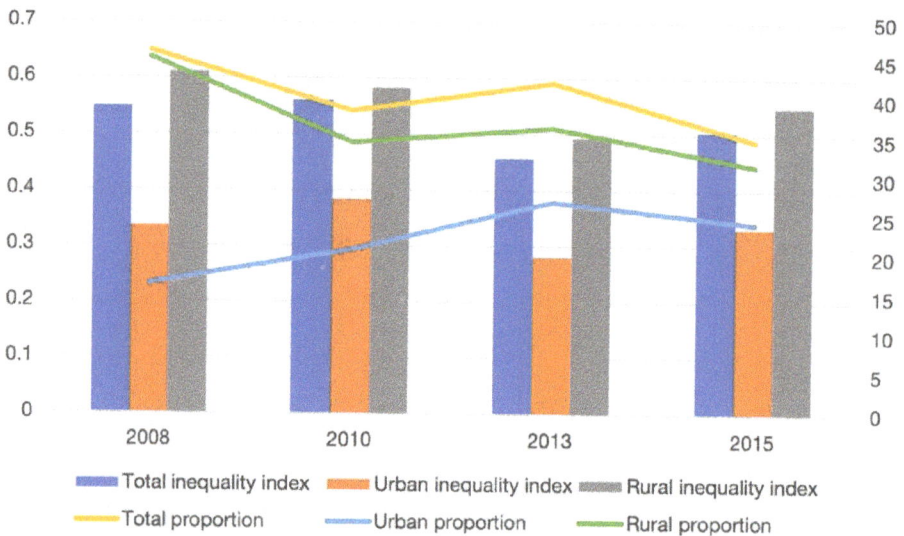

Figure 4.13 China's income inequality index and the proportion of inequality of opportunity
Source: Li (2019).

The new technological revolution will help close the urban–rural inequality gap in several ways. First, advances in agricultural technology (related to animal breeding, fertiliser use, irrigation, and so on) have a direct effect on increasing agricultural output and rural residents' incomes. The adoption of information and communication technologies (ICTs) such as mobile devices can also lower transaction costs, increasing market opportunities for the rural population (World Bank 2019). Second, significant improvements in rural education and investment in human capital will reduce the urban–rural income gap (Wang and Fan 2005). Finally, the revolution in information technology and the resulting changes to business and social security models will help boost rural economies (Picot and Lorenz 2010). The internet has a significant blocking effect on the income gap between urban and rural residents in China (Guo and Zhang 2019), of which inclusive digital finance is a very good example (Jia 2019).

However, various problems of inequality and imbalance may eventually become even more prominent. First, the extent to which technological changes can promote industry differs between cities, and the populations of unsuccessful cities will likely decrease rapidly. Second, the manufacturing industry is still an important sector for absorbing employment in China's central and western regions. In the short and medium terms, these regions may continue to suffer from the income-damaging effects of industrial transformation and face competition from emerging countries in Southeast Asia and Africa when undertaking industrial transfers from eastern China. The income gap between China's western and eastern regions may thus be widened. Finally, repetitive or low-skill work will be replaced with automation technologies. Due to the polarisation of service industry incomes, increases in market concentration and an increase in income gaps within large companies brought about by the technological revolution, income inequality within cities may be exacerbated in the short term.

The trend and outlook for China's urbanisation

China has now entered the late stage of its urbanisation acceleration period. According to general development laws, the leading industries driving urbanisation will shift to those in the service sector. Metropolitan areas will become the main spaces for population agglomeration, and population migration will gradually shift from rural–urban to intercity migration. Urban development will shift from rapid quantitative expansion to high-quality development. From the perspective of the macro-socioeconomic landscape, China will enter the ranks of upper-middle-income countries by 2035. Its economic, social and industrial structures will experience major changes, entering the high-quality development stage driven by service industries and led by consumption. China's road to urbanisation will be marked by improved quality and efficiency, scientific development models, continuous optimisation of urban systems and modernisation of governance systems.

The general trend of urbanisation between 2020 and 2050

By 2019, the urbanisation rate in China reached 60.6 per cent—higher than previous estimates by the Chinese Academy of Social Sciences (CASS). International experience shows that when countries achieve middle-income status, urbanisation rates will reach approximately 50 per cent, while all high-income countries display urbanisation rates above 70 per cent. According to our forecast, China's urbanisation rate will reach 72.4 per cent in 2035 and its per capita GDP will reach US$36,000 (World Bank, DRC and People's Republic of China 2014). Morgan Stanley's *The Rise of China's Super-Cities: New Era of Urbanisation* report predicted that China's urbanisation rate would reach 75 per cent by 2030. At the stage of high-quality and high-income development, China's economic and industrial structures will be more balanced and effective, innovation will play a more important role as a driver of development and the mechanism for urban agglomeration—in which large and small and medium-sized cities develop synergistically—will become more formalised.

China's urbanisation has entered a stage focused on the pursuit of high-quality development

Ray M. Northam (1979) showed that the urbanisation process could be summarised as a slightly flattened S-shaped curve. He took a rate of above 70 per cent as the indicator of the terminal stage of urbanisation (Table 4.1), while arguing that when the urbanisation rate exceeds 70 per cent, economic development will be dominated by tertiary and knowledge-intensive high-tech industries. Population growth will shift to a 'low birth rate and low mortality rate' pattern, the population growth rate will stabilise and differences between urban and rural areas will become smaller. According to the experiences of developed countries, the main driver of the terminal stage of urbanisation is the third technological revolution, represented by information technology, and globalisation. The information technology revolution then magnifies the differences between regions within a country and enterprises allocate resources and organise production nationally according to these differences. At this stage, there will be new divisions of production between cities.

At China's current stage of urbanisation, the competitiveness of cities and the vitality of their leading industries increasingly depend on the advantages acquired by the development of education, scientific research and institutional mechanisms, while the traditional advantages of geography and natural resources have already been relatively weakened. The various systems and policies of the city have taken basic shape and urban management has increasingly become subject to legal and standardised processes, making adjustment and reform difficult. For example, Zhao et al. (2015) compared the level of innovation in Shenzhen and Shanghai and found that, although Shanghai has more abundant educational resources, greater investment in social research and development and economic aggregates, Shenzhen is better than Shanghai in terms of patent output, the performance of strategic emerging industry development and innovative enterprise development. The main reasons for these differences are that Shenzhen has a better commercial atmosphere, a higher degree of marketisation, a more complete industrial support system, a more innovative and business-friendly financial system and more inclusive cultural environment. Therefore, in the late stage of urbanisation in China, more intensive institutional reforms are needed to further enhance cities' competitiveness and industrial vitality.

Table 4.1 Characteristics of and problems with the three stages of urbanisation

	Level and speed of urbanisation	Drivers of urbanisation	Industrial structure	Problems and trends
Initial stage	10–30%; population slowly gathers in cities	Light-industry development	Mainly agriculture, supplemented by light industry	Insufficient infrastructure, the urban death rate exceeds the rural rate
Accelerating stage	30–50%; population accelerating towards urban agglomeration	Heavy and chemical industry development	Heavy and chemical industries	Traffic congestion, housing shortages, environmental degradation, and suburbanisation trend
	50–70%; urban population growth slows	Producer and life services	Equal emphasis on heavy and chemical industries and service industry	Urban infrastructure and sanitation conditions begin to improve
Late stage	70% or above; the proportion of urban population in the total stabilises	Informatisation and globalisation	Service and high-tech industries	Coexistence of agglomeration and dispersion

China's urbanisation development prospects

At present, China's urbanisation has entered the new era of its development, and 2020–50 will be a crucial period. In the first half of urbanisation, the development of cities was focused chiefly on growth rates. However, with the transformation and upgrading of urban industries, cities will in future focus on the requirements for high-quality development, including improving the quality and efficiency of urbanisation and forming a low-carbon, green and efficient urban development model, while continuing to modernise urban governance.

Urbanisation quality and efficiency have improved significantly

The new technological revolution will improve the quality and efficiency of development of Chinese cities. Cities with an economy of scale and complete infrastructure will attract innovative elements such as technology, knowledge, human talent and funds. Relying on a city's huge consumer market, industry can smoothly shift from labour intensive to knowledge and technology intensive, thus enhancing regional economic vitality. A number of new industries, enterprises and products will emerge and effectively guarantee the long-term competitiveness of the city.

The urban development model is more scientific and reasonable

By 2050, China's urban spatial resources will likely be better utilised, urban planning will be more refined and the urban environment more liveable. Cities will no longer blindly expand in size or rely on land transfers to promote urban construction. In the future, the development of Chinese cities will ideally be focused on social, economic and ecological quality. City managers should also be more focused on guiding urban spatial planning, maintaining a reasonable and moderate development intensity and sustaining harmony between humans and nature. They should establish a sustainable investment and financing model and the focus of investment will have to shift to enhancing the city's overall competitiveness and meeting a higher level of residents' needs. The investment and financing system will be market-oriented and use policy funds such as local bonds, local fiscal revenue and development finance to attract social capital.

Continuous optimisation of urban systems and patterns

From 2020 to 2050, the main body of spatial development will be urban agglomerations, and the effect of the coordinated development of large, medium and small cities will be fully manifest. By 2050, China's three major urban agglomerations are expected to be home to 30 per cent of the population and generate more than 60 per cent of GDP. At the same time, in areas where resources and environmental carrying capacities are stronger—such as Chengdu–Chongqing, the Central Plain and the middle reaches of the Yangtze River in China's west and centre, as well as Harbin–Changchun in the north-east—several urban agglomerations will have been cultivated to promote a balance between population and economic distribution. It is estimated that, by 2050, China's 19 urban agglomerations will attract more than 80 per cent of the country's urban population and occupy about 65 per cent of the country's urban construction land.

The modernisation level of the urban governance system is improved

Deep integration of the internet, big data, artificial intelligence and other technologies with urban governance systems can greatly improve China's urban management, improve the intelligence, convenience and proximity of public services and effectively resolve various 'urban diseases'. City management centres will encourage more citizens to participate in urban management and community self-governance activities. Social security, education, medical care and infrastructure will be further improved.

Strategic choices to promote high-quality development of Chinese cities

According to the 'three-step' deployment proposed at the Nineteenth National Congress of the Chinese Communist Party, a 'well-off society' will be built by 2020, socialist modernisation will have been achieved by 2035 and a modernised socialist country will have been established by 2050. In the next stage of urbanisation, China must establish goals of high-efficiency, low-carbon, green and inclusive development for industry, socioeconomic systems, markets and technology to construct a new path of urbanisation. The development and application of new technological innovation represent a new opportunity for China, while the potential of its huge domestic market and the institutional dividend brought about by new rounds of reform and opening up are unique driving mechanisms of urbanisation.

Strengthening the supporting effect of industries

At the end of 2018, the added value of China's service industry accounted for only 53.3 per cent of GDP, which was still far below the average level of 74 per cent for developed countries. The service industry is the largest contributor to employment. In the process of urbanisation, population agglomeration, changes in lifestyle and improvements in living standards will serve to expand the demand for consumer services. The optimal allocation of production factors, the linkage of the three industrial sectors and refinement of the social divisions of production will also expand the demand for services. In addition, with further improvements in technology and mechanisation levels in agriculture and changes in agricultural production organisation and business models, agricultural productivity will continue to increase, providing a relatively sufficient labour force for the urban sector.

Active integration in the new technological revolution to enhance cities' innovation capability

After years of hard work, China's overall levels of technological advancement and capacity for innovation have been significantly improved. Some important fields are among the best in the world and some industries are now positioned at the high end of the global value chain. Applications and breakthroughs are showing up in the new generation of information technology, typified by advances in artificial intelligence, quantum information, mobile communications, the Internet of Things and blockchain technology. Since the 2018 Central Economic Working Conference, policies and implementation plans related to the 'new infrastructure' have been deployed and promoted. On the demand side, new infrastructure will help stabilise growth and employment, serve consumption upgrades and better meet the Chinese population's need for a better life. On the supply side, new infrastructure will create the basic conditions for innovation and development, especially as China moves to seize the heights of global technological innovation. For example: since 2014, Shanghai has accelerated the construction of a 'science and innovation centre with global influence' and introduced a series of measures such as '22 Options on Scientific and Technological Innovation' and 'Implementation Opinions on Promoting the Development of New Generation Artificial Intelligence'. In May 2020, the Shanghai Municipal Government issued the 'Shanghai Action Plan for Promoting New Infrastructure Construction (2020–2022)', involving 48 major projects and an estimated total investment of RMB270 billion.

Making full use of the development potential of a large domestic market

To advance the process of urbanisation, China must make full use and unleash the potential of its massive domestic market. The increase in the level of urbanisation and public services has led to the continuous expansion of urban consumer groups and the upgrading of the consumption structure and potential, which have provided continued impetus for economic development. There is still a lot of room for regional rebalancing in the urbanisation process. The Yangtze River Delta, Pearl River Delta and other regions embarked early on a high-quality development track, while the development advantages of megacities such as Beijing, Shanghai, Guangzhou and Shenzhen continue to increase. Additionally, large cities such as Hangzhou, Nanjing, Wuhan, Zhengzhou, Chengdu and Xi'an have also already formed new regional growth poles.

Unlocking the institutional dividends brought by the new round of reform and opening up

In the middle and late stages of urbanisation, the institutional barriers that hinder development still exist and the institutional dividends of reform and opening up are still vast. First, it is necessary to realise the marketisation of migrant workers and the equalisation of basic public services through the reform of the household registration system (*hukou*) to rapidly increase China's total factor productivity. Second, the factor market should be reformed by removing the barriers to the free flow of labour, land, capital, technology, information and other factors. The interactive two-way flow of factors between urban and rural areas should be actively encouraged. Next, industrial competitiveness should be promoted by reforming monopolistic industries, breaking both administrative and natural monopolies. The principle of competitive neutrality should be introduced to improve industrial competitiveness. Finally, the international competitiveness of Chinese cities can be improved by implementing a proactive opening policy. This includes seizing the opportunity of a new round of major projects exemplified by the Belt and Road Initiative, the Hainan Free Trade Island and Shanghai Free Trade Zone, as well as the opening and further expansion of the service and high-end manufacturing industries.

Conclusions

China's urbanisation model is endogenous to its economic development path and model of industrial structural change. Since the period of reform and opening up, China's economy has rapidly integrated into the global economic system and its urban industrial structure has undergone transformation and upgrading. The new technological revolution and high-quality development of China's economy will provide significant opportunities for high-quality urbanisation in China. In the next stage, China must establish a goal of high-efficiency, low-carbon, green and inclusive urbanisation for industry, socioeconomic systems, markets and technology to build a new urban development path. The new technological revolution will effectively transform and upgrade cities' traditional manufacturing industries and generate a large number of new industries that are technology and knowledge intensive, especially in the services sector. China's huge domestic market potential and the institutional dividends brought by the new round of reform and opening up will be a unique driving force of urbanisation.

References

21st Century Economic Research Institute (2020), *Report on the High-Quality Development of Chinese Cities in 2020,* [In Chinese], Beijing.

Chen, M. (2018), Activating the 'era of parity' in photovoltaics, [In Chinese], *China Electric Power Enterprise Management* (6).

Chen, Q. (2009), *Grasp the Historical Opportunity of New Energy Vehicles*, [In Chinese], Research Report, Beijing: State Council Development Research Center.

China National Petroleum Corporation (CNPC) (2017), *China Energy Outlook 2050*, Beijing: CNPC.

Chinese Academy of Social Sciences (CASS) and United Nations Human Settlement Program (UN-Habitat) (2019), *Global Urban Competitiveness Report*, Shenzhen: CASS and UN-Habitat.

Deng, Y. (2015), Research on the evolution and coordination of the intercity rail and the spatial structure of urban agglomeration, PhD thesis, Northern Jiaotong University, Beijing.

Guo, J. and Gao, S. (2018), *The Realization Path of the Zero-Carbon Smart Green Energy System in Xiong'an New Area*, [In Chinese], Research Report, Beijing: Development Research Center of the State Council.

Guo, J. and Zhang, Y. (2019), Can the internet block the widening income gap between urban and rural residents? An empirical study based on China's provincial panel data, *Shanghai Economy* 6.

Jia, J. (2019), Digital dividend or digital gap? How can digital inclusive finance narrow the income gap?, *Journal of Regional Financial Research* 12.

Li, Y. (2019), *The Formation Mechanism and Countermeasures for the Evolution of Inequality of Opportunity in My Country's Income Distribution*, [In Chinese], Research Report, Beijing: Development Research Center of the State Council.

Liu, S. (2001), *Beijing City Structure Improvement: Problems and Countermeasures*, [In Chinese], Research Report, Beijing: Development Research Center of the State Council.

Morgan Stanley (2019), *The Rise of China's Super-Cities: New Era of Urbanisation*, New York: Morgan Stanley.

Niu, Z. (2017), A study on the influence of big data on the modernisation of governance: A case study in Hebi Municipality, Henan Province, PhD thesis, China Agricultural University, Beijing.

Northam, R. M. (1979), *Urban Geography*. New York: John Wiley.

Picot, A. and Lorenz, J. (2010), *ICT for the Next Five Billion People: Information and Communication for Sustainable Development*, Berlin: Springer-Verlag. doi. org/10.1007/978-3-642-12225-5.

School of Transportation Engineering (2019), *Transformation of Transportation Technology and Urbanization in China*, [In Chinese], Shanghai: Tongji University.

State Infrastructure Commission of the People's Republic of China (1980), *Summary of National Urban Planning Conference*, [in Chinese], available from: www.mohurd.gov.cn/ wjfb/200611/t20061101_155448.html.

Wang, X. and Fan, G. (2005), Analysis of the trend and influencing factors of China's income gap, *Economic Research Journal* (10).

World Bank (2007), *Structural Change and Energy Use: Evidence from China's Provinces*, China Working Paper Series No. 6, Washington, DC: World Bank Group.

World Bank (2019), *Improving the Measurement of Rural Women's Employment: Global Momentum and Survey Research Priorities*, Policy Research Working Paper, Washington, DC: World Bank Group.

World Bank, Development Research Center (DRC) and the People's Republic of China (2014), *Urban China: Toward Efficient, Inclusive, and Sustainable Urbanization*. Washington, DC: World Bank.

Yang, R. and Yang, C. (2019), The high-quality development measurement of the Yangtze River Economic Belt and the evolution of time and space, *Journal of Central China Normal University* 53(5).

Zhao, C., Zhu, H. and Huang, S. (2015), *Innovative Breakthrough: Why Shenzhen?*, [In Chinese], Research Report, Beijing: Development Research Center of the State Council.

Zheng, J., Sun, X., Jia, L. and Zhou, Y. (2019), Electric passenger vehicle sales and carbon dioxide emission reduction potential in China's leading markets, *Journal of Cleaner Production* 243: 118607. doi.org/10.1016/j.jclepro.2019.118607.

Zhou, Y. (2018), *Several Recommendations on the Development of New Energy Automobile Industry*, [In Chinese], Research Report, Beijing: Development Research Center of the State Council.

5

Revenue-neutral tax reform in China

Yanchao Xu and Shawn Xiaoguang Chen

Introduction

As China's decades-long phenomenal economic growth gradually loses momentum, the tension between cutting taxes to promote growth and maintaining fiscal revenue looms large for the country's governments. From 1978 to 2011, the average growth rate of China's economy was more than 9 per cent. Since 2012, it has entered the so-called 'new normal' of declining growth. Over the past three years, the downward pressure has further strengthened. The new domestic and international economic situation has brought challenges to fiscal and monetary policies. Fiscal and tax reforms characterised by tax and fee reductions (*jianfei jiangshui*) have emerged as key policies for three reasons. First, expansionary monetary policy is already bounded by global low interest rates. Additionally, monetary policy is expected to remain stable due to concerns about asset bubbles and inflation. Second, conventional fiscal stimulus through public investment is already subject to diminishing marginal effects. Third, the general consensus holds that many businesses in China are suffocating from rising costs and high taxes. Therefore, reducing taxes and fees seems to be an inevitable policy choice for Chinese governments.

To reduce the burden on firms and restore market vitality, the Central Committee of the Chinese Communist Party and the State Council have continued in recent years to introduce policies and measures to cut taxes and fees.[1] However, given the current economic situation and the fiscal and taxation systems, these tax cuts led to a decline in revenue. On 1 May 2018, the value-added tax (VAT) rate for manufacturing and other industries decreased from 17 per cent to 16 per cent and the rate for transportation and other industries decreased from 11 per cent to 10 per cent. The scale of VAT reduction from May to December 2018 was about RMB270 billion. Based on this rough calculation, if the VAT is reduced by 1 percentage point, China's annual tax revenue will drop by RMB462.86 billion, which is 7.52 per cent of China's domestic VAT revenue in 2018 and 2.5 per cent of the national general public budget. The amount exceeds the government's total expenditure on culture, sport and media, and is close to its total expenditure on environmental protection. On 1 April 2019, the Ministry of Finance, the State Taxation Administration and the General Administration of Customs released 'Circular No. 39 of 2019', stipulating that, for general VAT taxpayers in China, taxable sales of imported goods would be adjusted from 16 per cent to 13 per cent; tax rates originally applicable at 10 per cent would be adjusted to 9 per cent. In a press conference held by the State Taxation Administration on 23 July 2019, Cai Zili, executive deputy director of the Taxation Reduction Office and director of the Department of Revenue Planning and Accounting, stated that, from April to June 2019, net VAT reductions reached RMB318.5 billion (State Taxation Administration of China 2019b). Based on our calculations, the net reduction of VAT in those three months exceeded total expenditure on energy conservation and environmental protection for the first half of 2019.

The decline in tax revenue may harm the economy. Due to rigid demand for local fiscal expenditure, 'tax reduction and fee reduction' may turn into 'tax reduction and fee increase'. This is not only consistent with the typical response of local governments, but also confirmed by recent tax and non-tax revenue data.[2] If this happens, the policy goal of stimulating business vitality through tax and fee reductions will be difficult to achieve. Guo (2019) believes ongoing tax and fee reductions will see

---

1   Especially since 1 April 2019, China's manufacturing VAT rate has been reduced from 16 per cent to 13 per cent. The VAT rates in construction and other industries have been reduced from 10 per cent to 9 per cent. On 22 March 2019, the *Economic Daily* asked in the headline to the story about the tariff reduction measures, 'Unclear: Do we mean "the largest tax cuts in history"?' (Sohu Technology 2019).

2   According to the Ministry of Finance's 'Financial Revenue and Expenditure in the First Half of 2019', released on 13 July 2019, national tax revenue in the first half of 2019 increased by 0.9 per cent year-on-year, and non-tax revenue increased by 21.4 per cent year-on-year (State Taxation Administration of China 2019a). On 10 May 2019, Premier Li Keqiang clearly emphasised at the panel discussion on the implementation of the tax reduction and fee reduction policy that '[we must] resolutely prevent the use of various names to arbitrarily charge fees, and we must not allow anyone to hinder tax reduction and fee reduction' (China Network of Court 2019). Guo (2019) shows that in total local government fiscal revenue, the proportion of the general public budget revenue fell from 46.4 per cent in 2015 to 40.5 per cent in 2018, while the proportion of government funding revenue continued to increase, from 22.1 per cent to 29.9 per cent.

the fiscal deficits and revenues of governments at all levels significantly affected and may trigger fiscal risks. Due to a lack of new tax sources, local governments will have to borrow in response to falling fiscal revenues, which may worsen local debt problems. Furthermore, the decline in tax revenue may lead local governments to reduce expenditure on education and public security, resulting in adverse effects on social equity, human capital accumulation and social stability.[3]

The main constraint facing China's fiscal policy is how to reduce taxes and fees while securing fiscal revenue. Scholars in China have proposed various policy solutions.[4] In this study, we propose a revenue-neutral reform characterised by 'rate cuts and productivity enhancement'—that is, by reducing the statutory tax rate ('rate cut'), strengthening tax enforcement and administration, reducing disparities in effective tax rates among firms and improving aggregate production efficiency ('productivity enhancement'), governments can maintain tax revenue from a greater tax base. This chapter combines the classic Allingham and Sandmo (1972) tax-evasion model, Hopenhayn's (2014) resource misallocation model and Olley and Pakes' (1996) productivity theory to analyse the feasibility of revenue-neutral reform. Based on the *National Statistics on Prefecture, City, and County Finance* for 2000 to 2007 (Ministry of Finance 2000–07), and annual firm-level data from the *Annual Survey of Industrial Production* (NBS 2000–07), we use the abolition of agricultural taxes in 2005 as a fiscal shock to county governments to study the impact on tax enforcement and subsequent allocation efficiency across firms. Based on the estimated key parameters from the reduced-form regressions, we estimate the lower bound for the VAT rate deduction under the revenue-neutral reform model. We show that improved tax enforcement can reduce the effective tax rate difference between firms and enhance aggregate productivity. The estimation results show that, in an ideal scenario where all firms uniformly pay the statutory tax rate, the rate can be reduced to around 13 per cent without changing tax revenue.

The preconditions of the revenue-neutral reform we propose are that China's tax enforcement and administration are subject to serious problems. Many empirical studies have provided direct evidence of the discretionary power of local governments, even when it comes to VAT collection, which is usually thought to be very strictly enforced. For example, Chen (2017b) used the abolition of China's agricultural taxes in 2005 as a quasi-natural experiment and found that the VAT rate of firms in counties with greater fiscal pressure after the reform increased significantly. Lu and Guo (2011) believe improvements in tax enforcement and administration are the main cause of increases in tax revenue.

---

3   After local government revenues decreased, education expenditures have decreased significantly.
4   For example, Guo (2019) proposed measures to address fiscal risks caused by tax and fee reductions by formulating fiscal consolidation strategies, strengthening fiscal governance and implementing tax expenditure budgets.

Moreover, weak tax enforcement leads to dispersion in effective tax rates across firms. Of course, we may expect this dispersion to gradually decrease with the simplification of tax rates and adoption of tax-collection technology; however, several recent studies show, surprisingly, that the dispersion in the effective tax rate across firms did not in fact decline between 2007 and 2017 (Bai et al. 2019; Lu 2019).

According to theories of misallocation (Restuccia and Rogerson 2008; Hsieh and Klenow 2009), dispersion in tax rates across firms can lead to the misallocation of resources among firms and reduce aggregate productivity. Chen (2017b) found that there is a big difference between the statutory VAT rate and the effective tax rate in China,[5] and the total factor productivity (TFP) loss caused by dispersion in the VAT rate was as high as 7.9 per cent.

Existing studies of tax and fee reductions in China mainly aim to reduce the burden on firms. Few have analysed resource allocation at the macro-level or aggregate productivity. Our study makes the following contributions to the literature: first, we theoretically study the feasibility of revenue-neutral reform and its underlying mechanisms, which are based on a positive feedback loop of 'lower tax rate → better tax enforcement and compliance → higher productivity → greater tax base → lower tax rate'. Second, using the estimates of key parameters, we calculate the lower bound of the statutory VAT rate that is able to sustain revenue-neutral reform.

The rest of the chapter is organised as follows: section two proposes a theoretical model; section three conducts the empirical work; section four quantifies the lower bound of the VAT rate deduction under the revenue-neutral reform; while section five concludes.

Theoretical model

This section proposes a model to explain the key mechanisms underlying the proposed revenue-neutral reform. The model includes firms' tax-evasion behaviour and production and governments' tax enforcement. The model features two mechanisms. On the one hand, strict tax enforcement and administration can reduce the dispersion in effective tax rates across firms, thereby improving the efficiency of resource allocation. On the other, a reduction in the statutory tax rate leads to better compliance, which consequently reduces effective tax rate disparities across firms and further improves aggregate productivity. In the end, 'rate reduction' and

---

5   Bai et al. (2019) use data from the 2007–15 China Tax Survey on corporate taxation inequality to show that, for Chinese companies, the actual tax rate has actually increased since 2009. Lu (2019) showed the discretionary tax enforcement in total taxation, VAT and corporate income tax using Chinese listed-company data for 2008–17, and suggested there is no downward trend in the actual tax rate.

'productivity enhancement' form a virtuous cycle. To verify whether the theoretical model is in line with China's current reality, we formulate testable propositions from the model to guide our empirical work.

Framework

Assume that all firms are facing the same statutory tax rate, t. Due to the lack of strict tax enforcement and administration, firms are evading tax to varying degrees; τ_t is the effective tax rate for company i.

Definition 1: Strict tax enforcement and administration refer to $\tau_i = t$ for $\forall i$. Lax tax enforcement and administration mean the following two conditions hold at the same time:

- The effective tax rate of some firms is lower than the statutory tax rate, $\tau_i \leq t$ for $\forall i$ and $\exists i$, such that $\tau_i < t$.
- There are dispersions in effective tax rates between firms—that is: $\text{var}(\tau_i) > 0$.[6]

We introduce the parameter $\varepsilon \in [0,+\infty)$, which represents the degree of tax enforcement and administration; $\text{var}(\tau_i)$ is a decreasing function in ε. When enforcement is very strict, we have $\varepsilon \rightarrow +\infty$, thus $\text{var}(\tau_i)$. When collection is abnormally lax, we have $\varepsilon \rightarrow 0$ and $\text{var}(\tau_i) \rightarrow +\infty$.

Let y_i be the output of firm i, p_i is the corresponding price, Y is total output and P the price, which is normalised to 1.

Government tax revenue is shown as Equation 5.1.

Equation 5.1

$$T = \Sigma_i \tau_i p_i y_i = \bar{\tau} PY$$

In Equation 5.1, $\bar{\tau} = \Sigma_i w_i \cdot \tau_i$ is the macro effective tax rate, which is the weighted average of the firm's effective tax rate, τ_i; the weight is $w_i = \dfrac{p_i y_i}{PY}$ and content is $\Sigma_i p_i y_i = PY$.

To facilitate analysis, we assume that the production function satisfies the form of AK; k_i is the capital stock of firm i and the total capital is $k = \Sigma_i k_i$.[7] The aggregate production function is $Y = TFP \cdot K$, where TFP represents the aggregate total factor productivity. If there is dispersion in effective tax rates between firms, the misallocation will reduce the TFP to a level lower than TFP^e at which resources are efficiently allocated. With $P = 1$, Equation 5.1 can be written as Equation 5.2.

---

6   We ignore the rare case of $\tau_i \leq t$ for $\forall i$, and $\text{var}(\tau_i) > 0$.
7   The conclusion of the Cobb–Douglas production function still holds. We use the AK model for convenience of exposition.

Equation 5.2

$T = \bar{\tau} \cdot TFP \cdot K$

In Equation 5.2, capital, K, is a function of the effective tax rate.

Under circumstances in which the effect of tax rate reduction on investment is small, tax revenue is at the rising part on the left side of the Laffer curve. There is a tension between tax rate reduction and maintaining tax revenue. To simplify the analysis, we make the following assumptions.

Assumption 1: $-d\ln K / d\ln\bar{\tau} < 1$. That is, the elasticity of net investment to the effective macro tax rate is less than 1, and the tax incentive for investment is small.

Generally, $\bar{\tau}$ is a function of the statutory tax rate, t. Additionally, the level of tax enforcement and administration, ε, also affects $\bar{\tau}$ and TFP. The relationships can be represented, respectively, by $\bar{\tau}(t;\varepsilon)$ and $TFP(\varepsilon)$, for which we formulate the following two assumptions.

Assumption 2: When tax collection is strict ($\varepsilon = +\infty$), we have $\bar{\tau}(t;\varepsilon) = t$. When tax collection is lax ($\varepsilon < +\infty$), we have $\bar{\tau}(0;\varepsilon) = 0$ if $t = 0$ and $\bar{\tau} = 0$; and, for a given tax enforcement intensity, ε, we have $\bar{\tau}(t;\varepsilon) < t$ and $0 < \partial\bar{\tau}(t;\varepsilon)/\partial t \leq 1$. That is, when the statutory tax rate is zero, the macro effective tax rate is also zero; the macro effective tax rate, $\bar{\tau}$, is lower than the statutory tax rate, t, and increases as the statutory tax rate rises.

Assumption 3: $\partial\bar{\tau}(t;\varepsilon)/\partial\varepsilon > 0$, $dTFP(\varepsilon)/d\varepsilon > 0$. Both the macro effective tax rate, $\bar{\tau}(t;\varepsilon)$, and $TFP(\varepsilon)$ increase as the tax enforcement intensity, ε, increases.

Based on Assumptions 1–3, we will analyse the properties of the Laffer curve when the tax enforcement intensity, ε, varies.

The Laffer curve reflects the relationship between tax, T, and the statutory tax rate, t, for a given level of tax enforcement and administration. According to the analysis above, we know: $T(t;\varepsilon) = \bar{\tau}(t;\varepsilon) \cdot TFP(\varepsilon) \cdot K(\bar{\tau}(t;\varepsilon))$.

Given the tax enforcement intensity, ε, the relationship between tax, $T(t;\varepsilon)$, and the statutory tax rate, t, is the Laffer curve, and $\partial\bar{\tau}(t;\varepsilon) / \partial t$ indicates the monotonicity of the Laffer curve. Given a statutory tax rate, t, the tax, $T(t;\varepsilon)$, changes with the tax enforcement intensity, ε, and different values of ε correspond to different Laffer curves.

Let the Laffer curve under strict tax-collection conditions ($\varepsilon = +\infty$) be $T^\varepsilon(t)$, and under lax collection conditions the Laffer curve is $T(t;\varepsilon)$. The following two propositions hold.

Proposition 1: Under Assumptions 1–3, the Laffer curve, $T(t;\varepsilon)$, monotonically increases with the statutory tax rate, t, and the Laffer curve with a low level of tax enforcement is located below that with a high level of enforcement.

Since the Laffer curve, $T(t;\varepsilon)$, increases monotonically with the statutory tax rate, t, lowering the tax rate will inevitably lead to lower taxes. However, Proposition 2 shows that, by strengthening tax enforcement and administration, the government can reduce tax rates and ensure that revenues remain unchanged, which means it is feasible to launch a revenue-neutral reform with tax rate reduction.

Proposition 2: Under the condition that the taxation income, $T(t;\varepsilon) \equiv \bar{T}$, is unchanged, we have $\Delta t = -\frac{\partial T/\partial \varepsilon}{\partial T/\partial t} \cdot \Delta\varepsilon$, and the statutory tax rate, t, and the tax enforcement intensity, ε, are inversely changed.

Propositions 1–2 can be shown in Figure 5.1, where the horizontal axis represents the statutory tax rate and the vertical axis is total tax revenue. $T^\varepsilon(t)$ represents the Laffer curve under completely strict management conditions. $T(t;\varepsilon_0)$ is the Laffer curve with statutory tax rate t and collection level ε_0. When the statutory tax rate is t_0, the total tax revenue is $\bar{T}$. The equilibrium point is at A. When the statutory tax rate is unchanged and the tax enforcement and administration level is increased from ε_0 to ε_1, the Laffer curve rises from $T(t;\varepsilon_0)$ to $T(t;\varepsilon_1)$, the equilibrium point becomes point B and the total tax revenue corresponding to point B is higher than $\bar{T}$. In a revenue-neutral reform, we can reduce the statutory tax rate to t_1 and move the equilibrium from point B to point C. As the equilibrium point changes from point A to point C, total tax revenue remains unchanged, the level of tax enforcement and administration increases from ε_0 to ε_1 and the statutory tax rate decreases from t_0 to t_1. The variation in T from point A to point B can be captured by $\partial T / \partial \varepsilon$, and that from point B to point C by $\partial T / \partial t$.

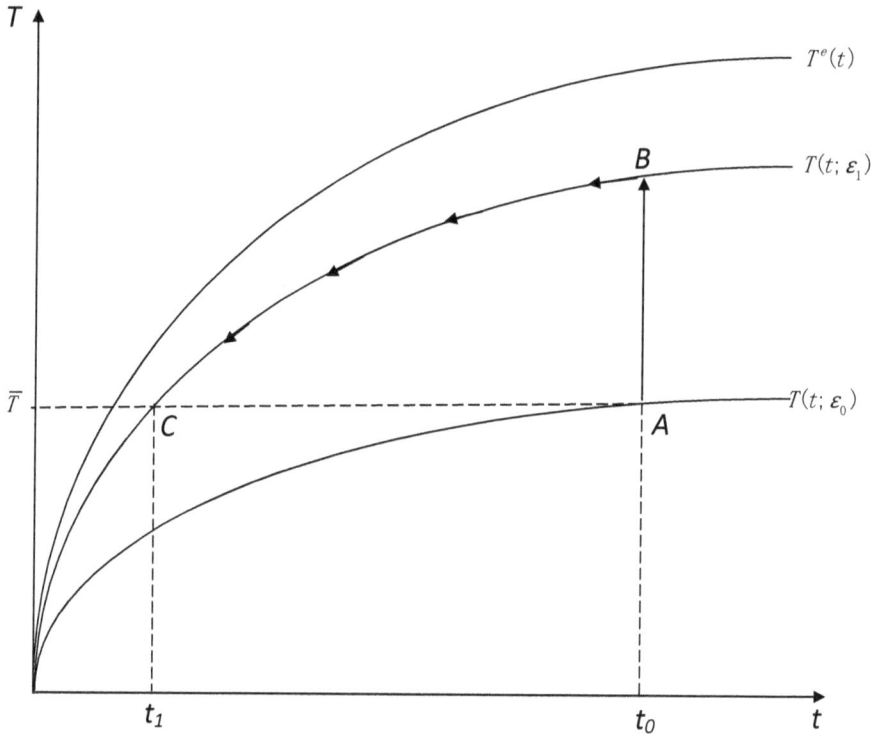

Figure 5.1 Tax enforcement and the Laffer curve
Source: Authors' calculations.

Micro-foundation of the Laffer curve

This section provides the micro-foundation for the Laffer curve shown in Figure 5.1. It consists of two parts: firms' tax evasion and firms' production. For analytical convenience, the model assumes that firms' tax evasion and production are handled by different departments. The financial department is responsible for taxation and the production department for hiring labour and producing goods.

Analysis of firms' tax evasion

Drawing on the classic model of Allingham and Sandmo (1972), this section analyses how the effective tax rate of a firm in the presence of tax evasion is affected by the following three policies of the tax department: tax audit (probability η_i), tax evasion penalty (variable F_i) and the statutory tax rate, t. In the model, the statutory tax, t, applies to all firms, but due to the existence of tax discretion and tax cost differences, η_i and F_i differ from firm to firm, resulting in different equilibrium effective tax rates, τ_i, across firms, further generating resource misallocation and loss of aggregate productivity.

Assuming the government levies taxes on total sales revenue, the sales revenue of firm i is s_i, the statutory tax base is t, the revenue reported by the firm to the tax department is x_i, and the amount of tax evasion by the firm is $t(s_i-x_i)$. The probability that the government will conduct tax audits on firms is η_i. In the presence of an audit, firms' tax evasion will be detected. Firms not only need to pay the tax in full, but also face a penalty of $F_i \cdot (s_i-x_i)$, where F_i is a fixed constant. For the sake of calculation, we assume that the utility function of the firms' financial department is Equation 5.3.

Equation 5.3

$$\max_{x_i}(1-\eta_i)u(c_n) = \eta_i u(c_f)$$

In Equation 5.3, $u(\cdot)$ is the state utility function; $c_n = s_t - tx_i$ is the after-tax income when tax evasion was not caught; otherwise, $c_f = (1-t)s_t - F_i \cdot (s_i-x_i)$ is the net income after tax payment and fines.

The firm's optimal tax declaration decision, x_i^*, is determined by the following first-order conditions (Equation 5.4).

Equation 5.4

$$\frac{(1-\eta_i)}{(F_i \eta_i)} = \frac{u'[(1-t)s_i - F \cdot t(s_i-x_i^*)]}{u'(s_i-tx_i^*)}$$

With x_i^*, the company's average effective tax rate is Equation 5.5.

Equation 5.5

$$\tau_i = [(1-\eta_i)\frac{x_i^*}{s_i} + \eta_i] \cdot t$$

Propositions 5–6 explain how the tax enforcement intensity, ε, affects the mean, $\bar{\tau}$, and variance, $var(\tau_i)$.

Assumption 4: Assuming $-\partial \ln w_i / \partial \ln \tau_i < 1$, the elasticity of the tax base to the effective tax rate is less than 1, $(w_i = \frac{p_i y_i}{PY}$ (please refer to Equation 5.1)).

Following the model above and Assumption 4, we can obtain Propositions 3–5. Combined with Assumption 5, we can get Propositions 6–7.

Proposition 3: As the statutory tax rate rises, the effective tax rate faced by firms increases, and the macro effective tax rate of the economy also rises. That means for any firm, i, there is $\partial \tau_i / \partial t > 0$. Combined with Assumption 4, we get $\partial \bar{\tau} / \partial t > 0$.

Proposition 4: Strengthening penalties and inspections can increase effective tax rates. That means for any firm, i, we have $\partial \tau_i / \partial F_i > 0$, $\partial \tau_i / \partial \eta_i > 0$.

Proposition 5: Treating all taxpayers fairly can reduce the difference in effective tax rates between firms—that is, $\partial F_i/\partial\varepsilon > 0$.

Propositions 4–5 imply $\partial\mathrm{var}(\tau_i)/\partial\mathrm{var}(F_i) > 0$ and $\partial\mathrm{var}(\tau_i)/\partial\mathrm{var}(\eta_i) > 0$.

Assumption 5: For any firm, i, we have $\partial F_i/\partial\varepsilon \geq 0$. For firm i, we have $\partial F_i/\partial\varepsilon > 0$ and $\partial\mathrm{var}(F_i)/\partial\varepsilon < 0$. For any firm, i, there is $\partial\eta_i/\partial\varepsilon \geq 0$, and there exists firm i, such that $\partial\eta_i/\partial\varepsilon > 0$ and $\partial\mathrm{var}(\eta_i)/\partial\varepsilon < 0$. That means, when tax enforcement, ε, is strengthened, the punishment for tax evasion, F_i, or the audit probability, η_i, would increase, and discretion over punishment or audit probabilities among firms is reduced.

Proposition 6: Under Assumptions 4–5, we have $\partial\bar{\tau}/\partial\varepsilon > 0$.

Proposition 7: Under Assumptions 4–5, we have $d\mathrm{var}(\tau_i)/d\varepsilon < 0$.

Firms' production decisions

This section analyses the relationship between the distribution of the effective tax rate, τ_i, across firms and the aggregate TFP of the economy. Firms' production function takes the form AK in Equation 5.6.

Equation 5.6

$$y_i = A_i k_i$$

In Equation 5.6, y_i is the total output of firm i and k_i is the capital stock. Assuming the firm is in a monopolistic competitive industry, the demand function of the firm is $p_i = Q^{-\theta}$.

The problem of profit maximisation is $\max_{k_i} (1-\tau_i)A_i{}^{(1-\theta)}k_i{}^{(1-\theta)}-rk_i$, in which τ_i is the effective tax rate of firm i. The solution to the problem above is $k_i = A_i{}^{\frac{(1-\theta)}{\theta}}(1-\tau_i)^{\frac{1}{\theta}}(1-\theta)^{\frac{1}{\theta}}r^{\frac{1}{\theta}}$.

Correspondingly, the optimal total output level of firm i is Equation 5.7.

Equation 5.7

$$y_i = A_i{}^{\frac{1}{\theta}}(1-\tau_i)^{\frac{1}{\theta}}(1-\theta)^{\frac{1}{\theta}}r^{\frac{1}{\theta}}$$

And the total capital of all firms is Equation 5.8.

Equation 5.8

$$K = \sum_{i=1}^{N} k_i = (1-\theta)^{\frac{1}{\theta}}r^{-\frac{1}{\theta}}\sum_{i=1}^{N} A_i{}^{\frac{(1-\theta)}{\theta}}(1-\tau_i)^{\frac{1}{\theta}}$$

According to Olley and Pakes's definition of *TFP*, we have Equation 5.9.

Equation 5.9

$$TFP = \sum_{i=1}^{N} \frac{y_i}{\sum_{i=1}^{N} y_i} \cdot A_i$$

By substituting Equation 5.7 into Equation 5.9, we can get Equation 5.10.

Equation 5.10

$$TFP = \frac{\sum_{i=1}^{N} A_i^{\frac{1+\theta}{\theta}} (1-\tau_i)^{\frac{1}{\theta}}}{\sum_{i=1}^{N} A_i^{\frac{1}{\theta}} (1-\tau_i)^{\frac{1}{\theta}}}$$

Assuming $\ln A_i$ and $\ln(1-\tau_i)$ follow a joint normal distribution, the correlation coefficient between the two variables is $-\rho(\rho>0)$. From Equation 5.10, we can prove that $\log TFP$ can be expressed as Equation 5.11.

Equation 5.11

$$\log TFP = \overline{\ln A_i} + \frac{2+\theta}{\theta} \, \mathrm{var}[\ln(A_i)] - \frac{\rho}{\theta} \, \sqrt{\mathrm{var}[\ln(A_i)]} \cdot \sqrt{\mathrm{var}[\ln(1-\tau_i)]}$$

Equation 5.11 shows that the larger the variance of the effective tax rate, the lower is the efficiency of resource allocation.

Impact of tax enforcement intensity, ε, on aggregate TFP

Based on the results of sections one and two, we have the following conclusions about the relationship between the level of tax enforcement and the aggregate *TFP*.

Proposition 8: $\partial \ln TFP / \partial \varepsilon > 0$.

So far, Propositions 3, 6 and 8 have provided microeconomic foundations for Assumptions 2–3 in section one.

Now we turn to the empirical test of three key hypotheses.

Empirical test

Hypotheses and empirical strategies

Based on the theoretical analyses in section two, we propose the following testable hypotheses.

Hypothesis 1: When the statutory tax rate remains unchanged, firms' effective tax rate rises as regional fiscal pressure increases (that is, Assumption 3).

Hypothesis 2: When the statutory tax rate remains unchanged, as regional fiscal pressure increases, the decrease in the percentage of production factors (capital stock, labour) is lower than the increased percentage of the effective tax rate (that is, Assumption 1).

Hypothesis 3: When the statutory tax rate is unchanged, the variance of the effective tax rate among firms reduces as regional fiscal pressure increases. And, when $\ln A_i$ and $\ln(1-\tau_i)$ are negatively correlated, the aggregate resource-allocation efficiency improves (that is, Assumption 3).

Chen (2016, 2017a) used the abolition of agricultural taxes as a quasi-natural experiment to verify Hypothesis 1. We use similar empirical strategies to test Hypotheses 2 and 3. We show the prerequisite of Hypothesis 3 ($\ln A_i$ and $\ln(1-\tau_i)$ are negatively correlated) in section three (relationships among the main variables).

Data sources

The empirical study in this chapter examines whether fiscal pressure has affected the differences in the effective VAT rates for China's manufacturing firms and ultimately improved the efficiency of manufacturing resource allocation. For this purpose, we use two datasets for our quantitative analysis: the *Annual Survey of Industrial Production* conducted by the National Bureau of Statistics of China (NBS 2000–07), which includes all state-owned and non-state-owned firms with annual sales of more than RMB5 million; and the *National Statistics on Prefecture, City, and County Finance* (Ministry of Finance 2000–07). The main reason for selecting these two datasets is that the former can relatively accurately calculate each firm's effective VAT rate and the latter can calculate the fiscal pressure faced by the local government.

Measurement of main variables

Exogenous fiscal pressure shock

Following Chen (2017a), we measure the fiscal pressure generated by the abolition of agricultural taxes in China in 2005 by Equation 5.12.

Equation 5.12

$$Agr_c = \frac{Agr\_tax_{c,2000-2004} + Subsidy_{c,2000-2004}}{Total\_tax_{c,2000-2004}} - \frac{Subsidy_{c,2005-2007}}{Total\_tax_{c,2005-2007}}$$

In Equation 5.12, $Agr\_tax_{c,2000-2004}$ is the sum of county-level agricultural taxes between 2000 and 2004; $Subsidy_{c,2000-2004}$ and $Subsidy_{c,2005-2007}$ represent the sums of transfer payments related to rural tax reform at the county level in 2000–04 and 2005–07, respectively; and $Total\_tax_{c,2000-2004}$ and $Total\_tax_{c,2005-2007}$ are the sums of tax revenue at the county level in 2000–04 and 2005–07, respectively.

We use $Agr_c \times Post_t$ to capture the shock of fiscal pressure across counties and over time, where $Post_t$ is the dummy variable indicating the year before and the year after the abolition of agricultural taxes, and $Post_t$ takes a value of 1 if $t > 2004$ and 0 otherwise.[8]

Effective VAT rate and its variance

Using firm-level data, we can obtain the effective VAT rate of each firm and further calculate the variance of the effective VAT rate among firms at the year–county–(two-digit) industry levels, as shown in Equation 5.13.

Equation 5.13

$$VarTau_{cjt} = Var[\ln(-\tau_{cjit})]$$

The subscripts c, j, t and i are county, (two-digit) industry, year and firm, respectively; τ_{cjit} is the effective VAT rate of each firm, which is defined as the firm-level 'Payable VAT/Value-added'.

Aggregate TFP

Following Bartelsman et al. (2013), we use the Olley and Pakes (1996) productivity decomposition method to calculate the TFP, as in Equation 5.14 (for notational convenience, we ignore the county and industry subscripts, c and j).

---

8   Although the abolition of agricultural taxes officially began on 1 January 2006, from the perspective of taxes data, the nationwide large-scale complete taxes deduction and exemption actually took place in 2005.

Equation 5.14

$$TFP_t = \overline{TFP}_t + \sum_{i=1}^{N}\left(s_{it}-\bar{s}_t\right)\left(TFP_{it}-\overline{TFP}_t\right)$$

In Equation 5.14, TFP_t is average productivity using the firm size as weights; $\overline{TFP}_t$ is the arithmetical average of the firm's productivity; and the last term, $\sum_{i=1}^{n}\left(s_{it}-\bar{s}_t\right)\left(TFP_{it}-\overline{TFP}_t\right)$, represents the efficiency of resource allocation, which we call 'OP covariance'. Among them, s_{it} is the proportion of the output of a single firm in total output; TFP_{it} is the productivity of firm i at time t; $\bar{s}_t$ is the average of s_{it} for each firm, i; and $\overline{TFP}_t$ is the average of TFP_{it} for each firm, i.

We use four methods to estimate the TFP_{it}: LP (Levinsohn and Petrin 2003), ordinary least squares (OLS), ACF (Ackerberg et al. 2015) and OP (Olley and Pakes 1996).

The aggregate TFP in our empirical study is measured by 'OP covariance', which is calculated by the second component on the right-hand side of Equation 5.14. Specifically, s_{it} is the proportion of the total output value of a single firm in the total output value at the year–county–(two-digit) industry levels; TFP_{it} is the logarithmic productivity of firm i in year t; and $\overline{TFP}_t$ is the year–county–(two-digit) industry arithmetical average of the logarithmic productivity of the firm. For simplicity, we use '$LOG(TFP)$ (OP covariance)' to represent the aggregate TFP in regression tables.

Control variables

The key control variables are:

1. The average of $\ln(1-\tau_{cijt})$. To be consistent with Equation 5.13, we first calculate $\ln(1-\tau_{cijt})$ for each firm, and then calculate the average of $\ln(1-\tau_{cijt})$ at the year–county–(two-digit) industry levels.

2. The Herfindal index, which is calculated based on the firm's sales income at the year—county–(two-digit) industry levels.

3. The logarithm of the year–county–(two-digit) industry average of firm-level output, which, for convenience, is simplified as 'LOG(Average output)' in the tables of regression results.

4. The average markup—first, we estimate the markup for each firm according to the method of De Loecker and Warzynski (2012), and then calculate the year–county–(two-digit) industry average of firm-level markup.

5. Export–sales ratio, which is defined as the 'total export/total sales income' at the year–county–(two-digit) industry level.

6. The logarithm of per capita capital stock within the same industry: we first calculate the total capital stock and labour force at the year–county–(two-digit) industry level, and then calculate the per capita capital stock and take the logarithm. For simplicity, we will use 'LOG(Per capita capital stock)' in the tables of regression results.

7. The proportion of capital of different ownership in total capital: first, we separately calculate the proportion of state-owned capital, collective capital and foreign capital in the total capital for each firm, and then calculate the average of the abovementioned proportions at the year–county–(two-digit) industry level. For simplicity, we will use 'State-owned capital share', 'Collective capital share' and 'Foreign capital share', respectively, in tables of regression results.

Descriptive statistics

Table 5.1 shows the descriptive statistics of all the measurements involved in the regressions at the year–county–(two-digit) industry level.

Table 5.1 Descriptive statistics of variables

Variable name	Sample size	Mean	Std dev.	Minimum	Maximum
Aggregate TFP (LP estimation)	72,523	0.0270	0.089	−1.500	1.8880
Aggregate TFP (OLS estimation)	72,523	0.0030	0.077	−1.389	1.7550
Aggregate TFP (ACF estimation)	72,523	0.0110	0.080	−0.961	1.3740
Aggregate TFP (OP estimation)	72,523	0.0150	0.082	−1.300	1.6990
VarTau	71,648	0.0156	0.027	0.000	0.1960
Agr×Post	68,980	0.0840	0.112	−0.646	1.2000
Agr	68,980	0.1580	0.158	−0.646	1.2000
FP	46,743	−0.0150	0.072	−0.277	0.2247
The average of $\ln(1-\tau_{cijt})$	72,523	−0.1370	0.085	−0.874	0.0000
The average markup	72,523	1.3350	0.446	0.669	42.0240
LOG(Average output)	72,523	10.3800	0.784	7.425	13.5520
LOG(Per capita capital stock)	72,523	3.8260	0.795	−1.350	8.2390
Herfindal index	72,523	0.3180	0.174	0.006	0.9840
Export–sales ratio	72,523	0.1110	0.198	0.000	0.9990
State-owned capital share	72,503	0.0590	0.136	0.000	1.0000
Collective capital share	72,503	0.1170	0.188	0.000	1.0000
Foreign capital share	72,503	0.1060	0.184	0.000	1.0000

Variation in key variables

Changes in fiscal pressure and effective VAT rate

Figure 5.2 suggests that the regions with the greatest increase in fiscal pressure have the greatest growth in the effective VAT rate. This is consistent with Chen (2017a).

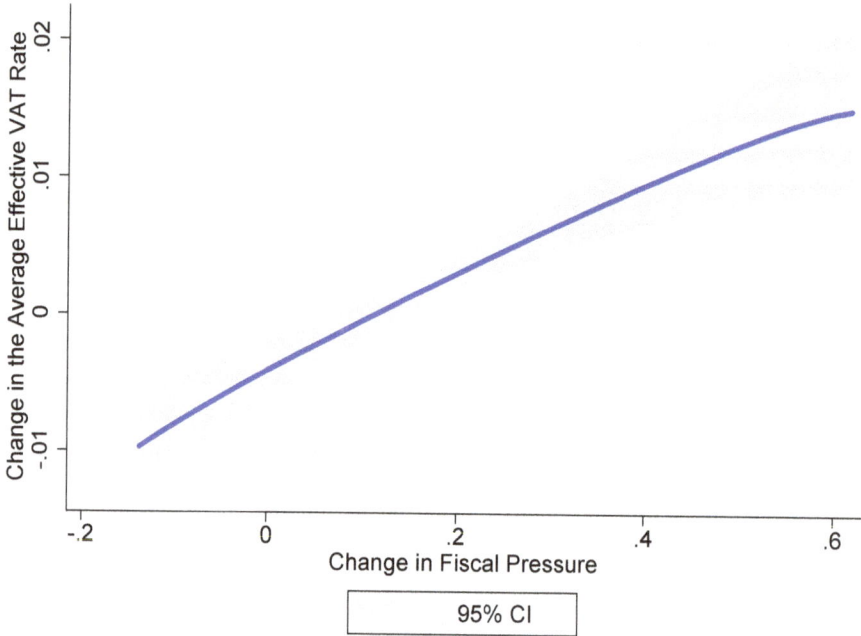

Figure 5.2 Changes in fiscal pressure and average effective VAT rate (comparison before and after reform)

Notes: Vertical axis variable: first, we calculate the average effective VAT rates at the county–(two-digit) industry level in 2005–07 and 2000–04, respectively, and then subtract the average for 2000–04 from that for 2005–07 for change over time of the average effective VAT rate. Horizontal axis variable: first, we calculate the averages of Agr*Post at the county–(two-digit) industry level in 2005–07 and 2000–04, respectively. We then subtract the average for 2000–04 from that for 2005–07 for the change over time in fiscal pressure. The shaded area in the graph is the 95 per cent confidence interval.

Source: Authors' calculations.

Changes in fiscal pressure and the variance of the effective VAT rate

Figure 5.3 shows that the regions with the greatest increase in fiscal pressure have the greatest reduction in the variance of the effective VAT rate.

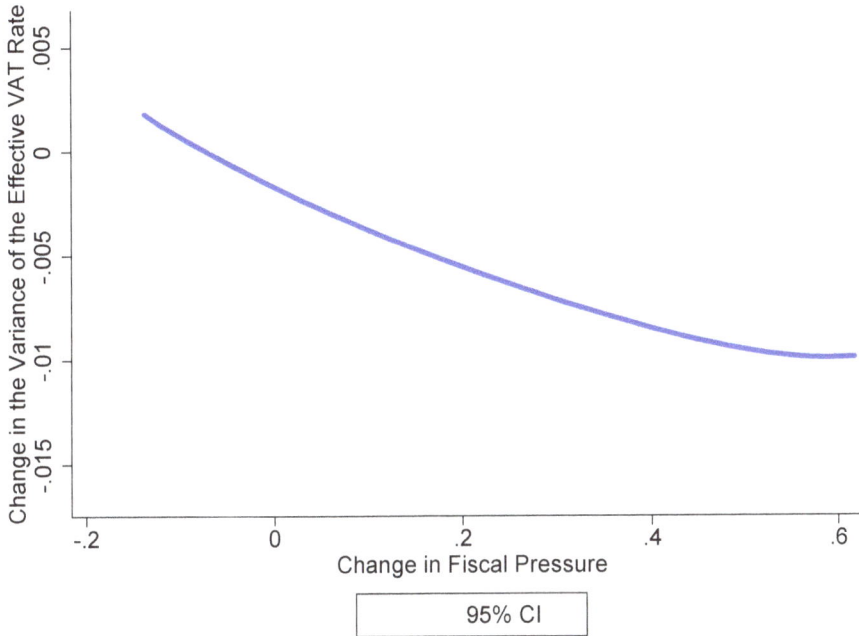

Figure 5.3 Changes in fiscal pressure and variance of the effective VAT rate (comparison before and after reform)

Notes: Vertical axis variable: first, we calculate the averages of the variance of the effective VAT rate at the county–(two-digit) industry level in 2005–07 and 2000–04, respectively. We then subtract the average for 2000–04 from that for 2005–07 for the change over time of the variance of the effective VAT rate. Horizontal axis variable: first, we calculate the averages of Agr*Post at the county–(two-digit) industry level in 2005–07 and 2000–04, respectively. We then subtract the average for 2000–04 from that for 2005–07 for the change over time in fiscal pressure. The shaded area in the graph represents the 95 per cent confidence interval.

Source: Authors' calculations.

Changes in fiscal pressure and aggregate TFP

Figure 5.4 shows the positive effects of fiscal pressure on the aggregate TFP, measured by four methods—LP, OLS, ACF and OP, respectively, in panels a, b, c and d.

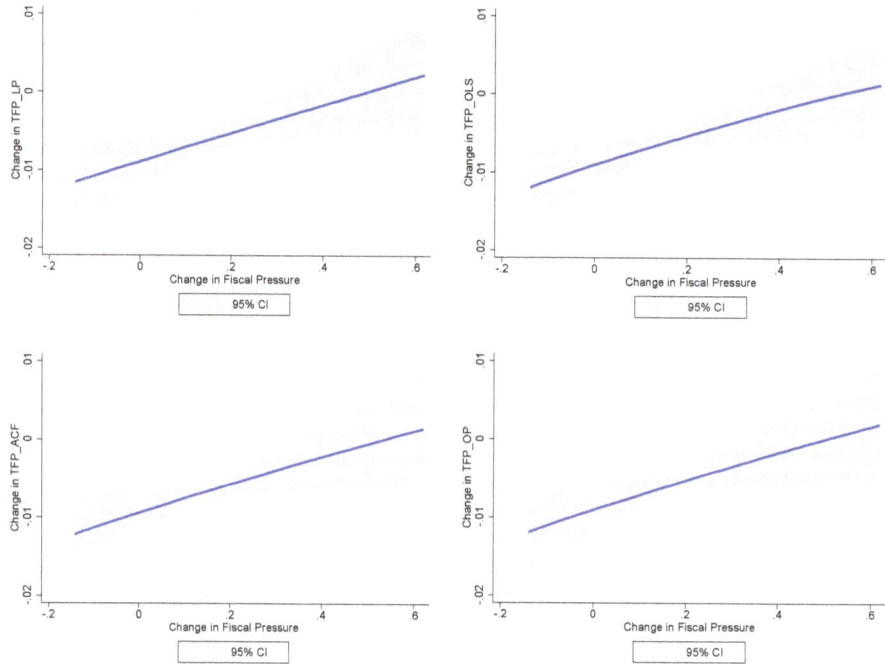

Figure 5.4 Changes in fiscal pressure and aggregate TFP (comparison before and after reform)

Notes: Vertical axis variables: first, we calculate the averages of the aggregate TFP (TFP_LP, TFP_OLS, TFP_ACF and TFP_OP) at the county–(two-digit) industry level in 2005–07 and 2000–04, based on the second component (OP covariance) on the right-hand side of Equation 5.3, and then separately subtract the average for 2000–04 from that for 2005–07, constructing variables of TFP_LP change, TFP_OLS change, TFP_ACF change and TFP_OP change. Horizontal axis variable: first, we calculate the averages of Agr*Post at the county–(two-digit) industry level in 2005–07 and 2000–04, respectively, and then subtract the average for 2000–04 from that for 2005–07. Following Equation 5.12, we get the measurement of fiscal pressure. The shaded area in the graph represents the 95 per cent confidence interval.

Source: Authors' calculations.

Correlation coefficient between $\ln A_i$ and $\ln(1-\tau_i)$

Proposition 8 and Hypothesis 3 suggest that strengthening tax enforcement can improve the aggregate TFP if $\ln A_i$ and $\ln(1-\tau_i)$ are negatively correlated. The data show that the correlation coefficient between $\ln A_i$ and $\ln(1-\tau_i)$ is approximately 0.022 (for the LP method), –0.027 (OLS method), –0.028 (ACF method) or –0.025 (OP method).

Regression specification

The difference-in-difference model is specified as Equation 5.15.

Equation 5.15

$$y_{cjt} = \alpha \times Agr_c \times Post_t + \beta \times Agr_c + X_{cjt} \times \theta + \gamma_t + \eta_{cj} + \varepsilon_{cjt}$$

In Equation 5.15, the subscripts c, j and t represent county, two-digit industry and year, respectively.[9] The dependent variable, y_{cjt}, is *VarTau* (variance of the effective VAT rate) and the aggregate *TFP* (OP covariance) (refer to Equations 5.13 and 5.14 for definition of the variables). The measurement for Agr_c on the right-hand side of Equation 5.15 is Equation 5.13. $Post_t$ is the dummy variable indicating the years since the abolition of agricultural taxes; it takes a value of 1 if $t > 2004$ and 0 otherwise; X_{cjt} is a control variable vector of firm characteristics ('county–industry–year' level); γ_t is the year fixed effects; η_{cj} is the county–industry fixed effects; ε_{cjt} is the random error. The parameter of interest is α.

Regression results

Fiscal pressure shock and variance of the effective VAT rate

The regression results are reported in Table 5.2. In column (1), we control for the year fixed effects and the average $\ln(1-\tau)$ at the industry level. The results show that the variance of the effective VAT rate decreases significantly (at the 5 per cent level) with the increase in fiscal pressure. Column (2) includes extra control variables. In column (3), we additionally control for the county–industry fixed effects. The estimates in columns (2)–(3) also show that the variance of the effective VAT rate among firms in the same industry decreases as the regional fiscal pressure increases. Columns (4) and (5) restrict the regression samples to those with the number of firms greater than three and greater than four, respectively, at the county–(two-digit) industry level, duplicating the regression in column (3).

Table 5.2 Fiscal pressure and variance of the effective VAT rate

	Dependent variable: VarTau (variance of the effective VAT rate)				
	(1)	**(2)**	**(3)**	**(4)**	**(5)**
Agr×Post	–0.006**	–0.007***	–0.009***	–0.008***	–0.007**
	(0.002)	(0.002)	(0.003)	(0.003)	(0.003)
Agr	0.000	0.006**			
	(0.002)	(0.002)			
Industry average ln(1-τ)	–0.195***	–0.198***	–0.267***	–0.262***	–0.249***
	(0.004)	(0.005)	(0.008)	(0.011)	(0.012)

9   In this chapter, enterprises are divided into the year–county–(two-digit) industry level, which shows the possibility that the number of enterprises at this level is very small. To avoid the estimation bias caused by this issue, we drop the samples to those in which the number of enterprises is not more than two. The average number of enterprises participating in the regressions is nine, the maximum is 479 and the minimum is three. To further test the sensitivity of the regressions, we conduct sensitivity analyses by retaining the samples of those with the number of enterprises not less than four and not less than five.

	Dependent variable: VarTau (variance of the effective VAT rate)				
	(1)	(2)	(3)	(4)	(5)
Average markup		−0.001**	−0.000	−0.000	−0.000
		(0.000)	(0.000)	(0.000)	(0.000)
LOG(Average output)		0.000*	0.001	0.001	0.000
		(0.000)	(0.000)	(0.000)	(0.000)
LOG(Per capita capital stock)		0.000*	−0.000*	−0.001*	−0.000
		(0.000)	(0.000)	(0.000)	(0.000)
Herfindal index		0.007***	−0.003***	−0.002*	−0.000
		(0.001)	(0.001)	(0.001)	(0.002)
Export–sales ratio		−0.001	0.002*	0.002	0.002
		(0.001)	(0.001)	(0.001)	(0.001)
State-owned capital share		−0.003***	−0.007***	−0.008***	−0.006***
		(0.001)	(0.001)	(0.002)	(0.002)
Collective capital share		0.002**	0.001	0.001	0.001
		(0.001)	(0.001)	(0.001)	(0.001)
Foreign capital share		0.013***	0.007***	0.006**	0.005**
		(0.001)	(0.002)	(0.002)	(0.002)
Constant term	−0.011***	−0.020***	−0.024***	−0.024***	−0.020***
	(0.001)	(0.002)	(0.003)	(0.004)	(0.004)
Year fixed effects	Yes	Yes	Yes	Yes	Yes
County–industry fixed effects	No	No	Yes	Yes	Yes
Number of firms	> 2	> 2	> 2	> 3	> 4
R-squared	0.378	0.388	0.629	0.631	0.636
Sample size	68,980	68,960	66,382	49,177	38,395

* significant at the 10 per cent level
** significant at the 5 per cent level
*** significant at the 1 per cent level
Note: Standard errors in parentheses, clustered at county level.

Fiscal pressure shock and change in aggregate TFP

Table 5.3 shows the regression results between fiscal pressure and the aggregate *TFP*. The productivity of firms in columns (1)–(4) is estimated by the methods of LP, OLS, ACF and OP, respectively. The regression in panel A of Table 5.3 restricts the samples to those with the number of firms greater than two in the same industry. It can be seen from the coefficients of the interaction term that aggregate productivity in the manufacturing industry significantly increases as the fiscal pressure increases. To further investigate whether the number of firms at the year–(two-digit) industry level would affect the regression results, we use the samples with the number of firms greater than three and greater than four at the year–(two-digit) industry level for regression. The results are displayed in panels B and C of Table 5.3, which are basically the same as panel A.

Table 5.3 Fiscal pressure and aggregate LOG(TFP) (OP covariance)

	Dependent variable: Aggregate LOG(TFP) (OP covariance)			
	(1)	(2)	(3)	(4)
TFP estimation method	LP	OLS	ACF	OP
	Panel A: Number of firms in the same industry is greater than 2			
Agr×Post	0.051***	0.039***	0.045***	0.048***
	(0.009)	(0.008)	(0.008)	(0.008)
Industry average ln(1-τ)	0.003	0.002	0.003	0.002
	(0.006)	(0.005)	(0.006)	(0.006)
Average markup	–0.017***	–0.015***	–0.016***	–0.017***
	(0.005)	(0.006)	(0.005)	(0.005)
LOG(Average output)	–0.025***	–0.020***	–0.023***	–0.023***
	(0.002)	(0.001)	(0.001)	(0.001)
LOG(Per capita capital stock)	–0.002**	–0.003***	–0.001	–0.002**
	(0.001)	(0.001)	(0.001)	(0.001)
Herfindal index	0.034***	–0.003	0.006	0.013**
	(0.006)	(0.005)	(0.006)	(0.006)
Export–sales ratio	0.009*	–0.003	0.002	0.004
	(0.005)	(0.004)	(0.004)	(0.004)
State-owned capital share	0.016***	0.005	0.010**	0.011**
	(0.005)	(0.005)	(0.005)	(0.005)
Collective capital share	–0.011***	–0.011***	–0.009***	–0.011***
	(0.004)	(0.003)	(0.003)	(0.003)
Foreign capital share	–0.017***	–0.010*	–0.012**	–0.014**
	(0.006)	(0.005)	(0.005)	(0.005)
Constant term	0.306***	0.247***	0.247***	0.283***
	(0.018)	(0.016)	(0.016)	(0.017)
Year fixed effects	Yes	Yes	Yes	Yes
County–industry fixed effects	Yes	Yes	Yes	Yes

	Dependent variable: Aggregate LOG(TFP) (OP covariance)			
	(1)	(2)	(3)	(4)
TFP estimation method	LP	OLS	ACF	OP
R-squared	0.433	0.469	0.443	0.437
Sample size	66382	66382	66382	66382
	Panel B: Number of firms in the same industry is greater than 3			
Agr×Post	0.057***	0.045***	0.051***	0.054***
	(0.012)	(0.009)	(0.010)	(0.011)
	Panel C: Number of firms in the same industry is greater than 4			
Agr×Post	0.053***	0.042***	0.048***	0.051***
	(0.013)	(0.010)	(0.012)	(0.012)

* significant at the 10 per cent level

** significant at the 5 per cent level

*** significant at the 1 per cent level

Notes: Standard errors in parentheses, clustered at county level. The control variables of regression in panels B and C are the same as those in panel A.

Dynamic effect

In this section, we show the dynamic effects of fiscal pressure on the variance of the effective tax rate (in Figure 5.5) and the aggregate *TFP* with annual change (in Figure 5.6). In Figures 5.5–5.6, *Befor4*, *Befor3*, *Befor2* and *Befor1* represent the interaction terms between *Agr* and year dummies for 2001, 2002, 2003 and 2004, respectively; *After1* and *After2* represent the interaction terms between *Agr* and year dummies for 2006 and 2007, respectively.

Dynamic effect of fiscal pressure and variance of the effective VAT rate

Figure 5.5 shows the dynamic effect of fiscal pressure on the variance of the effective VAT rate is not significant before the reform. But after a year of reform it has a significant, negative effect on the variance of the effective VAT rate.

Dynamic effects of fiscal pressure and aggregate TFP

Figure 5.6 depicts the dynamic effect of fiscal pressure on aggregate *TFP* measured by the covariance of OP based on firms' *TFP* estimated by four methods: LP, OLS, ACF and OP. The figure shows that the effect is not significant before the reform, but there is a remarkable, positive impact of fiscal pressure on the aggregate *TFP* in the year of reform. Moreover, the effect gradually increases over time.

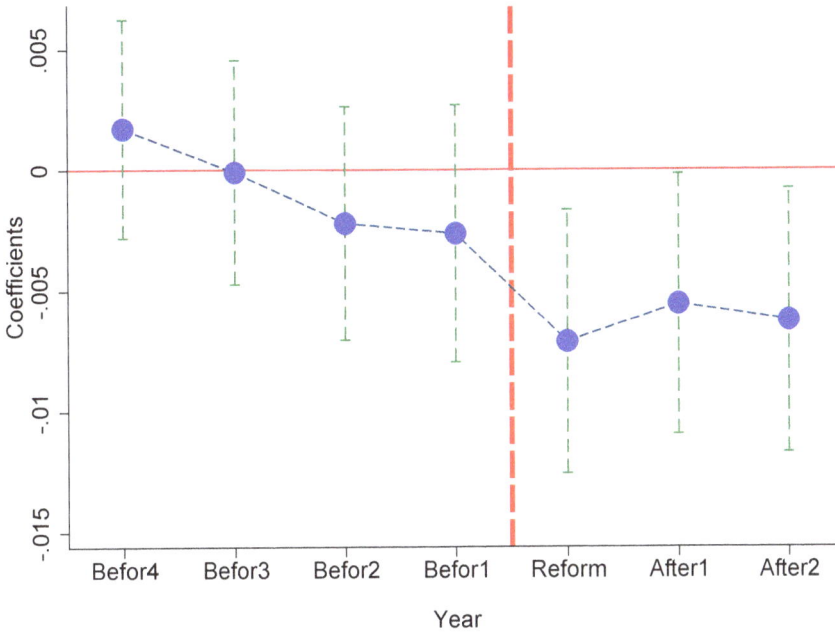

Figure 5.5 Dynamic effect of fiscal pressure and variance of the effective VAT rate

Notes: The longitudinal line represents the 95 per cent confidence interval; Befor4, Befor3, Befor2 and Befor1 represent the effect in the fourth, third, second and first year before the reform, respectively. 'Reform' represents the effect in the year of reform. After1 and After2 represent the effect in the first and second years after the reform, respectively.

Source: Data for the regression are from NBS (2000–07) and the *County Public Finance Statistics Yearbook of China* (2000–07).

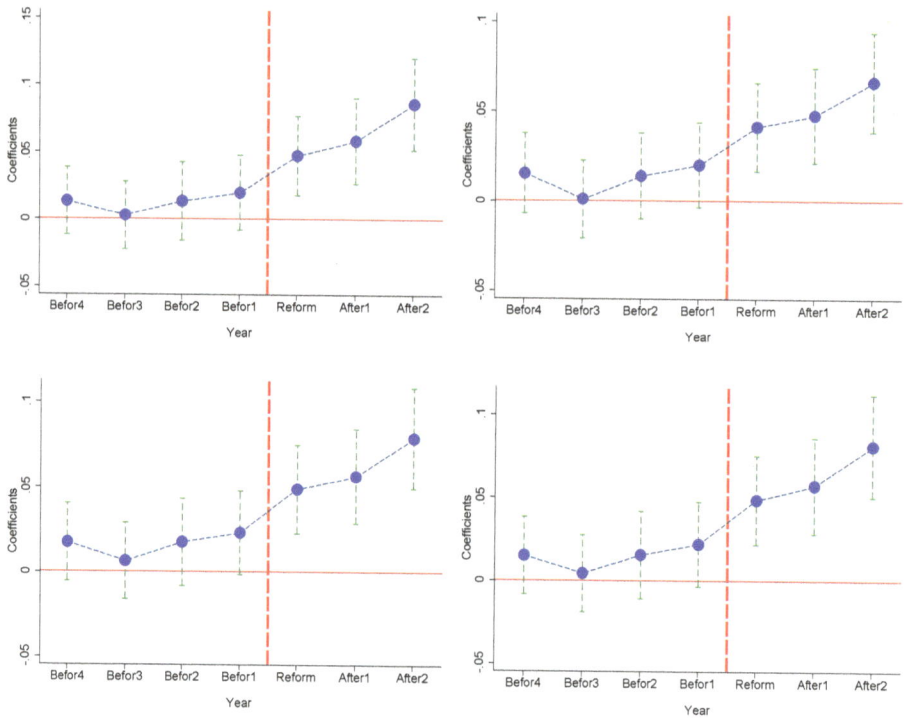

Figure 5.6 Dynamic effect of fiscal pressure and aggregate LOG(TFP) (covariance of OP)

Notes: The vertical axis indicators of a, b, c and d are total *TFP*—namely, the LOG(*TFP*) (covariance of OP), which is calculated by using the four methods of LP, OLS, ACF and OP, respectively, according to the second term on the right-hand side of Equation 5.14; vertical line segments represent 95 per cent confidence intervals; Befor4, Befor3, Befor2 and Befor1 represent the effect in the fourth, third, second and first year before the reform, respectively; 'Reform' represents the effect in the year of reform; After1 and After2 represent the effect in the first and second years after reform, respectively.

Source: Data for the regression are from NBS (2000–07) and the *County Public Finance Statistics Yearbook of China* (2000–07).

By how much can China reduce the VAT rate?

In this section, we quantitatively estimate the extent to which the VAT rate can be reduced in revenue-neutral reform.

Theoretical analysis

The theoretical model in section two shows that the tax revenue $T(t;\varepsilon) = \tau(t;\varepsilon) \cdot TFP(\varepsilon) \cdot K(\bar{\tau}(t;\varepsilon))$. The relationship between t and ε can be expressed as Equation 5.16.

Equation 5.16

$$\Delta t = -\frac{\partial T / \partial \varepsilon}{\partial T / \partial t} \cdot \Delta \varepsilon$$

Equation 5.16 is the basis for calculating the range of feasible reduction in the statutory tax rate, t, under the 'tax-neutral' reform. However, since the change in the tax enforcement level, $\Delta \varepsilon$, is not observable, we need to transform Equation 5.16 into expressions of observable variables and estimable parameters in the following way.

First, when t is constant, $\bar{\tau}$ and ε correspond to each other one-to-one, so $\partial T / \partial \varepsilon$ in Equation 5.16, can be written as Equation 5.17.

Equation 5.17

$$\partial T / \partial \varepsilon = dT / d\bar{\tau} \cdot \partial \bar{\tau} / \partial \varepsilon = \left[\left(1 - \eta_{\bar{\tau}}^K\right) + \eta_{\bar{\tau}}^{TFP} \right] \cdot \frac{T}{\bar{\tau}} \cdot \partial \bar{\tau} / \partial \varepsilon$$

Second, when ε is constant, $\bar{\tau}$ corresponds to t one-by-one, and $\partial T / \partial t$ in Equation 5.16 can be written as Equation 5.18.

Equation 5.18

$$\partial T / \partial t = dT / d\bar{\tau} \cdot \partial \bar{\tau} / \partial t = \left(1 - \eta_{\bar{\tau}}^K\right) \cdot \frac{T}{\bar{\tau}} \cdot \partial \bar{\tau} / \partial t$$

In Equations 5.17 and 5.18, the two elasticities are defined as $\eta_{\bar{\tau}}^K \triangleq -\frac{dlnK}{dln\bar{\tau}}$, $\eta_{\bar{\tau}}^{TFP} \triangleq -\frac{dlnTFP/dln\varepsilon}{\partial ln\bar{\tau}/\partial ln\varepsilon}$, respectively.

Under the condition that t is constant, we know $\Delta \varepsilon = (\partial \bar{\tau}(t,\varepsilon)/\partial \varepsilon)^{-1} \cdot \Delta \bar{\tau}$. Combining Equations 5.16–5.18, we get Equation 5.19.

Equation 5.19

$$\Delta t = -\frac{\left[\left(1 - \eta_{\bar{\tau}}^K\right) + \eta_{\bar{\tau}}^{TFP} \right]}{\left(1 - \eta_{\bar{\tau}}^K\right) \cdot \partial \bar{\tau} / \partial t} \cdot \Delta \bar{\tau}$$

In Equation 5.19, $\Delta \bar{\tau}$ is the change in the effective tax rate caused by the change in the tax enforcement level, ε, which can be observed. For convenience of description, we define the parameters as Equation 5.20.

Equation 5.20

$$\lambda \triangleq -\frac{\Delta t}{\Delta \bar{\tau}}\bigg|_{T = \bar{\tau}} = \frac{\left[\left(1 - \eta_{\bar{\tau}}^K\right) + \eta_{\bar{\tau}}^{TFP} \right]}{\left(1 - \eta_{\bar{\tau}}^K\right) \cdot \partial \bar{\tau} / \partial t}$$

The economic meaning of λ is that, on the premise that the government's tax revenue remains unchanged, the effective tax rate, $\bar{\tau}$, can be increased 1 percentage point by strengthening tax enforcement, and the statutory tax rate, t, can be reduced by λ percentage point.

Estimation of parameters

Equation 5.20 shows that the feasible range of reduction of the statutory tax rate, t, in the 'tax-neutral reform' depends on $\eta_{\bar{\tau}}^K$ and $\eta_{\bar{\tau}}^{TFP}$. These two elasticities can be inferred from the previous regression results. Specifically, the fiscal pressure, ΔAgr, in the quasi-natural experiment of abolishing agricultural taxes can be used as an exogenous driver of the change in the tax enforcement level, ε. $\eta_{\bar{\tau}}^K$ and $\eta_{\bar{\tau}}^{TFP}$ can be estimated by the following two expressions: $\eta_{\bar{\tau}}^{TFP} = \dfrac{\Delta \ln TFP / \Delta Agr}{\Delta \ln \bar{\tau} / \Delta Agr}$ and $\eta_{\bar{\tau}}^K = \dfrac{\Delta \ln K / \Delta Agr}{\Delta \ln \bar{\tau} / \Delta Agr}$.

Estimation of elasticity $\eta_{\bar{\tau}}^{TFP}$,

First, according to the regression results in Table 5.3, we know that $\Delta \ln TFP / \Delta Agr = 0.046$. Second, we use Equation 5.15 with the effective VAT rate, τ_{ijct}, as the explained variable. The regression results are shown in columns (1) and (2) of Table 5.4. Column (1) controls the fixed time effect, the fixed effect of the firm and the logarithmic value-added per capita of the firm. Column (2) additionally controls the relative scale of firms in the same industry, *Markup*, the proportion of firms' exports in total sales revenue, the proportion of capital under different ownership in the total capital of firms and the interaction term of county–(two-digit) industry. The coefficient of $Agr \times Post$ (that is $\Delta \bar{\tau} / \Delta Agr$) in column (2) is 0.048. Given the average value of the effective VAT rate for 2005–07 is about 12 per cent, we know $\Delta \ln \bar{\tau} / \Delta Agr = \left(\dfrac{\Delta \bar{\tau}}{\Delta Agr} \right) / \bar{\tau} = 0.4$. Therefore, $\eta_{\bar{\tau}}^{TFP} = 0.046 / 0.4 \approx 0.1$.

Estimation of elasticity $\eta_{\bar{\tau}}^K$,

$\eta_{\bar{\tau}}^K$ is the elasticity of the input of a firm's production factors to the effective tax rate of that firm. The input factors include both capital and labour.

We use Equation 5.15 to estimate the impact of fiscal pressure on capital stock and the labour force. Table 5.4 reports the results. The explained variables of columns (3) and (4) are the logarithmic number of employees in the firm. And the explained variables of columns (5) and (6) are the logarithmic capital stock of the firm. Columns (3) and (5) do not include control variables at the firm level, and the impact of fiscal pressure on factors of production is not statistically significant. Columns (4) and (6) include extra controls, including the relative size of firms in the same industry, the markup, the proportion of the firm's exports in total sales revenue and the proportion of capital under different ownership in the firm's total capital. The regression results still show that the impact of fiscal pressure on production factors is not statistically significant.[10]

Table 5.4 suggests that $\Delta lnL/\Delta Agr \approx \Delta lnK/\Delta lnAgr \approx 0$.

According to the definition of the elasticity, we know $\eta_\tau^L = \eta_\tau^K \approx 0$ and η_τ^K is not negative. From Equation 5.20, a greater η_τ^K implies a bigger λ, which consequently leaves more room to cut the statutory tax rate, t, in the 'tax-neutral reform'.

Table 5.4 The impact of fiscal pressure on the actual VAT rate and factors of production[11]

Explained variable	(1)	(2)	(3)	(4)	(5)	(6)
	Effective rate of VAT		Logarithmic employment		Logarithmic capital stock	
Agr×Post	0.048*** (0.009)	0.048*** (0.009)	−0.017 (0.038)	−0.029 (0.038)	0.038 (0.072)	0.027 (0.068)
Logarithmic value-added per capita of firms	−0.038*** (0.001)	−0.043*** (0.001)				
Relative scale of firms in the same industry		0.154*** (0.007)		2.028*** (0.054)		2.812*** (0.051)
Markup		−0.001** (0.000)		0.021*** (0.003)		0.035*** (0.005)
Proportion of firm's exports in total sales revenue		0.019*** (0.002)		−0.029*** (0.011)		−0.046** (0.019)
Average value of state-owned assets in the firm's total assets		−0.012*** (0.001)		0.110*** (0.006)		0.199*** (0.013)
Average proportion of collective assets in the firm's total assets		−0.000 (0.001)		0.009* (0.005)		0.012 (0.008)
The average proportion of foreign capital in a firm's total assets		−0.003 (0.002)		0.046*** (0.007)		0.046*** (0.013)
Constant term	0.273*** (0.004)	0.137*** (0.006)	4.705*** (0.003)	2.634*** (0.055)	8.191*** (0.006)	5.312*** (0.053)
Whether to control the fixed effect of the year	Yes	Yes	Yes	Yes	Yes	Yes
Whether to control county–industry fixed effects	No	Yes	No	Yes	No	Yes

10 This may be because the samples we used did not cover a long period and the adjustment of production factors was relatively slow in the short term, and had not yet shown an effect.

11 The reason the regression does not control firms' logarithmic value-added per capita when the explained variables are a logarithm of the number of employees and a logarithm of the capital stock is that the logarithmic value-added per capita of firms is used as the outcome variable of the factor input and is placed in the control variables of the regression.

Explained variable	(1)	(2)	(3)	(4)	(5)	(6)
	Effective rate of VAT		Logarithmic employment		Logarithmic capital stock	
Whether to control the fixed effect of firms	Yes	Yes	Yes	Yes	Yes	Yes
R-squared	0.622	0.625	0.916	0.922	0.867	0.873
Sample size	732,019	727,874	732,046	727,898	732,046	727,898

* significant at the 10 per cent level

** significant at the 5 per cent level

*** significant at the 1 per cent level

Notes: Standard errors in parentheses. The standard error calculation of the regression uses a clustering method—clustering to the county level.

A simple calculation of tax reduction range

From the results in section five, we know that $\eta_{\bar{\tau}}^{TFP} = 0.1$, $\eta_{\bar{\tau}}^{L} = \eta_{\bar{\tau}}^{K} \approx 0$. Substitute these into Equation 5.20 and we get Equation 5.21.

Equation 5.21

$$\lambda = \frac{1.1}{\partial\bar{\tau}/\partial t}$$

We cannot directly estimate $\partial\bar{\tau}/\partial t$ for the VAT, but we know that, in our sample period, the statutory rate of the VAT is 17 per cent; and, given $\partial\bar{\tau}/\partial t = 1$, the minimum value of λ is 1.1, under the condition that tax revenue is kept constant, and the statutory tax rate for a single VAT, which is managed according to the law, is 14.38 per cent. We set the tax rate as the upper limit of the optimal VAT rate under tax-neutral conditions.

In addition, although there is no accurate estimate of VAT, $\partial\bar{\tau}/\partial t$, at present, this chapter attempts to use the 'Corporate Income Tax Unification' of 2008 to make a rough estimate of $\partial\bar{\tau}/\partial t$. In 2008, the corporate income tax unification was implemented to unify the statutory tax rate among domestic and foreign firms. In response to the decrease in the statutory tax rate for domestic firms, we found their effective tax rate decreased after the reform, which is consistent with the theoretical assumption. Specifically, the statutory rate of income tax for domestic firms decreased from 33 per cent in 2007 to 25 per cent (a drop of 8 percentage points). In 2008 and 2007, the average income tax rates of state-owned and domestic firms above designated size were 14.7 per cent and 16 per cent, respectively (down by 1.3

percentage points). Therefore, $\partial \bar{\tau}/\partial t \approx 1.3/8 = 0.163$. Substituting the above result into Equation 5.22, we get $\lambda \approx 6.75$, which implies that the lowest possible statutory VAT rate to sustain revenue-neutral reform is 12.65 per cent.[12]

To sum up, under tax-neutral reform, if the VAT is administered as a single statutory tax rate, the rate can be reduced to at least 14.38 per cent. Moreover, if we additionally take into account better tax compliance following the institution of lower tax rates, as suggested by the corporate income tax unification, the statutory rate of the VAT can be reduced to 12.65 per cent.

Conclusion

China's economic growth rate has been declining in recent years, leading Chinese local and provincial governments to attempt to stimulate the economy through cutting taxes. However, this leads to a decline in government revenue, raising concerns about fiscal risk and debt problems for local governments. To solve this tension, we propose a revenue-neutral reform through improving tax enforcement, cutting statutory tax rates and enhancing aggregate productivity.

Our theoretical model explains the mechanisms underlying the revenue-neutral reform. To test the theory, we made use of the abolition of agricultural taxes in 2005 as a 'quasi-natural experiment' to study how improvements in tax enforcement can lead to a smaller dispersion in the effective tax rate across firms and to greater aggregate productivity. Based on the estimates of several key elasticities, we estimated the extent of the VAT rate cut, with our results showing that the statutory VAT rate can be reduced to at least 14.38 per cent. Moreover, it can be reduced further, to 12.65 per cent, when the improvement of firms' tax compliance in response to the statutory tax rate cut is taken into account. The results imply that the latest standard VAT rate of 13 per cent, adopted in April 2019, may be sustainable for maintaining government revenue as long as governments continue to improve tax enforcement. The proposed reform may encounter several problems in its implementation. First, strengthening tax enforcement will increase the tax burden on some firms, leading to opposition to the reform. Second, the efficiency of resource allocation is difficult to observe in the short term and at the local level. The central government must take a holistic and long-term perspective to harvest the final fruits of reform. Third, strengthening tax enforcement is consistent with the notion of 'tax by law', which is different from strengthening tax enforcement on firms to make up for the deficit due to the shortfall in revenue.

---

12   It is possible the effect of the income tax unification policy did not fully reflect the year of reform. We calculated the average corporate income tax rates of state-owned and domestic enterprises above designated size in 2010 at 11.7 per cent, then, $\partial \bar{\tau}/\partial t \approx 0.525$, $\lambda \approx 2.095$. At this time, under the condition of tax neutrality, the optimal VAT rate for the government to fully collect and administer in accordance with the law is about 13.6 per cent.

In summation, the revenue-neutral reform that we propose may help not only solve current public revenue distress, but also facilitate structural reform and the transformation of the Chinese economy towards high-quality development. It may also help to make China's fiscal and tax systems become the 'foundation and important pillars of state governance', as proposed in the report of the Nineteenth National Congress of the Chinese Communist Party.

References

Ackerberg, D., Caves, K. and Frazer, G. (2015), Identification properties of recent production function estimators, *Econometrica* 83(6): 2411–51. doi.org/10.3982/ECTA13408.

Allingham, M. and Sandmo, A. (1972), Income tax evasion: A theoretical analysis, *Journal of Public Economics* 1(3–4): 323–38. doi.org/10.1016/0047-2727(72)90010-2.

Bai, C., Li, Y. and Wu, B. (2019), *Inequality in corporate taxation: Trends, status quo, and reasons*, Working Paper, Economics Department of Tsinghua University.

Bartelsman, E., Haltiwanger, J. and Scarpetta, S. (2013), Cross-country differences in productivity: The role of allocation and selection, *American Economic Review* 103(1): 305–34. doi.org/10.1257/aer.103.1.305.

Cai, H.B. and Liu, Q. (2009), Competition and corporate tax avoidance: Evidence from Chinese industrial firms, *The Economic Journal* 119(4): 764–95. doi.org/10.1111/j.1468-0297.2009.02217.x.

Chen, S.X.G. (2016), Fiscal pressure, tax administration and regional inequality, *Social Sciences in China* (4): 53–70.

Chen, S.X.G. (2017a), The effect of a fiscal squeeze on tax enforcement: Evidence from a natural experiment in China, *Journal of Public Economics* 147(March): 62–76. doi.org/10.1016/j.jpubeco.2017.01.001.

Chen, S.X.G. (2017b), VAT rate dispersion and TFP loss in China's manufacturing sector, *Economic Letters* 155(June): 49–54. doi.org/10.1016/j.econlet.2017.03.008.

China Network of Court (2019), Make the tax reduction and fee reduction policy more affordable and enterprises will stimulate the vitality of market players, [in Chinese]. Available from: www.chinacourt.org/article/detail/2019/05/id/3886036.shtml.

County Public Finance Statistics Yearbook of China (2000–07), Beijing: China Financial and Economic Publishing House.

De Loecker, J. and Warzynski, F. (2012), Markups and firm-level export status, *American Economic Review* 102(6): 2437–71. doi.org/10.1257/aer.102.6.2437.

Gao, P.Y. (2006), The mystery of the continuous and rapid growth of China's taxation, *Economic Research Journal* (12).

Gao, P.Y. (2008), Accelerating the process of VAT transformation, *China State Finance* (1).

Guo, J. and Li, T. (2009), Tax competition among local governments in China research: Empirical research based on provincial panel data in China, *World Management* (11).

Guo, Q.W. (2019), The potential financial impact and risk prevention of tax and fee reduction, *World Management* (6).

Hopenhayn, H.A. (2014), Firms, misallocation, and aggregate productivity: A review, *Annual Review of Economics* 6(August): 735–70. doi.org/10.1146/annurev-economics-082912-110223.

Hsieh, C.T. and Klenow, P.J. (2009), Misallocation and manufacturing TFP in China and India, *Quarterly Journal of Economics* 124(4): 1403–48. doi.org/10.1162/qjec.2009.124.4.1403.

Levinsohn, J. and Petrin, A. (2003), Estimating production functions using inputs to control for unobservables, *Review of Economic Studies* 70(2): 317–42. doi.org/10.1111/1467-937X.00246.

Long, X.N., Zhu, L.Y., Cai, W.X. and Li, S.M. (2014), Empirical analysis of tax competition among county governments in China based on spatial econometric models, *Economic Research Journal* (8).

Lu, B.Y. (2019), *Report on tax burdens of Chinese companies: Estimation based on data of listed companies*, Report on Public Finance No. 8, Beijing: Chongyang Institute for Financial Studies, Renmin University of China.

Lu, B.Y. and Guo, Q.W. (2011), The source of China's rapid tax growth: An explanation in the framework of tax capacity and tax efforts, *Social Sciences in China* (2).

Mao, J., Zhao, J. and Huang, C.Y. (2014), Effects of China's VAT system transition on firms' investment and employment: Empirical evidence from the 2008–2009 national tax surveys, *Finance and Trade Economy* (16.2).

Ministry of Finance (2000–07), *National statistics on prefecture, city, and county finance*, Beijing: China Finance Press.

National Bureau of Statistics of China (NBS) (2000–07), *Annual survey of industrial production*, Beijing: China Statistics Press.

Nie, H.H. and Jia, R.X. (2011), Productivity and resource misallocation of China's manufacturing firms, *The Journal of World Economy* 7: 27–42.

Olley, G.S. and Pakes, A. (1996), The dynamics of productivity in the telecommunication equipment industry, *Econometrica* 64(6): 1263–97. doi.org/10.2307/2171831.

Qiao, B.Y., Fan, J.Y. and Peng, Y.M. (2006), Intergovernmental transfer payments and local government efforts, *World Management* (3).

Restuccia, D. and Rogerson, R. (2008), Policy distortions and aggregate productivity with heterogeneous establishments, *Review of Economic Dynamics* 11(4): 707–20. doi.org/10.1016/j.red.2008.05.002.

Sohu Technology (2019), How does the history of the largest tax cut take effect? [in Chinese]. Available from: https://www.sohu.com/a/302991116_289823.

State Taxation Administration of China (2019a), *Financial Revenue and Expenditure in the First Half of 2019*, [in Chinese]. Available from: gks.mof.gov.cn/tongjishuju/201907/t20190716_3301309.htm.

State Taxation Administration of China (2019b), *Tax Revenues Organized by Taxation Departments across the Country in the First Half of 2019*, [in Chinese]. Available from: www.chinatax.gov.cn/chinatax/n810214/n810641/n2985871/n2985918/c4539995/content.html.

Wei, S.J. (2019), How to prevent debt crisis during the tax reform?, *Fudan Financial Review* 4.

Xu, W. and Chen, B.K. (2016), Tax incentives and firm investment: Based on the natural experiment of VAT transformation in 2004–2009, *World Management* (5).

Yin, H., Liu, D. and Li, S.G. (2015), Comparison of the estimation methods for firm TFP, *World Economic Papers* 1(4): 1–21.

Yin, H. and Zhu, H. (2011), A study of productive expenditure bias in county-level finance in China, *Social Sciences in China* (1).

Zhou, L.A., Liu, C. and Li, L. (2011), Tax efforts, taxation institutions and the mystery of tax growth, *China Economic Quarterly* 1(1).

6

Innovation and its growth effects in China

Sizhong Sun

Introduction

Innovation plays a central role in a country's economic development. Successful innovations create new ideas that help society progress. For a business, a successful innovation is likely to boost its competitive advantage, by reducing the marginal cost of production via process innovation, for example, or by increasing demand for its products via product innovation. Innovation can facilitate resource allocation[1] and is one of the drivers of sustainable growth. Policymakers frequently employ a number of measures, such as subsidies or tax credits, to encourage innovation.

One can view innovation as a production process—namely, using a set of inputs (for example, research and development) to produce a set of outputs (for example, new products). As such, innovation has both an input perspective, such as research and development (R&D) expenditure and R&D researchers, and an output perspective, including patents. The Organisation for Economic Co-operation and Development (OECD 2018) defines four types of innovation in the *Oslo Manual*—product, process, marketing and organisational innovation—which are classifications more concerned with the output perspective.

Owing to the importance of innovation, researchers have investigated it from various dimensions, one of which is the determinants of innovative activities. For R&D— the input perspective of innovation—previous studies exploring its determinants include Belderbos et al. (2013) in Europe, Japan and the United States; Hammadou

---

1   For example, Acemoglu et al. (2011) find that patents—an output of innovative activities—improve resource allocation via encouraging experimentation and knowledge transfer.

et al. (2014) in 14 European countries; Okamuro et al. (2011) in Japan; López (2008) in Spain; Chun and Mun (2012) in South Korea; and Kastl et al. (2013) in Italy.

From the output perspective, patents are extensively examined in the existing literature. To name a few, Fischer et al. (1994) studied firms' patent behaviour in the Austrian manufacturing sector, while Nicholas (2011) studied patenting behaviour in the United States during the 1920s. Gedik (2012) and Aldieri (2011) utilised patent citations to capture knowledge diffusion in Australia and the United States, respectively. Buesa et al. (2010) explored the determinants of regional innovation in Europe, where they treated R&D as the input and patents as the output of a knowledge production function. Chan (2010) studied the international patent application decisions of nine agricultural biotechnology firms from 1990 to 2000, while Figueroa and Serrano (2013) investigated the determinants of patent sale and acquisition decisions by small and large firms.

Compared with the studies of R&D and patents, there is less research exploring product, process, marketing and organisational innovation. For some examples, however, Gorodnichenko and Schnitzer (2013) investigated how financial constraints influenced a firm's innovation activities, including product innovation, in Europe in 2002 and 2005, where they found a negative impact from financial constraints on domestically owned firms' ability to innovate. The relative lack of studies on these four types of innovation, despite their clear conceptualisation, is possibly due to lack of data, particularly in developing countries.

In this chapter, I explore innovation in China from both the input (R&D) and the output (patents and the aforementioned four types of innovation) perspectives at both the national and the industry levels. In particular, I focus on the role of innovation in driving economic growth in terms of gross domestic product (GDP) and industrial output.

In so doing, this chapter contributes to the existing literature in two respects. First, it aims to provide an updated and comprehensive picture of innovation in China at an aggregate level, utilising the available industry and national data. An understanding of innovation in China will help readers to better assess China's economic potential in the future. Second, this chapter aims to evaluate the contribution of innovation to economic growth in China. Since the beginning of the reform and opening up four decades ago, the Chinese economy has been growing at impressive speed, and factors such as institutional reform and the release of cheap labour from the agricultural sector have arguably played important roles in this growth. Currently China has attained the status of an advanced developing economy and is now facing the middle-income trap. Some of these factors may no longer be the source of economic growth. For example, with China's potential arrival at its Lewis turning point (for discussions, see, among others, Cai 2010; Garnaut and Huang 2006;

Minami and Ma 2010), a labour shortage has become a binding constraint on economic growth. In light of such constraints, innovation can be a sustainable source of economic growth for China in the future.

The rest of this chapter is organised into five sections. In section two, I briefly survey existing studies, focusing on those that cover China. Section three presents an update of innovation in China from the dimensions of R&D, patents, as well as product, process, marketing and organisational innovation. In section four, utilising an autoregressive distributed lag (ARDL) model, I explore the role of R&D and patents in China's economic growth in both the short and the long terms. In section five, I assess the impacts of innovation on industrial output, utilising industry panel data, and finally, section six will conclude the chapter.

Related literature

Researchers frequently explore innovation from two perspectives. The first is to examine factors that affect innovation activities—see, for example, Anwar and Sun (2013), Zhou (2014) and Zhou and Song (2016) on the determinants of R&D in China. The second is to investigate the impacts of innovation activities. My study is related less to the first perspective than to the second. As such, I briefly survey existing studies that explore the second perspective in this section, focusing on those involving China.

R&D is a dimension of innovation that has been extensively explored. Using a rich dataset covering the population of China's large and medium-sized manufacturing enterprises, Jefferson et al. (2006) find that R&D expenditure promotes firms' product innovation, productivity and profitability. Li and Lu (2018) find that R&D promotes the green-sophistication of Chinese exports. Zhang and Xie (2020) examine the impacts of R&D investment and product innovation on China's export performance, and find that these innovation activities promote export propensity, but not export intensity. Similarly, Wu et al. (2020) find that innovation activity, measured in terms of R&D expenditure, promotes export-extensive, but not export-intensive, margins. In the mining sector, Rafiq et al. (2016) find that Chinese mining firms with R&D activities have higher profitability and sales revenues than those without. Similarly, Sun and Anwar (2019) observe that domestic firms in China's iron ore mining industry that conduct R&D are, on average, more productive and have higher sales revenue. Chinese government R&D programs are also found to promote firms' innovation outputs, including the number of patents and revenue from new product sales (Guo et al. 2016).

Hu et al. (2017) find that the correlation between patents and labour productivity has weakened, despite a surge in patent applications in China. The increase in applications does not mean that patent quality, measured in terms of citations, is high. Fisch et al. (2017) observe that, compared with the United States, Europe, Japan and South Korea, Chinese patents have lower value in terms of citations, with similar findings made by Boeing and Mueller (2019).

Dai and Cheng (2018) assess the effect of product innovation on firm markup and productivity, using a large sample of Chinese manufacturing firms. They find significantly positive impacts on firm markup and revenue productivity by product innovation, but its influence on adjusted productivity is negative or insignificant. Zhu et al. (2021) link product and process innovation to employment in China, where they find process innovation serves to promote employment, while product innovation dampens employment.

Many studies on innovation activities in China explore the regional dimension. Chen and Guan (2010) utilise a method of data envelopment analysis to measure the efficiency of China's regional innovation systems, finding a low level of efficiency. Similarly, Bai (2013) estimates the regional innovation efficiency in China from 1998 to 2007 using a stochastic frontier approach and finds low innovation efficiency. Fu et al. (2012) investigate the path-dependent evolution of regional innovation systems in Shenzhen and Dongguan.

Fan et al. (2012) assess the regional innovation inequality in China from 1995 to 2006, finding R&D to be one of the major drivers of increases in inequality. Huang et al. (2010) find double-threshold effects for regional innovation on the productivity spillovers from foreign direct investment in 29 Chinese provinces between 1985 and 2008. Using a multi-agent-based simulation, Wang et al. (2014) show that policies can promote the process of innovation diffusion, which in turn boosts the economies of less-developed regions, particularly in central China.

Fu and Mu (2014) explore the policy choices in the extended national innovation performance framework, while Liu et al. (2011) and Wu (2012) assess the evolution of China's innovation policies. Fan (2014) critically reviews the studies of China's innovation capability, including the development pathway of its national innovation system.

The research in this chapter has three distinct features that distinguish it from these existing studies. First, it covers more types of innovation activities, including R&D, patent, product, process, marketing and organisational innovation. Second, it analyses China's innovation activities and their growth effects at the industry and national levels. Third, it does not cover the regional dimension of innovation activities.

Overview of innovation in China

Over the past few years, innovation in China—in terms of inputs (R&D) and outputs (for example, patents)—has been on a rising trajectory. Figure 6.1 shows the trend for both R&D expenditure and the number of full-time-equivalent R&D researchers. The top-left panel of Figure 6.1 suggests that the number of full-time-equivalent R&D researchers has been growing at increasing speed, to reach 4.61 million in 2019. The increasing R&D personnel will, not surprisingly, contribute to the growth of innovation outputs, which in turn will boost economic growth. The trend for R&D expenditure (as a share of GDP), shown in the top-right panel of Figure 6.1, appears different to that for the number of R&D researchers. First, it pursued a downward trend before 1997, reaching a low of 0.5 per cent in 1994; second, after 1997, R&D expenditure began to rise substantially, reaching a peak of 2.2 per cent in 2019. However, its growth rate appears to be declining. From 1989 to 2019, R&D expenditure (as a share of GDP) increased more than threefold, from 0.7 per cent in 1989 to 2.2 per cent in 2019. Despite the figure appearing relatively modest (less than 2.2 per cent), the increasingly large size of the Chinese economy (GDP) implies a large volume of R&D investment.

The accelerating growth rate in the number of R&D researchers, coupled with the declining growth rate of R&D expenditure (relative to GDP), suggests an increased share of spending on R&D personnel. The bottom-left panel of Figure 6.1 shows the association between the number of R&D researchers and R&D expenditure— appearing to confirm this. We can observe that a 1 per cent increase in R&D expenditure is associated with a more than 1 per cent increase in the number of R&D researchers when R&D expenditure is at a high level. Nevertheless, despite the link between the number of R&D researchers and R&D expenditure, their growth rates do not appear to be substantially linked (the bottom-right panel of Figure 6.1).

In Figure 6.2, I examine patent applications made by both residents and non-residents and associate them with the number of R&D researchers and expenditure levels. The top-left panel of Figure 6.2 exhibits the time trends of patent applications of residents and non-residents, from which three features emerge. First, patent applications by both residents and non-residents exhibit an increasing trend— consistent with the rise in R&D expenditure and researcher numbers in Figure 6.1. Second, the number of patent applications before 2000, from residents and non-residents, is relatively modest and the growth trend is less obvious compared with that of the post-2000 period—once again, consistent with the pattern of inputs (R&D expenditure and researchers). As is observable in Figure 6.1, both R&D expenditure and the number of researchers grew substantially faster after 2000 than in the preceding period. Third, the number of patent applications made by residents has come to dominate that made by non-residents since 2005, with the gap increasing over the years (also see the top-right panel of Figure 6.1). Clearly therefore, residents have come to play an increasingly crucial role in innovation in China.

The association between residents' patent applications and R&D inputs (expenditure and number of researchers) also differs from that for non-residents. The bottom-left panel of Figure 6.2 plots the number of patent applications against the number of R&D researchers and displays the corresponding fitting curves. For residents' patent applications, the convex and upward sloping fitting curve suggests a positive correlation with the number of R&D researchers and that the degree of association becomes higher at higher numbers of researchers. In contrast, despite the similarly positive correlation for non-residents' patent applications, the fitting curve is concave, indicating that a unit increase in the number of R&D researchers is associated with a smaller increase in the number of non-residents' patent applications. The bottom-right panel of Figure 6.2 presents the associations with R&D expenditure. For residents' patent applications, we can observe a pattern similar to their association with the number of R&D researchers. In contrast, the fitting curve of the scatter plot between non-residents' patent applications and R&D expenditure becomes linear. Therefore, R&D inputs appear to be differentially associated with patent applications by residents and non-residents.

Figure 6.3 provides a snapshot of product, process, organisational and marketing innovation by displaying the distributions of the share of enterprises (above designated size) that engaged in these four types of innovation in two-digit industries in 2018. The dots and horizontal bars in Figure 6.1 represent the median and mean of these shares, respectively. On average, 22.92 per cent of enterprises above designated size conducted product innovation, 26.62 per cent conducted process innovation, 26.91 per cent conducted organisational innovation and 23.4 per cent conducted marketing innovation. Comparing the means with the medians in Figure 6.3, we can observe that they are close to each other in all four distributions, suggesting symmetrical distributions. Comparing the means and medians across the four innovation types, we can see that more firms conducted organisational and process innovation than marketing and product innovation.

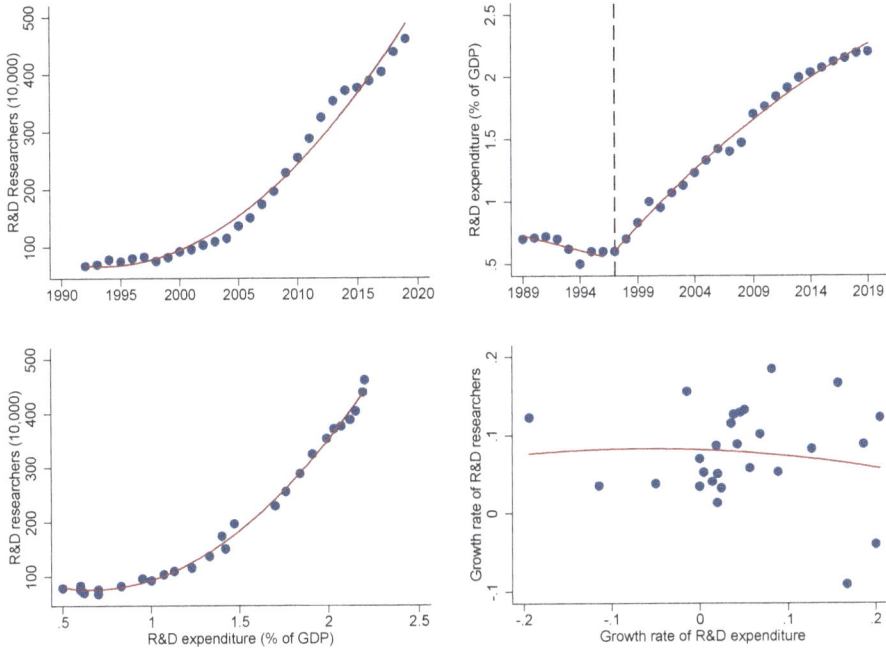

Figure 6.1 R&D expenditure and number of full-time-equivalent R&D researchers

Source: NBS (2021).

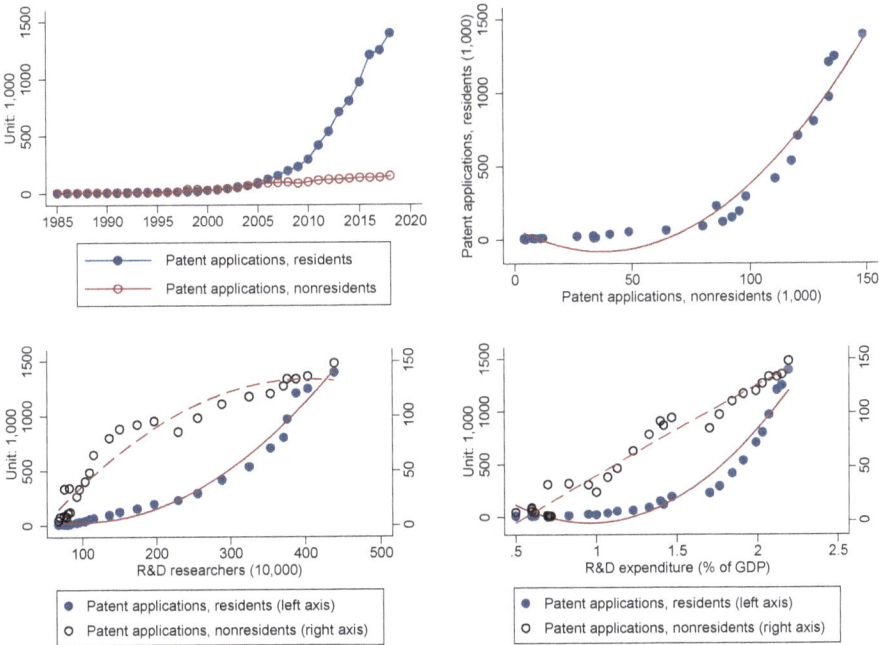

Figure 6.2 Patent applications

Sources: NBS (2021); World Bank (2021).

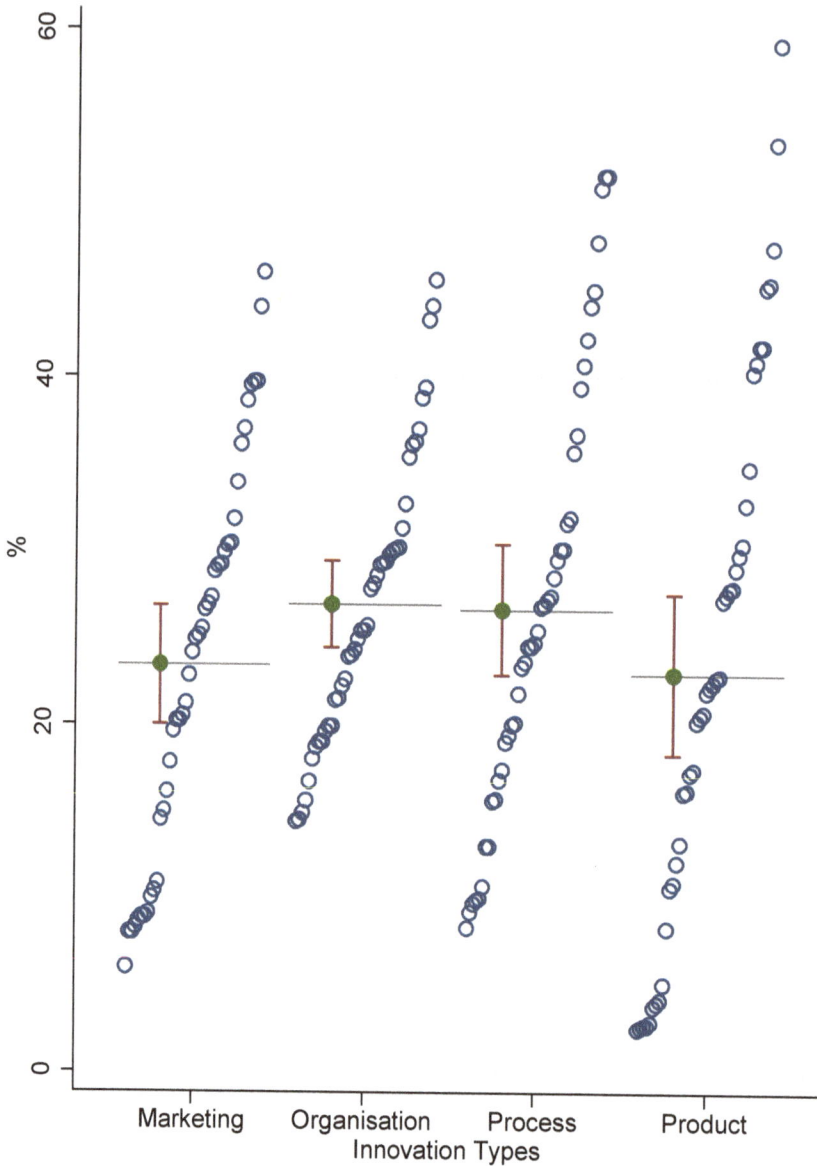

Figure 6.3 Share of enterprises (above designated size) conducting product, process, organisational and marketing innovation, by industry, 2018 (per cent)
Source: NBS (2021).

For product innovation, the instrumentation manufacturing industry has the highest share of enterprises conducting product innovation (59.2 per cent). In contrast, the coal mining and washing industry reports the lowest share of enterprises with product innovation (2.5 per cent). Among enterprises conducting process innovation, the instrumentation manufacturing industry again registers the highest share, with 51.6 per cent, while the mining sector displays the lowest share, with the coal mining and washing industry at 9.2 per cent and other mining industries at 8.3 per cent. The instrumentation manufacturing industry continues to also occupy the top position in organisational innovation, registering a share of 45.6 per cent. In contrast, the nonmetallic mining and dressing sector reports the lowest share, of 14.4 per cent. In marketing innovation, the industries with the highest and lowest shares are the pharmaceutical manufacturing industry and the ferrous metal mining and dressing industry, with shares of 46 and 6 per cent, respectively, while the instrumentation manufacturing industry has the second-highest share of enterprises with marketing innovation, at 44 per cent. Generally, the mining sector exhibits lower shares across all four types of innovation when compared with the manufacturing sector.

Owing to data availability, I am able to examine the dynamics of product innovation in terms of the number of new-product projects across industries between 2011 and 2018. Figure 6.4 presents these distributions across the eight years in question. Here we can observe two patterns: first, the average number of new-product projects (the curve with circles in Figure 6.4) exhibits a weak upward trend, which becomes more obvious after 2015, with the median (the bars in the boxes in Figure 6.4) exhibiting a similar pattern; second, the means are substantially higher than the medians in all eight years, due to some industries having large numbers of new-product projects (the outliers in Figure 6.4).

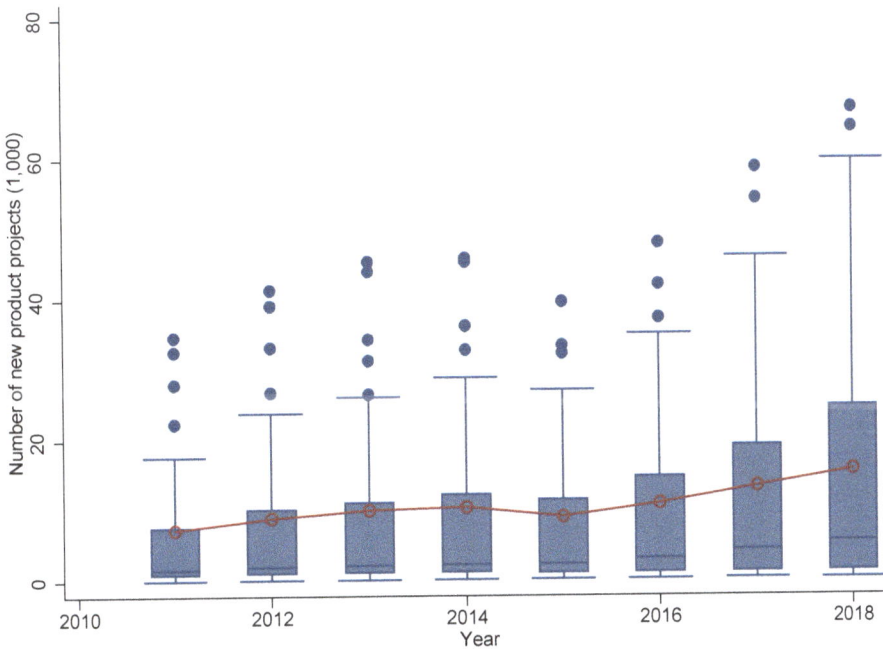

Figure 6.4 Distributions of the number of new-product projects, 2011–2018

Source: NBS (2021).

In summary, innovation activities are on a rising trajectory in China, whether measured in terms of inputs (R&D expenditure and researchers) or outputs (patents and product, process, organisational and marketing innovation). With these rising trends, it is important to investigate how they affect the Chinese economy. Therefore, in the next two sections, I examine the impact of innovation on national GDP and on industrial outputs at the industry level.

Innovation and GDP

To investigate the impact of innovation on economic growth in China, I utilise the aggregate production function framework; and, since the data are a time series from 1989 to 2019, an autoregressive distributed lag model is used in the estimations, as in Equation 6.1.

Equation 6.1

$$\Delta lnY_t = \alpha_0 + \sum_{p=1}^{P} \alpha_1^p lnY_{t-p} + \alpha_2 lnI_t + \alpha_3 lnK_t + \alpha_4 lnL_t$$

$$+ \sum_{q=-Q}^{Q} \alpha_5^q \Delta lnI_{t-p} + \sum_{q=-Q}^{Q} \alpha_6^q \Delta lnL_{t-p}$$

$$+ \sum_{q=-Q}^{Q} \alpha_7^q \Delta lnK_{t-p} + \varepsilon_t$$

In Equation 6.1, Y, I, L and K represent GDP, innovation, labour and capital, respectively; Δ is the difference operator; ε is the error term; and P and Q are the lag lengths. In the estimations, due to the small sample size, I set $P = 1$ in most estimations. If the error terms exhibit autocorrelation in an estimation, I instead set $P = 2$. The lag length, Q, is also set to 1 in the estimations, and sometimes no lead is used. Conceptually, it is possible that some right-hand-side variables are endogenous. For example, on the one hand, innovation promotes economic growth, while on the other, higher economic growth is likely to lead to higher innovation as economic growth facilitates investment in innovation. The lags and leads of differenced lnL, lnK and lnI are intended to absorb such possible correlations with the error term. Innovation is captured by four dimensions in the regressions—namely, the number of full-time-equivalent R&D researchers, R&D expenditure (as a share of GDP), the number of patent applications by residents and the number of patent applications by non-residents. Note that, in the ARDL model, the long-run impact of innovation can be measured by $\alpha_2 / (-\Sigma_{p=1}^{P} \alpha_1^p)$.

The data on GDP are sourced from the *World Development Indicators* (*WDI*) (World Bank 2021), which are in constant 2010 US dollars. The labour force (unit: 10,000) acts as a proxy for labour, sourced from the National Bureau of Statistics of China (NBS 2021). Data on capital are the gross fixed capital formation (percentage of gross national income, or GNI), calculated as the ratio of total investment in fixed assets against GNI, which are also sourced from the NBS. For innovation, data on R&D expenditure (percentage of GDP) and the number of full-time-equivalent R&D researchers (unit: 10,000 persons per year) are obtained from the NBS, while data on patent applications by residents and non-residents are sourced from the *WDI*. I first test the stationarity of the time series (*lnY*, *lnI*, *lnL* and *LnK*), and Table 6.1 reports the results. Except *lnL*, the other series are all I(1) and *lnL* is I(0). Therefore, an ARDL model is appropriate in this case.

Table 6.2 reports the estimation results, for which labour and capital are not included. In the estimations, a number of diagnostic tests were conducted, which verify the validity of the estimations. For example, for the regression where innovation is measured as the number of full-time-equivalent R&D researchers (column [1] of Table 6.2), the Ramsey regression equation specification error test (RESET test) finds a test statistic of 1.09 (*p*-value of 0.3829), which fails to reject the null hypothesis that the model has no omitted variables. The Breusch–Pagan test for heteroskedasticity obtains a test statistic of 8.76 (*p*-value of 0.119), suggesting no presence of heteroskedasticity. The Dickey–Fuller test of the predicted residuals obtains a test statistic of –3.093 (with drift, and *p*-value of 0.0027), confirming that the residuals are stationary (I(0)). Durbin's alternative test for autocorrelation finds a test statistic of 4.593 with *p*-value of 0.0321, which fails to reject the null hypothesis of no first-order autocorrelation at the 1 per cent level. The Breusch–Godfrey Lagrange multiplier (LM) test for autocorrelation also fails to reject the null of no serial correlation from orders one to five at the 1 per cent level.

The LM test for autoregressive conditional heteroskedasticity (ARCH) fails to reject the null of no ARCH effects from orders one to five at the 1 per cent level. I also plot the cumulative sums of the recursive residuals and their squares from the regression, which stay within their 95 per cent confidence bands, confirming the stability of the regression (graph not reported to save space). For the other regressions, including those where I include *lnL* and *lnK* in Table 6.4, the same diagnostic tests are applied and, when applicable, adjustments are made to accommodate the findings of these tests. For example, in column [3] of Table 6.2, the standard errors are robust as the Breusch–Pagan test rejects the null of no heteroskedasticity at the 1 per cent level. These diagnostic tests are not reported, to save space, but are available on request.

In the four regressions in Table 6.2, the estimated coefficients of innovation are statistically nonsignificant at the 5 per cent level for regressions [1], [3] and [4]. In contrast, the innovation coefficient is estimated to be positive and significant at the 5 per cent level in regression [2]. The nonsignificant estimates appear to suggest that innovation measured in terms of the number of R&D researchers and patent applications of residents and non-residents plays a less important role in economic growth in the short term. In the four regressions, some of the estimated coefficients of the lags of differenced innovation are statistically significant, suggesting a time lag for innovation. The significant estimate of the coefficient of innovation, measured in terms of R&D expenditure as a share of GDP, is likely to capture the short-term growth effect for non-innovation-related spending.

In the long run, the situations are different. In all four regressions, the estimated coefficients of innovation are positive and statistically significant at the 5 per cent level, suggesting that innovation promotes economic growth in the long run. For R&D researchers, a 1 per cent increase in the number of full-time-equivalent R&D researchers results in a 0.69 per cent increase in aggregate output. The impact of R&D spending is even bigger, with an elasticity of 1.34. It is interesting to compare the long-run coefficient of residents' patent applications with that of non-residents. Despite both being significantly positive, the magnitude of the coefficient for non-residents' patent applications is higher, suggesting that non-residents' patent applications play a greater role in boosting economic growth.

In Table 6.2, the regressions do not control for the roles of labour and capital. I report the regression results that control for labour and capital inputs in Table 6.3. Capital, labour and innovation are highly correlated (pairwise correlation > 0.86). With the small sample size, the multicollinearity issue is a concern. To address this, I first project labour on to the subspace spanned by an innovation measure and a vector of 1 to obtain a vector of labour measure that is orthogonal to the innovation measure and used in the regression. Second, I project capital to the subspace spanned by innovation, orthogonalised labour and a vector of 1, from which I obtain an orthogonalised capital for the regressions.

Comparing the regression results of Table 6.3 with those of Table 6.2, unsurprisingly, we can observe differences in terms of the magnitude of the estimated coefficients. In particular, the short-run coefficient of innovation, measured in terms of R&D expenditure, now becomes statistically insignificant at the 5 per cent level. Nevertheless, the pattern in which innovation, measured in any one of the four dimensions, plays an insignificant role in economic growth in the short run while promoting economic growth in the long run continues to hold even after labour and capital are controlled in the regressions. Thus, the findings in Table 6.2 are robust.

Table 6.1 Unit root tests

Variables	Levels				First difference				Results
	ADF		PP		ADF		PP		
	Constant	Constant + trend	Constant	Constant + trend	Constant	Constant + Trend	Constant	Constant + trend	
lnY	−1.216	−2.287	−1.298	−0.789	−3.809	−3.918	−2.751	−2.934	I(1)
lnI [1]	0.603	−1.771	0.421	−1.845	−3.924	−3.891	−3.938	−3.914	I(1)
lnI [2]	−0.114	−2.125	−0.235	−2.257	−4.520	−4.453	−4.539	−4.476	I(1)
lnI [3]	1.348	−2.457	1.052	−2.425	−4.660	−4.547	−4.670	−4.571	I(1)
lnI [4]	−0.699	−1.504	−0.686	−1.603	−5.477	−5.423	−5.482	−5.431	I(1)
lnL	−3.566	−2.219	−4.343	−2.293	−4.953	−5.964	−5.003	−5.992	I(0)
lnK	−0.976	−1.287	−1.062	−1.782	−2.955	−2.896	−2.942	−2.880	I(1)

Notes: The null hypothesis is that the series contains a unit root; for lnY, one year lag is used; [1] is the number of R&D researchers; [2] is R&D expenditure; [3] is patent applications by residents; and [4] is patent applications by non-residents.

Sources: Author's estimations using data from World Bank (2021); NBS (2021).

Table 6.2 Regression results

	[1]		[2]		[3]		[4]	
	Coef.	S.E.	Coef.	S.E.	Coef.	S.E.	Coef.	S.E.
lnYt-1	−0.05*	0.03	0.58***	0.09	0.68***	0.19	0.88***	0.18
lnYt-2			−0.63***	0.09	−0.71***	0.20	−1.38***	0.32
lnYt-3							0.49**	0.18
lnIt	0.04	0.03	0.06***	0.02	0.01	0.01	0.01	0.01
Constant	1.38*	0.69	1.41***	0.30	0.84	0.64	0.41	0.38
Long-run coefficient								
lnI	0.69***	0.22	1.34***	0.10	0.37***	0.09	0.63***	0.19
N	25.00		28.00		31.00		30.00	
F	6.44		18.25		7.29		5.01	
Adj. R2	0.53		0.79		0.51		0.49	

*** significant at the 1 per cent level

** significant at the 5 per cent level

* significant at the 10 per cent level

Notes: In [1], innovation is measured as the number of full-time-equivalent R&D researchers; in [2], innovation is R&D expenditure as a share of GDP; in [3], innovation is the number of residents' patent applications, and the standard errors are robust; in [4], innovation is the number of non-residents' patent applications. The coefficients of lags and leads of differenced terms are not reported, to save space.

Sources: Author's estimations using data from World Bank (2021); NBS (2021).

Table 6.3 Regression results with capital and labour

	[1]		[2]		[3]		[4]	
	Coef.	S.E.	Coef.	S.E.	Coef.	S.E.	Coef.	S.E.
lnYt-1	0.05	0.08	0.49***	0.15	−0.11**	0.04	−0.17***	0.05
lnYt-2			−0.57***	0.13				
lnIt	−0.08	0.08	0.12	0.09	0.04**	0.02	0.10***	0.04
lnLt	−0.39	0.49	0.00	0.43	0.20**	0.09	0.28***	0.09
lnKt	0.20***	0.06	0.02	0.05	0.07	0.07	0.17**	0.06
Constant	−0.95	1.86	2.43	1.51	2.80***	0.98	3.84***	1.16
Long-run coefficients								
lnI	1.58*	0.88	1.45***	0.18	0.40***	0.03	0.62***	0.01
lnL	7.55**	3.41	1.62	4.46	1.86***	0.49	1.62***	0.23
lnK	−3.48	6.65	0.39	0.40	0.85	0.78	0.99***	0.08
N	25.00		28.00		32.00		32.00	
F	8.06		10.22		4.7		5.62	
Adj. R2	0.75		0.79		0.54		0.60	

*** significant at the 1 per cent level

** significant at the 5 per cent level

* significant at the 10 per cent level

Notes: In [1], innovation is measured as the number of full-time-equivalent R&D researchers; in [2], innovation is R&D expenditure as a share of GDP; in [3], innovation is the number of residents' patent applications; in [4], innovation is the number of non-residents' patent applications. The coefficients of lags and leads of differenced terms are not reported, to save space.

Sources: Author's estimations using data from World Bank (2021); NBS (2021).

Industry analysis

Similar to the national-level analysis, the industry-level analysis also starts with the aggregate production function framework, where the industry output is a function of capital, labour and a measure of innovation. Unlike the ARDL model in section four, since we are using balanced panel data, here we utilise the fixed-effect estimator in the regressions. The empirical model is Equation 6.2.

Equation 6.2

$$lnY_{it} = \beta_0 + \beta_1 lnI_{it} + \beta_2 lnK_{it-2} + \beta_3 lnK_{it-2} + \zeta_i + \epsilon_{it}$$

In Equation 6.2, Y, I, K and L are the industry output (revenue), a measure of innovation, capital and labour, respectively; ε is the error term; ζ is the unobserved industry fixed effect that can be correlated with the inputs (K, L and I); and the subscripts i and t denote industry and year, respectively. The inputs in the right-hand side of the equation can be endogenous. So, for K and L, I use the two-year lag to alleviate the possible endogeneity of capital and labour. For innovation, I utilise two years lead of the level and difference of the innovation measure as the excluded instruments.[2]

The industry panel data are sourced from the NBS and the *China Industry Statistical Yearbook* (NBS 2011–17) and cover 28 two-digit industries over six years (2012–18). The two-digit industries are aggregates of enterprises above a designated size, and as such do not include all firms in the relevant industry. The industry output (revenue, unit: RMB100 million) is deflated using the ex-factory price index of industrial producers (1985 = 100). Capital is proxied by the total assets in the industry (unit: RMB100 million), which is deflated by using the fixed-asset investment price index (1990 = 100). Labour is measured as the average number of workers in each industry (unit: 1,000 persons), data for which are sourced from the *China Industry Statistical Yearbook* (NBS 2011–17).

I use four indicators to measure innovation: the number of new-product projects, full-time-equivalent R&D researchers, R&D projects and valid invention patents. These four indicators capture both the input and the output perspectives of innovation activities, and Table 6.4 presents the summary statistics of these variables. We can observe substantial variations for all variables, which allow for identification of the impact of innovation. For example, on average, industries have revenues of almost RMB110 billion with a standard deviation of more than RMB100 billion. The revenue for the highest industry is more than 490 times that of the lowest industry.

Table 6.5 presents the regression results, where the first two columns (FE [1] and FE [2]) are fixed-effect estimations assuming exogeneity of explanatory variables and the second two columns (IV FE [1] and IV FE [2]) account for the potential endogeneity of innovation. In the IV FE estimations, I check the relevance and validity of excluded instruments by the under-identification (the Kleibergen–Paap rk LM test), weak identification (the Kleibergen–Paap rk Wald F test) and over-identification tests (the Hansen J test), and in all regressions the excluded instruments are relevant and valid. For example, in the regression with capital, labour and the number of new-product projects, the Kleibergen–Paap rk LM test statistic is 40.58 (p-value < 0.01), rejecting the null hypothesis that excluded instruments are irrelevant. The Kleibergen–Paap rk Wald F test statistic is 102.85—higher than the critical value of the Stock–Yogo weak identification test (10 per cent maximal IV size: 19.93). The Hansen J statistic is 0.735 (p-value of 0.3914), suggesting the excluded instruments are valid.

---

2   Except for the regression with the number of full-time-equivalent R&D researchers, capital and labour (the right column of panel [2] in Table 6.5), where the excluded instruments are four years lead of innovation and three years lead of differenced innovation as the two years lead instruments do not pass the Hansen J test.

In all regressions, the estimated coefficients of innovation, measured for any of the four indicators, are positive and statistically significant at the 1 per cent level. The significantly positive estimates suggest that innovation promotes industrial development in China. A 1 per cent increase in the number of new-product projects and the number of valid invention patents results in an approximately 0.8 per cent increase in the industrial output. Similarly, a 1 per cent increase in the number of full-time-equivalent R&D researchers and the number of R&D projects leads to an approximately 1 per cent increase in industrial output. Note that, despite the fact the magnitudes of the estimated coefficients of innovation exhibit some variation, they are generally consistent with each other in the sense that one estimate is not too far away from the others.

Therefore, as with the findings from national-level analysis, the industry-level analysis also confirms the growth effect of innovation, which is robust to different measures of innovation activity. Note that the industry panel data only cover seven years, and our regressions here estimate the long-run effect of innovation, rather than examining the short-run dynamics.

In Table 6.5, due to issues of data availability, process, marketing and organisational innovation are not examined. For process innovation, the available data cover 21 two-digit industries in the manufacturing sector over three years (2016–18). For marketing and organisational innovation, the data are cross-sectional, covering 28 two-digit industries in 2018. Table 6.6 reports the estimation results for process innovation, where the excluded instruments are its one-year lead of level and one-year lag of differenced process innovation. The statistical tests suggest these instruments are relevant, valid and not weak. Table 6.7 reports the regression results for marketing and organisational innovations, where I assume exogeneity of innovations, and therefore the estimated coefficients measure association, rather than causality. In both tables, the process, marketing and organisational innovations are measured as the shares of the number of innovating firms in the two-digit industries (percentage).

In Table 6.6, the estimated coefficient of process innovation is 0.01, which is statistically significant at the 1 per cent level. A 1 per cent increase in the share of firms that conduct process innovation results in a 0.01 per cent increase in industry output. In Table 6.7, the coefficients of marketing and organisational innovation are estimated to be 0.06 and 0.07, respectively, both of which are statistically significant at the 1 per cent level. The estimates suggest that both marketing and organisational innovations are positively associated with industry output. Therefore, with this smaller sample, we continue to observe significant growth effects from innovation.

Table 6.4 Summary statistics

Variable	Mean	Std dev.	Min.	Max.
Yt	1,093.7110	1,000.8160	8.58	4,222.00
Kt-2	25,645.9900	24,167.5000	1,882.30	134,531.40
Lt-2	244.1529	212.3263	13.13	909.26
npp	11,163.2600	15,076.9000	65.00	67,027.00
ferdr	73,200.9100	99,088.3900	566.80	552,618.00
rdp	10,263.7800	12,696.4100	85.00	52,317.00
nip	19,176.2400	40,928.2400	49.00	300,369.00

Notes: N = 196; Y_t = unit = RMB100 billion (current price); K_{t-2} = unit = RMB100 billion (current price); L_{t-2} = unit = 10,000; npp = number of new-product projects; ferdr = number of full-time-equivalent R&D researchers; rdp = number of R&D projects; nip = number of valid invention patents.

Source: NBS (2021).

Table 6.5 Industry estimation results

	FE [1]		FE [2]		IV FE [1]		IV FE [2]	
	Coef.	S.E.	Coef.	S.E.	Coef.	S.E.	Coef.	S.E.
[1] Innovation: Number of new-product projects								
lnI_t	0.68***	0.04	0.53***	0.06	0.76***	0.07	0.80***	0.10
lnK_{t-2}			−0.08	0.13			0.03	0.12
lnL_{t-2}			0.35***	0.11			−0.22	0.14
N	196.00		196.00		182.00		182.00	
F	341.92		144.40		102.09		105.94	
Centred R^2	0.73		0.74		0.63		0.62	
K-P rk LM					26.81		40.58	
K-P rk Wald F					52.23		102.85	
Hansen J					0.02		0.74	
[2] Innovation: Number of full-time-equivalent R&D researchers								
lnI_t	0.77***	0.04	0.76***	0.09	1.10***	0.12	0.34***	0.13
lnK_{t-2}			−0.23*	0.13			0.38***	0.09
lnL_{t-2}			0.21	0.13			0.19	0.17
N	196.00		196.00		182.00		168.00	
F	438.03		154.28		88.01		557.19	
Centred R^2	0.73		0.74		0.38		0.80	
K-P rk LM					27.51		18.91	
K-P rk Wald F					35.91		14.61	
Hansen J					0.53		6.06	

	FE [1]		FE [2]		IV FE [1]		IV FE [2]	
	Coef.	S.E.	Coef.	S.E.	Coef.	S.E.	Coef.	S.E.
[3] Innovation: Number of R&D projects								
lnl_t	0.78***	0.04	0.66***	0.07	1.07***	0.12	1.17***	0.15
lnK_{t-2}			−0.22*	0.13			−0.25**	0.12
lnL_{t-2}			0.37***	0.11			−0.31*	0.17
N	196.00		196.00		182.00		182.00	
F	440.66		173.36		81.15		86.47	
Centred R^2	0.72		0.74		0.43		0.51	
K-P rk LM					27.60		41.24	
K-P rk Wald F					37.57		81.17	
Hansen J					0.05		9.80	
[4] Innovation: Number of valid invention patents								
lnl_t	0.64***	0.03	0.44***	0.04	0.79***	0.08	0.98***	0.16
lnK_{t-2}			−0.31**	0.15			−0.48***	0.18
lnL_{t-2}			0.66***	0.11			0.00	0.18
N	196.00		196.00		182.00		182.00	
F	333.29		149.03		93.05		74.56	
Centred R^2	0.65		0.71		0.45		0.35	
K-P rk LM					29.92		37.86	
K-P rk Wald F					63.77		45.74	
Hansen J					3.57		0.67	

*** significant at the 1 per cent level

** significant at the 5 per cent level

* significant at the 10 per cent level

Notes: Standard errors are robust to heteroskedasticity and autocorrelation; K-P rk LM = Kleibergen–Paap rk LM test statistic; K-P rk Wald F = Kleibergen–Paap rk Wald F test statistic; year dummies are dropped in the regression due to multicollinearity.

Source: Author's estimations using data from NBS (2021).

Table 6.6 Industry estimation results: Process innovation

	FE				IV FE			
	Coef.	S.E.	Coef.	S.E.	Coef.	S.E.	Coef.	S.E.
lnl_t	−0.0020	0.02	−0.003	0.01	0.08***	0.01	0.01***	0.00
lnK_{t-2}			0.060	0.31			0.71***	0.04
lnL_{t-2}			0.720***	0.23			0.27***	0.05
N	63.0000		63.000		54.00		54.00	
F	0.0100		33.730		29.01		54.00	
Centred R^2	0.0003		0.440		−0.27		0.97	

	FE				IV FE			
	Coef.	S.E.	Coef.	S.E.	Coef.	S.E.	Coef.	S.E.
K-P rk LM					17.02		17.63	
K-P rk Wald F					73.29		78.84	
Hansen J					5.04		1.63	

*** significant at the 1 per cent level

** significant at the 5 per cent level

* significant at the 10 per cent level

Notes: Standard errors are robust to heteroskedasticity and autocorrelation; K-P rk LM = Kleibergen–Paap rk LM test statistic; K-P rk Wald F = Kleibergen–Paap rk Wald F test statistic; year dummies are dropped in the regression due to multicollinearity.

Source: Author's estimations using data from NBS (2021).

Table 6.7 Industry estimation results: Marketing and organisational innovation

	[1] Marketing				[2] Organisational			
	Coef.	S.E.	Coef.	S.E.	Coef.	S.E.	Coef.	S.E.
$\ln I_t$	0.09***	0.02	0.06***	0.01	0.11***	0.02	0.07***	0.02
$\ln K_{t-2}$			–0.02	0.34			–0.33	0.40
$\ln L_{t-2}$			0.78***	0.22			1.08***	0.28
Constant	2.88***	0.48	–0.26	1.91	2.12***	0.69	0.51	2.00
N	28.00		28.00		28.00		28.00	
F	27.26		36.27		23.51		34.18	
Centred R^2	0.50		0.75		0.38		0.72	

*** significant at the 1 per cent level

** significant at the 5 per cent level

* significant at the 10 per cent level

Note: Standard errors are robust to heteroskedasticity.

Source: Author's estimations using data from NBS (2021).

Concluding remarks

This chapter aims to provide an update of aggregate innovation activity in China. In light of the increasingly binding resource constraints—for example, depletion of cheap labour released from the agricultural sector—innovation is likely to play an important role in China's future economic development. Therefore, it is important to examine innovation in China to gain a better understanding of the country's future growth trajectory. I focus on the growth effects of innovation in China from several dimensions—namely, the input perspective of R&D expenditure and the number of R&D researchers, as well as the output perspective of patents and product, process, organisational and marketing innovation.

The main message of this chapter is threefold: first, innovation in China is on a growth trajectory, with this growth showing little evidence of slowing; second, innovation appears to promote economic growth in the long run at both the national and the industry levels; and third, there is a lack of a short-run growth effect from innovation at the national level. With four decades of economic growth, China is paying more and more attention to innovation, which is likely to become a new source of future economic growth. This study utilises aggregate national and industry data. Future studies, on the other hand, will be able to explore disaggregated data at the firm or project level to provide a picture of innovation in China from an alternative angle.

References

Acemoglu, D., Bimpikis, K. and Ozdaglar, A. (2011), Experimentation, patents, and innovation, *American Economic Journal: Microeconomics* 3(1): 37–77. doi.org/10.1257/mic.3.1.37.

Aldieri, L. (2011), Technological and geographical proximity effects on knowledge spillovers: Evidence from the US patent citations, *Economics of Innovation and New Technology* 20(6): 597–607. doi.org/10.1080/10438599.2011.554632.

Anwar, S. and Sun, S. (2013), Foreign entry and firm R&D: Evidence from Chinese manufacturing industries, *R&D Management* 43(4): 303–17. doi.org/10.1111/radm.12009.

Bai, J. (2013), On regional innovation efficiency: Evidence from panel data of China's different provinces, *Regional Studies* 47(5): 773–88. doi.org/10.1080/00343404.2011.591784.

Belderbos, R., Leten, B. and Suzuki, S. (2013), How global is R&D? Firm-level determinants of home-country bias in R&D, *Journal of International Business Studies* 44(8): 765–86. doi.org/10.1057/jibs.2013.33.

Boeing, P. and Mueller, E. (2019), Measuring China's patent quality: Development and validation of ISR indices, *China Economic Review* 57: 101331. doi.org/10.1016/j.chieco.2019.101331.

Buesa, M., Heijs, J. and Baumert, T. (2010), The determinants of regional innovation in Europe: A combined factorial and regression knowledge production function approach, *Research Policy* 39(6): 722–35. doi.org/10.1016/j.respol.2010.02.016.

Cai, F. (2010), Demographic transition, demographic dividend, and Lewis turning point in China, *China Economic Journal* 3(2): 107–19. doi.org/10.1080/17538963.2010.511899.

Chan, H.P. (2010), The determinants of international patenting for nine agricultural biotechnology firms, *The Journal of Industrial Economics* 58(2): 247–78. doi.org/10.1111/j.1467-6451.2010.00420.x.

Chen, K. and Guan, J. (2010), Measuring the efficiency of China's regional innovation systems: Application of network data envelopment analysis (DEA), *Regional Studies* 46(3): 355–77. doi.org/10.1080/00343404.2010.497479.

Chun, H. and Mun, S.-B. (2012), Determinants of R&D cooperation in small and medium-sized enterprises, *Small Business Economics* 39(2): 419–36. doi.org/10.1007/s11187-010-9312-5.

Dai, X. and Cheng, L. (2018), The impact of product innovation on firm-level markup and productivity: Evidence from China, *Applied Economics* 50(42): 4570–81. doi.org/10.1080/00036846.2018.1458195.

Fan, P. (2014), Innovation in China, *Journal of Economic Surveys* 28(4): 725–45. doi.org/10.1111/joes.12083.

Fan, P., Wan, G. and Lu, M. (2012), China's regional inequality in innovation capability, 1995–2006, *China & World Economy* 20(3): 16–36. doi.org/10.1111/j.1749-124X.2012.01285.x.

Figueroa, N. and Serrano, C.J. (2013), *Patent trading flows of small and large firms*, NBER Working Paper Series No. 18982, Cambridge, MA: National Bureau of Economic Research. doi.org/10.3386/w18982.

Fisch, C., Sandner, P. and Regner, L. (2017), The value of Chinese patents: An empirical investigation of citation lags, *China Economic Review* 45: 22–34. doi.org/10.1016/j.chieco.2017.05.011.

Fischer, M.M., Fröhlich, J. and Gassler, H. (1994), An exploration into the determinants of patent activities: Some empirical evidence for Austria, *Regional Studies* 28(1): 1–12. doi.org/10.1080/00343409412331348026.

Fu, W., Diez, J.R. and Schiller, D. (2012), Regional innovation systems within a transitional context: Evolutionary comparison of the electronics industry in Shenzhen and Dongguan since the opening of China, *Journal of Economic Surveys* 26(3): 534–50. doi.org/10.1111/j.1467-6419.2012.00721.x.

Fu, X. and Mu, R. (2014), Enhancing China's innovation performance: The policy choices, *China & World Economy* 22(2): 42–60. doi.org/10.1111/j.1749-124X.2014.12061.x.

Garnaut, R. and Huang, Y. (2006), Continued rapid growth and the turning point in China's development, in R. Garnaut and L. Song (eds), *The Turning Point in China's Economic Development*, 12–34, Canberra: ANU Press. doi.org/10.22459/TPCED.08.2006.02.

Gedik, Y. (2012), Geographical localisation of knowledge spillovers by Australian patent citations, *Economic Papers: A Journal of Applied Economics and Policy* 31(2): 173–81. doi.org/10.1111/j.1759-3441.2012.00172.x.

Gorodnichenko, Y. and Schnitzer, M. (2013), Financial constraints and innovation: Why poor countries don't catch up, *Journal of the European Economic Association* 11(5): 1115–52. doi.org/10.1111/jeea.12033.

Guo, D., Guo, Y. and Jiang, K. (2016), Government-subsidised R&D and firm innovation: Evidence from China, *Research Policy* 45(6): 1129–44. doi.org/10.1016/j.respol.2016.03.002.

Hammadou, H., Paty, S. and Savona, M. (2014), Strategic interactions in public R&D across European countries: A spatial econometric analysis, *Research Policy* 43(7): 1217–26. doi.org/10.1016/j.respol.2014.01.011.

Hu, A.G.Z., Zhang, P. and Zhao, L. (2017), China as number one? Evidence from China's most recent patenting surge, *Journal of Development Economics* 124: 107–19. doi.org/10.1016/j.jdeveco.2016.09.004.

Huang, L., Liu, X. and Xu, L. (2010), Regional innovation and spillover effects of foreign direct investment in China: A threshold approach, *Regional Studies* 46(5): 583–96. doi.org/10.1080/00343404.2010.520694.

Jefferson, G.H., Bai, H., Guan, X. and Yu, X. (2006), R&D performance in Chinese industry, *Economics of Innovation and New Technology* 15(4–5): 345–66. doi.org/10.1080/10438590500512851.

Kastl, J., Martimort, D. and Piccolo, S. (2013), Delegation, ownership concentration and R&D spending: Evidence from Italy, *The Journal of Industrial Economics* 61(1): 84–107. doi.org/10.1111/joie.12012.

Li, C. and Lu, J. (2018), R&D, financing constraints and export green-sophistication in China, *China Economic Review* 47: 234–44. doi.org/10.1016/j.chieco.2017.08.007.

Liu, F.-C., Simon, D.F., Sun, Y.-T. and Cao, C. (2011), China's innovation policies: Evolution, institutional structure, and trajectory, *Research Policy* 40(7): 917–31. doi.org/10.1016/j.respol.2011.05.005.

López, A. (2008), Determinants of R&D cooperation: Evidence from Spanish manufacturing firms, *International Journal of Industrial Organization* 26(1): 113–36. doi.org/10.1016/j.ijindorg.2006.09.006.

Minami, R. and Ma, X. (2010), The Lewis turning point of Chinese economy: Comparison with Japanese experience, *China Economic Journal* 3(2): 163–79. doi.org/10.1080/17538963.2010.511912.

National Bureau of Statistics of China (NBS) (2011–17), *China Industry Statistical Yearbook*, Beijing: China Statistics Press.

National Bureau of Statistics of China (NBS) (2021), *Annual Data*. Beijing: National Bureau of Statistics China. Available from: data.stats.gov.cn/easyquery.htm?cn=C01.

Nicholas, T.O.M. (2011), Did R&D firms used to patent? Evidence from the first innovation surveys, *The Journal of Economic History* 71(4): 1032–59.

Okamuro, H., Kato, M. and Honjo, Y. (2011), Determinants of R&D cooperation in Japanese start-ups, *Research Policy* 40(5): 728–38. doi.org/10.1016/j.respol.2011.01.012.

Organisation for Economic Co-operation and Development (OECD) (2018), *Oslo Manual 2018: Guidelines for collecting, reporting and using data on innovation*, 4th edn, Paris: OECD. Available from: www.oecd.org/science/oslo-manual-2018-97892643 04604-en.htm.

Rafiq, S., Salim, R. and Smyth, R. (2016), The moderating role of firm age in the relationship between R&D expenditure and financial performance: Evidence from Chinese and US mining firms, *Economic Modelling* 56: 122–32. doi.org/10.1016/j.econmod.2016.04.003.

Sun, S. and Anwar, S. (2019), R&D activities and FDI in China's iron ore mining industry, *Economic Analysis and Policy* 62: 47–56. doi.org/10.1016/j.eap.2019.01.003.

Wang, Z., Yao, Z., Gu, G., Hu, F. and Dai, X. (2014), Multi-agent-based simulation on technology innovation-diffusion in China, *Papers in Regional Science* 93(2): 385–408.

World Bank (2021), *World Development Indicators*, Washington, DC: The World Bank Group. Available from: datatopics.worldbank.org/world-development-indicators/.

Wu, F., Wu, H. and Zhang, X. (2020), How does innovation activity affect firm export behavior? Evidence from China, *Emerging Markets Finance and Trade* 56(8): 1730–51. doi.org/10.1080/1540496X.2019.1694889.

Wu, X. (2012), The evolution of innovation policy in China: A brief introduction, *Australian Economic Review* 45(4): 463–66. doi.org/10.1111/j.1467-8462.2012.00706.x.

Zhang, D. and Xie, Y. (2020), Synergistic effects of in-house and contracted R&D on export performance: Evidence from China, *Applied Economics Letters* 27(1): 9–13. doi.org/10.1080/13504851.2019.1605582.

Zhou, Y. (2014), Role of institutional quality in determining the R&D investment of Chinese firms, *China & World Economy* 22(4): 60–82. doi.org/10.1111/j.1749-124X.2014.12075.x.

Zhou, Y. and Song, L. (2016), International trade and R&D investment: Evidence from Chinese manufacturing firms, *China & World Economy* 24(1): 63–84. doi.org/10.1111/cwe.12144.

Zhu, C., Qiu, Z. and Liu, F. (2021), Does innovation stimulate employment? Evidence from China, *Economic Modelling* 94: 1007–17. doi.org/10.1016/j.econmod.2020.02.041.

7

Conditions in China's corporate sector

Joel Bowman[1]

Introduction

The conditions in China's corporate sector are important for Chinese economic growth and financial stability and have significant implications for China's major trading partners, including Australia. Chinese business investment has been an important source of economic growth and has driven demand for resource commodities. However, by the same token, the corporate sector has been the largest contributor to nonfinancial-sector leverage, and corporate debt remains high by international standards. Analysis of the activities and financial health of China's companies is also helpful for forming assessments about the broader trajectory of the Chinese economy and the effectiveness of government policies affecting businesses.

A range of previous studies has examined conditions in China's corporate sector.[2] These analyses have documented the decline in corporate profitability and the rise in leverage since 2008–09, which stemmed from the rapid increase in debt-funded investment that formed part of the Chinese Government's stimulus response to the Global Financial Crisis (GFC).

---

1   This chapter provides an update on a *RBA Bulletin* article (Bowman 2019). The views expressed in this chapter are those of the author and should not be attributed to the Reserve Bank of Australia. The author thanks Eden Hatzvi for his helpful suggestions.
2   These include Lam et al. (2017); Laurenceson and Ma (2019); Read (2017); Roberts and Zurawski (2016); and Zhang et al. (2015).

157

This chapter provides an update on recent developments by drawing on official industrial survey data. However, the official data cover only a limited number of industries and are restricted to companies above a certain size.[3] Therefore, for more detailed analysis, this chapter uses alternative data derived from the financial statements of listed companies. As of mid-2020, more than 3,700 nonfinancial companies were listed on the Shanghai and Shenzhen stock exchanges, with a combined value of RMB68 trillion (US$10 trillion) in assets.[4] Listed companies represent a relatively small but growing share of China's broader corporate sector; these firms accounted for around 10 per cent of nonfinancial corporate debt in 2019.

Profitability has declined, driven by the private sector

A range of indicators suggests that growth in revenue and profits of Chinese firms has slowed in the past few years. The profitability of industrial firms captured in the official industrial survey had been trending lower following the 2008–09 stimulus. In large part, this downward trend reflected the fact that returns to new large capital outlays declined following the large boost to investment that occurred during the period of stimulus. Profitability rebounded in 2016 and 2017 following government efforts to reduce overcapacity, leverage and the cost of doing business, under the policy framework of 'Supply-Side Structural Reform' (see Boulter 2018). However, in the past few years, growth in revenue and profits has moderated again and the return on assets has trended sharply lower (Figure 7.1).

The decline in profitability since 2015 has been driven by private companies, albeit the profitability of private firms still remains higher than that of state-owned enterprises (SOEs) (Figure 7.2).[5] In contrast, the profitability of SOEs has been trending higher. The more granular data reported by listed companies also suggest that the slowing of profitability in recent years has been driven by private companies, particularly smaller firms, and that the profitability of SOEs has been trending higher (Figure 7.3).[6]

---

3   China's National Bureau of Statistics (NBS) publishes aggregate data on the financial position of industrial (mining, manufacturing and utilities), real estate and construction firms with an annual revenue exceeding RMB20 million.

4   The data are sourced from financial statements collated by Wind Information and include all nonfinancial 'A' shares listed on the Shanghai and Shenzhen stock exchanges. The sample is unbalanced, so it includes all companies listed on the exchange at each point in time.

5   The work identifies state versus private firms using the ownership classification scheme from China's NBS. State firms are reflected by 'state-holding enterprises', which include SOEs, state-funded corporations and state-owned joint-operation enterprises for which the percentage of state assets is larger than that of any other single shareholder of the same enterprise.

6   This work identifies state versus private among listed firms using the ownership classification scheme from Wind Information. State companies include those classified as local or central state-owned companies and public enterprises. The ownership classification is time invariant.

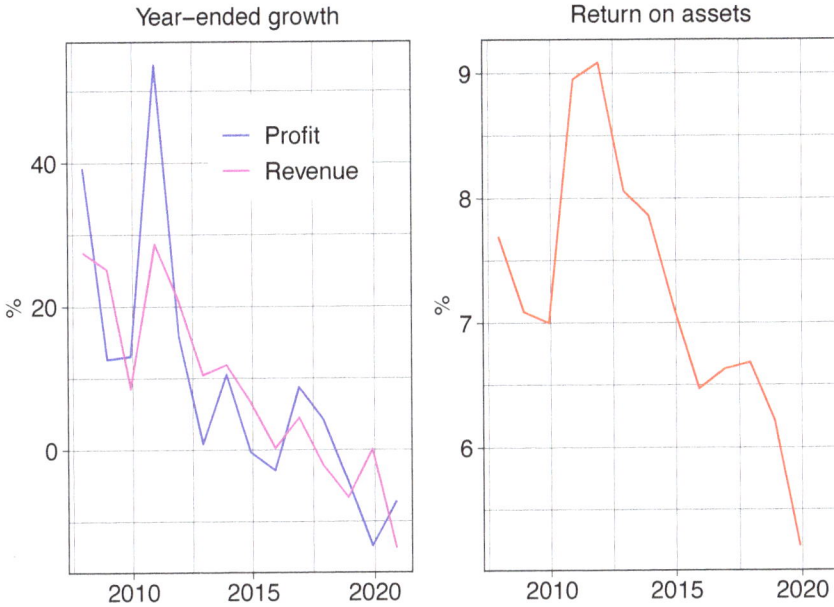

Figure 7.1 Industrial sector financial indicators

Notes: The latest observation in the left-hand panel is based on the year-to-date data until April. Return on assets is estimated as total profits divided by total assets.

Sources: Author's calculations; CEIC Data.

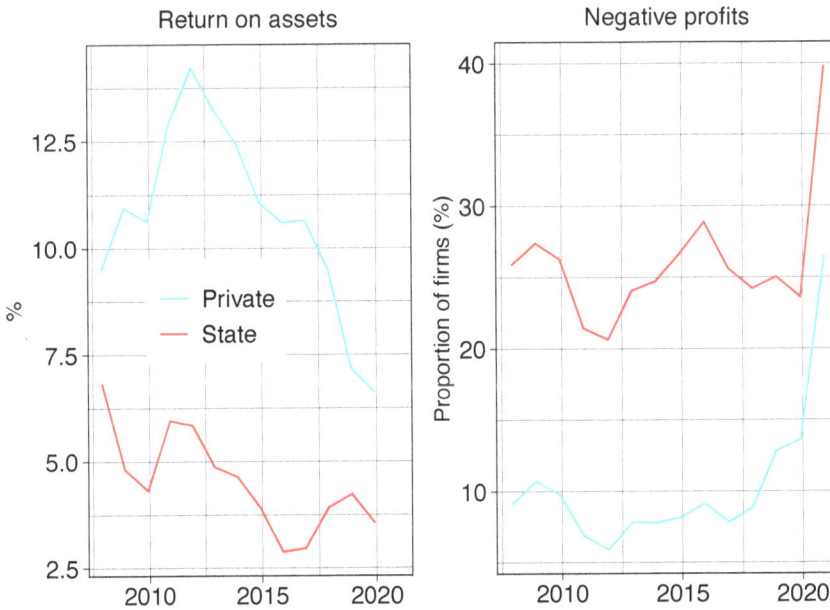

Figure 7.2 Industrial sector profitability

Notes: Return on assets is estimated as total profits divided by total assets. The latest observation in the right-hand panel is based on data up to April.

Sources: Author's calculations; CEIC Data.

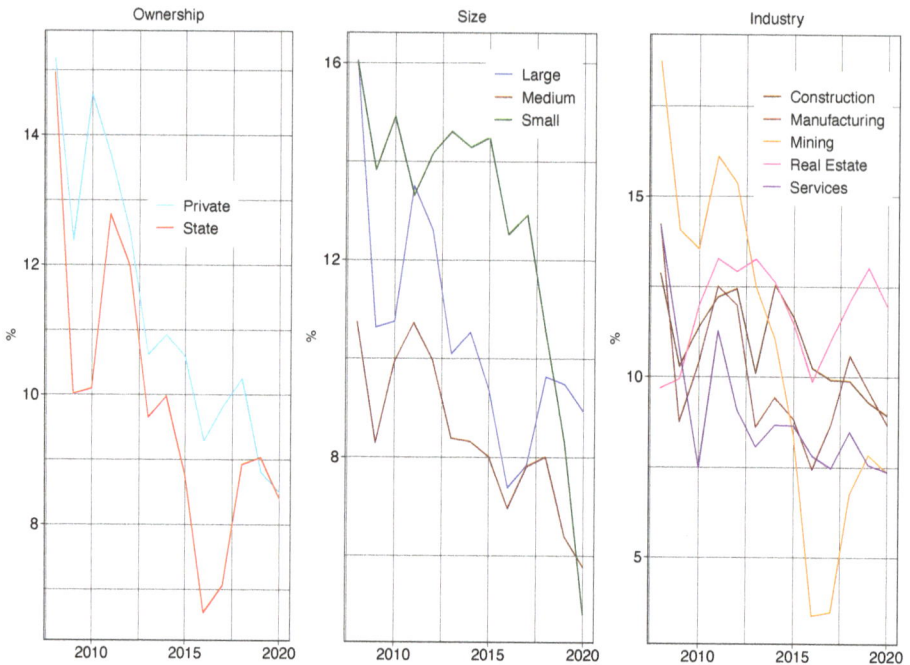

Figure 7.3 Listed company profitability (return on equity)

Notes: Return on equity is estimated as total profits (excluding goodwill loss) divided by total equity. Firms with negative equity are excluded. Enterprises are grouped by size into small (assets less than RMB1 billion or approximately US$140 million), medium (assets greater than RMB1 billion but less than RMB6 billion or US$140–850 million) and large (assets greater than RMB6 billion or US$850 million). The China Securities Regulatory Commission (CSRC) Industry Classification is used.

Sources: Author's calculations; Wind Information.

It is likely that the profitability of SOEs has continued to be supported by the government's implementation of supply-side structural reform, since the high leverage and excess capacity characterising these firms made them the primary target of these policies. SOEs have responded by reducing their investment expenditure and excess capacity. This is evident in SOE-dominated industries, such as mining. The exception has been for SOEs in the construction industry: their return on equity has declined as they reduced their leverage, but their profits relative to assets have been little changed.

The decline in profitability of private companies appears to have been exacerbated by efforts by Chinese regulators to reduce risks in the financial system; these efforts have resulted in a squeeze on less-regulated sources of credit, on which private firms are more reliant. The deterioration in profitability is also likely to be related to a broader slowdown in global manufacturing and trade that has weakened the cash flow of export-oriented firms (which are concentrated among smaller private firms).

The profitability of listed firms in the manufacturing and service industries, which are dominated by private firms, has generally declined. The slowdown in revenue and profits has occurred across all the subcomponents of manufacturing. The profitability of car manufacturers has also been severely affected by tighter emissions standards, which have forced manufacturers to reduce production of models designed to old standards faster than they can increase production of cars designed to the new standards (Cui 2019). The falling profitability of listed service industry firms appears to be related to slowing growth in consumer spending; the decline in profitability has been particularly acute for the accommodation, entertainment and retail industries.

More recently, the effect of the COVID-19 pandemic can be seen in these data. The imposition of restrictions on activity led to a further contraction in revenue growth and the proportion of firms recording losses rose materially for both private firms and SOEs in 2020.

The private sector is most exposed to the global trade slowdown

The deteriorating profitability of private companies in China is partly related to global developments. The global slowdown in trade, underpinned by weaker growth in some advanced economies and the US–China trade and technology dispute, is likely to have weighed on corporate cash flows, particularly for export-oriented manufacturing firms. Exports rebounded strongly in 2020, reflecting increased demand for personal protective equipment, medical supplies and goods needed for remote work; China has benefited from being one of the first economies to restart production following the onset of COVID-19. However, export growth in China may resume its decline as some of this pandemic-related demand dissipates and because of the sharp decline in global growth in 2020.

Listed private companies receive a higher proportion of their revenue from offshore than SOEs, and this has been increasingly the case over time. This is reflected in the fact that the proportion of China's exports coming from the private sector increased from 5 per cent in 2000 to 50 per cent in 2019, while the contribution from SOEs declined (Figure 7.4).

The slowdown in Chinese exports has weighed on employment in China's industrial sector (particularly manufacturing) (Figure 7.5). Export-oriented firms are more labour intensive than firms with low export exposure, and export-oriented firms have responded to the slowdown in trade by reducing their labour intensity (Bowman 2019).

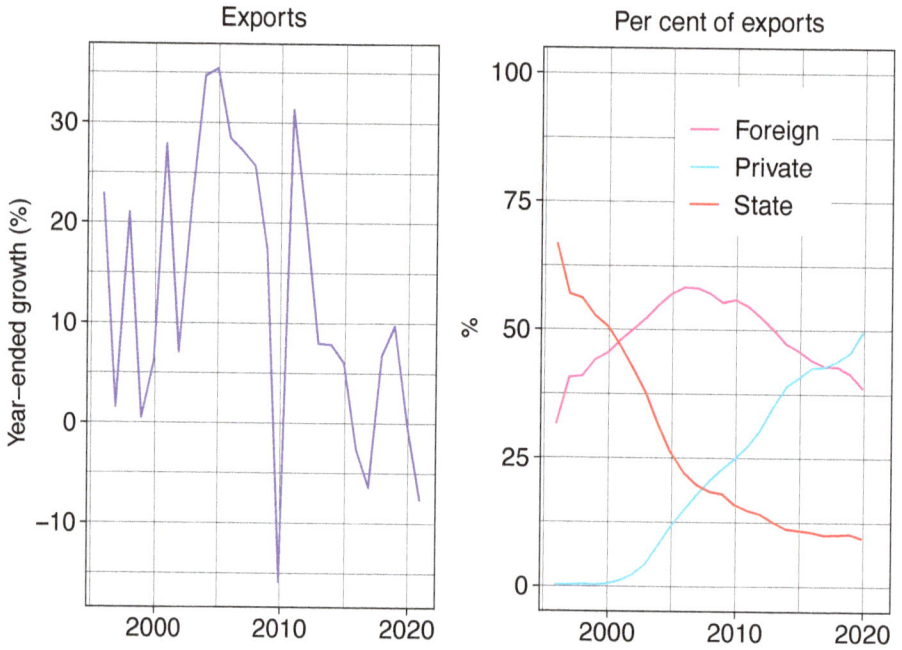

Figure 7.4 Exports

Note: The latest observation in the left-hand panel is based on the year-to-date data up to May.

Sources: Author's calculations; CEIC Data.

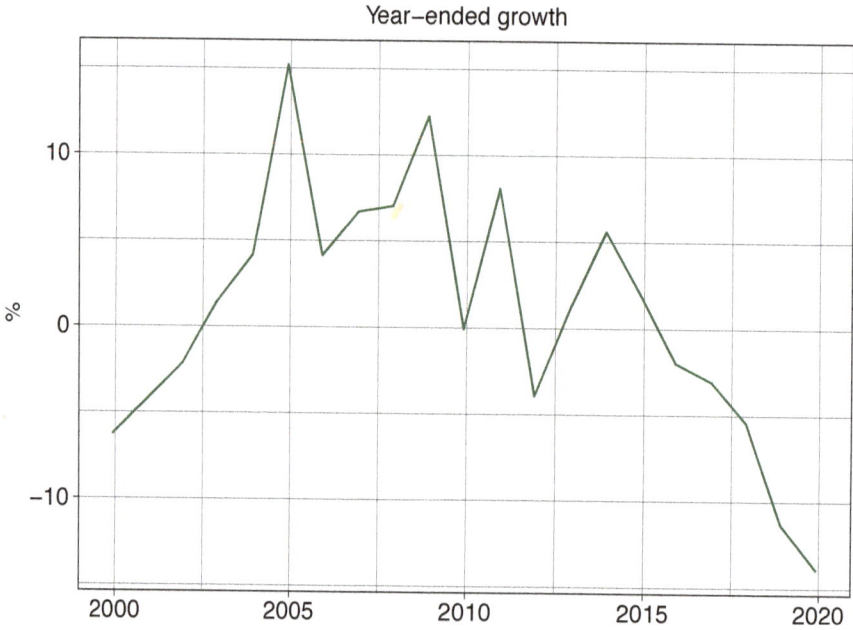

Figure 7.5 Industrial employment

Sources: Author's calculations; CEIC Data.

Corporate leverage has declined

Corporate sector leverage, measured by the debt-to-equity ratio, has declined in the past few years (Figure 7.6).[7] The amount of leverage among SOEs has declined, reflecting the success of supply-side policies, which were reinforced by the introduction of deleveraging as a key performance metric for centrally supervised SOEs (State Council 2018).

Leverage has been declining over recent years in the construction and mining industries, driven largely by SOEs. The reduction in excess capacity as a result of supply-side structural reform is likely to have contributed to increased profitability in the remaining firms, increasing their scope to reduce their leverage. The reduction in leverage among listed construction firms has also been supported by cash flows being directed away from capital expenditure and towards debt repayment. Leverage in the manufacturing and service industries—which are dominated by private firms—has moderated since the early 2010s but has been stable for the past few years.

Leverage remains elevated in the real estate industry, having increased strongly over a number of years, but has declined since 2017 (Figure 7.7). However, conventional leverage measures, such as the debt-to-equity ratio, do not fully capture the financial risks facing property developers because they exclude non-debt liabilities such as presold apartments. Accounting for both debt and nondebt liabilities, data on financing flows for both listed and unlisted Chinese real estate developers suggest they had at least RMB25 trillion in debt outstanding by mid-2019 (27 per cent of GDP).[8] The authorities have imposed restrictions to curb the amount of financing directed to the real estate sector amid concerns that financing to other industries may be 'crowded out' (Guo 2019).

Developers have responded by increasing their use of presale funding, while delaying construction and extending delivery times to reduce near-term expenditure (Kemp et al. 2020). This has increased the risk that developers could face financial pressure should they encounter a shortage of funding needed to deliver presold homes. Increased regulation of real estate financing may help prevent leverage from ratcheting up further but may also increase the sector's vulnerability to a negative shock.

---

7   The decline in corporate leverage is also evident with the Bank for International Settlements (BIS) measure of China's nonfinancial corporate debt as a percentage of GDP, which declined from 160 per cent in 2016 to 149 per cent in 2019.

8   This consists of RMB11 trillion of bank loans, RMB3 trillion of trust loans, RMB2 trillion of entrusted loans, RMB4 trillion of bonds outstanding and RMB6 trillion in deposits and advance payments.

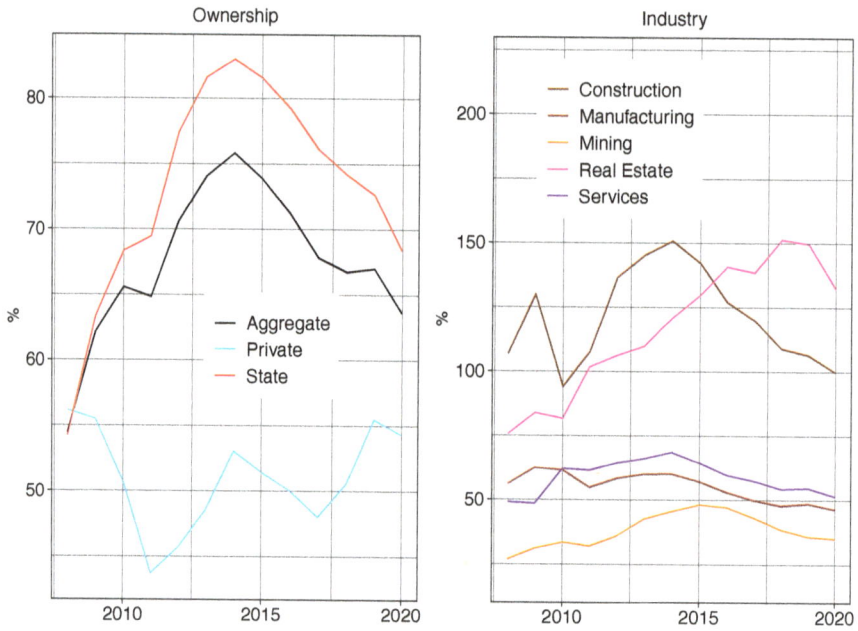

Figure 7.6 Listed company leverage (debt to equity)

Notes: Debt to equity is estimated as total debt (interest-bearing liabilities) divided by total equity. Firms with negative equity are excluded.

Sources: Author's calculations; Wind Information.

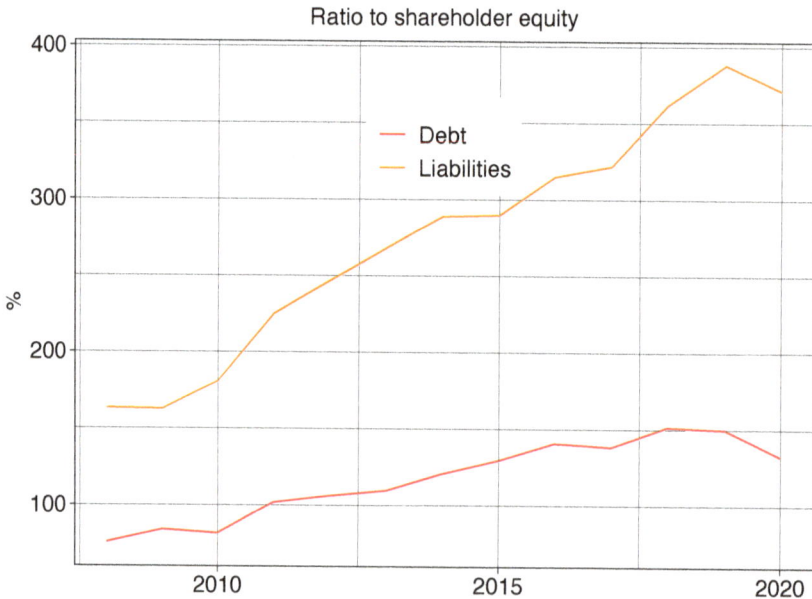

Figure 7.7 Listed real estate company leverage

Note: Firms with negative equity are excluded.

Sources: Author's calculations; Wind Information.

Financial conditions for smaller firms tightened pre-COVID-19

Funding conditions tightened for smaller firms (predominately privately owned) pre-COVID-19 in response to the authorities' deleveraging campaign. This campaign predominantly targeted shadow banking and small banks in China, both of which disproportionately lend to smaller firms. In response, loans to small firms had been growing at a slower pace than broader loan growth (Figure 7.8). The cause of the comparably slower growth of loans to small firms appears to be supply driven, as survey measures suggest loan demand has increased for smaller firms since 2018.

The tighter financing conditions have also been evident in listed company data, as the implied interest rate for smaller firms has increased more rapidly compared with that for larger firms over the past few years (Figure 7.9).

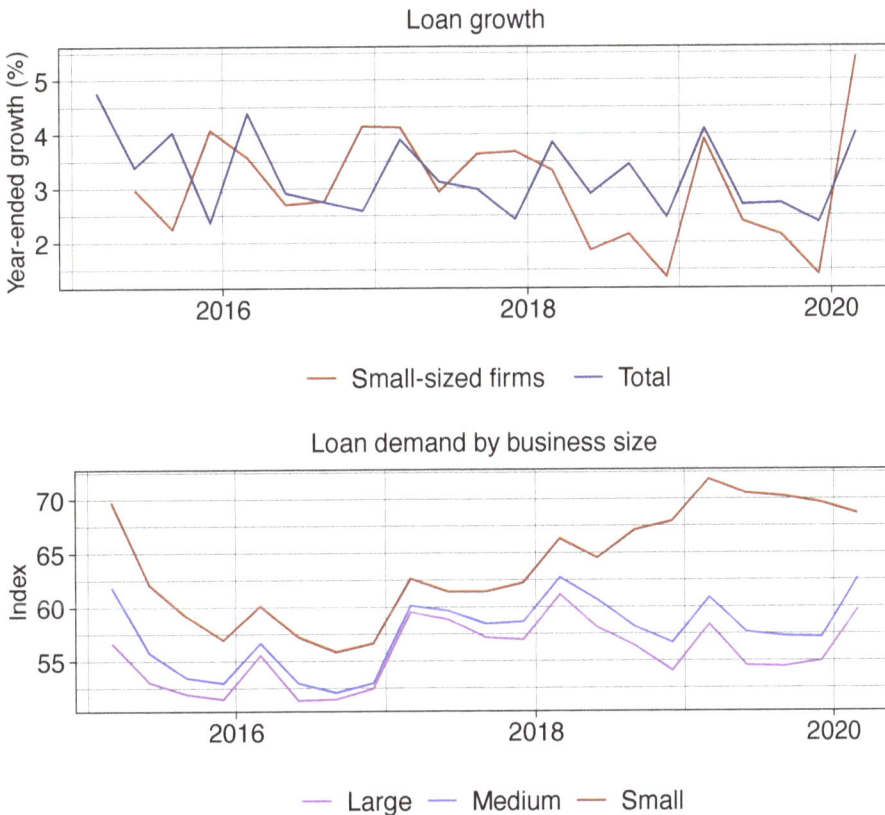

Figure 7.8 Loan growth and demand

Note: Loan demand proxied by the Banking Climate Index, which is estimated using survey responses collected by the People's Bank of China.

Sources: Author's calculations; CEIC Data.

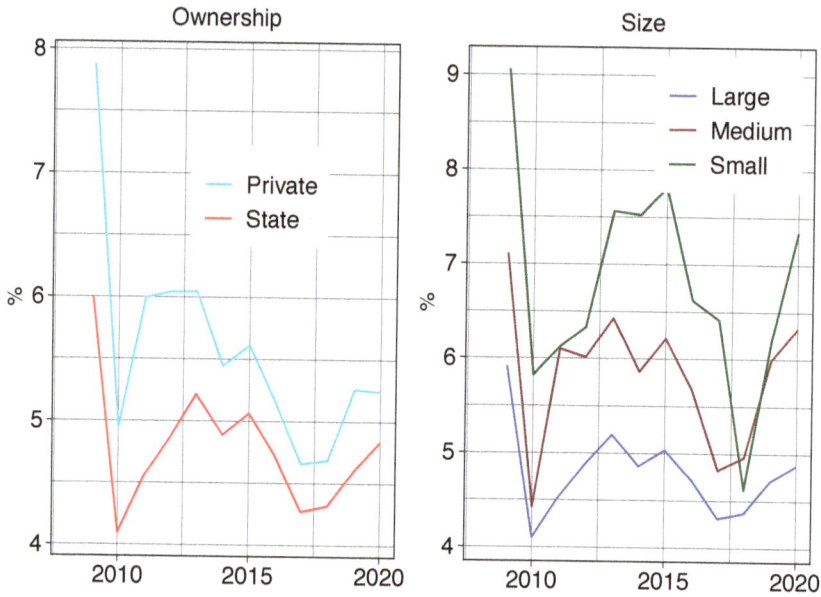

Figure 7.9 Listed company implied interest rates

Notes: Estimated as ratio of annual interest expense to average debt in the current and previous years. Firms with negative equity or debt are excluded.

Sources: Author's calculations; Wind Information.

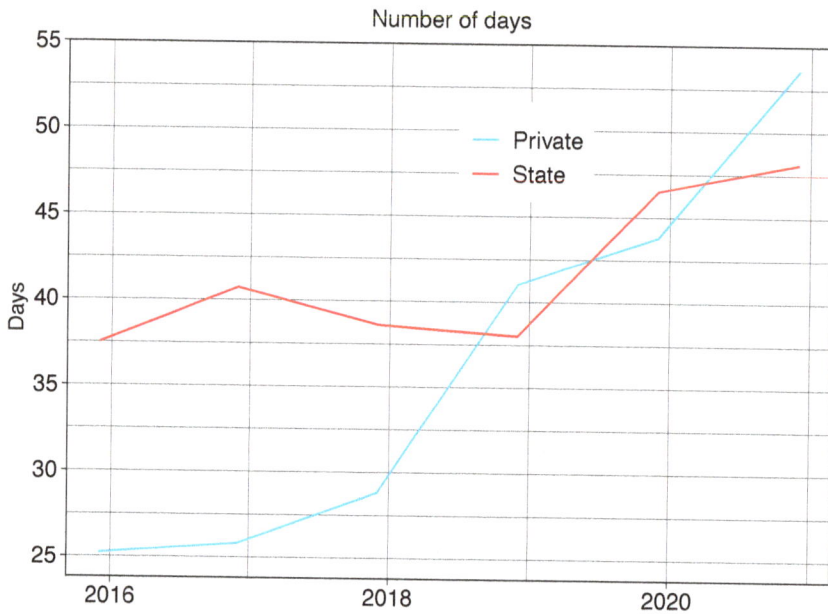

Figure 7.10 Industrial sector accounts receivable average payback

Notes: Measures the average number of days in which accounts receivable are collected. The last observation is for April 2020.

Source: CEIC Data.

The tightening of financing conditions of smaller private firms has been exacerbated by developments in trade credit. SOEs improved their own liquidity positions by delaying payments to private suppliers. This has resulted in a sharp rise in the average number of days before accounts receivable are collected for private firms (Figure 7.10).

The owners of listed private companies, especially smaller firms, have responded to this tightening of financial conditions by pledging an increasing proportion of their equity as collateral to obtain funding.[9] The tightening of financial conditions has also contributed to a rise in corporate bond defaults by private enterprises (albeit from low levels).

Authorities have responded to recent trends

The Chinese authorities have enacted a number of easing measures in response to these trends and to the broader effects of COVID-19. These measures are focused on easing the financial pressures facing private firms, particularly small enterprises. Some of the key measures announced to date include the following:[10]

- Financial regulators have instructed banks to increase lending to private enterprises (Guo 2018). This has included the setting of targets for the growth rate of small and micro-enterprise loans for large commercial banks. The authorities also announced in May 2020 that loan repayments for small and medium enterprises should be extended as much as possible (Li 2020).
- The People's Bank of China (PBC) has introduced a number of new measures to support the flow of credit, particularly to smaller firms, including a number of targeted reductions in the reserve requirement ratio and reduced interest rates on some of its lending operations. The authorities also expanded the PBC's relending facility.[11]
- Fiscal authorities have extended tax and fee reduction policies for small businesses. This includes exempting small businesses from making contributions to old-age insurance, unemployment insurance and work-injury compensation insurance schemes. The authorities will also reduce or cancel value-added taxes (VATs) for small-scale taxpayers. The payment of corporate income taxes by small businesses will be postponed until 2021 (STA 2020).

---

9   For further details, see IMF (2019).
10   Further details on the financing problems for smaller private businesses and the policy response in China are articulated in PBC and CBIRC (2019).
11   The relending facility enables banks to obtain funding from the PBC in exchange for loans they have extended to certain customers—typically, small businesses.

- Central SOEs must reduce rents for small firms, particularly those heavily affected by the COVID-19 pandemic (SASAC 2020).
- China's Premier, Li Keqiang (2018), has instructed SOEs that they 'must resolutely put an end to the arrears of private enterprise accounts', to reduce the rising stock of accounts receivable owing to private companies.

The authorities have also supported the broader corporate sector by steadily increasing the amount of direct government subsidies (Figure 7.11), a rising portion of which has been directed towards larger enterprises, particularly in the manufacturing industry. The authorities may also provide support to companies through other measures. For example, access to funding is cheaper and more readily available for SOEs compared with private firms, in part due to the widespread perception of implicit guarantees (Bunny 2020). The recent rise in private firms' borrowing costs, particularly smaller firms, has occurred despite efforts by the authorities to lower these costs. This suggests that easing financial conditions for smaller private firms may prove to be a challenging task for the authorities in practice.

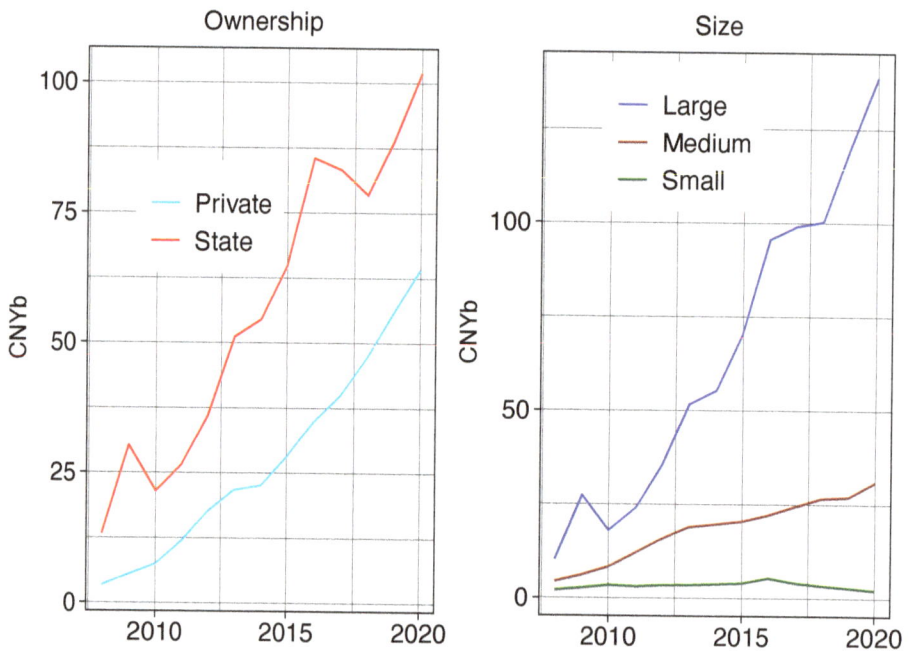

Figure 7.11 Listed company direct government subsidies

Notes: Enterprises are grouped by size into small (assets less than RMB1 billion or approximately US$140 million), medium (assets greater than RMB1 billion but less than RMB6 billion or US$140–850 million) and large (assets greater than RMB6 billion or US$850 million).

Sources: Author's calculations; Wind Information.

Improving the efficiency of the corporate sector

The Chinese authorities have announced a range of measures in recent years that, if successfully implemented, will improve the efficiency of China's corporate sector. These include:

- Promoting the market-based allocation of land, labour and capital so that efficient firms can readily access the necessary factors of production (State Council 2020). The Chinese authorities intend to increase the market-based allocation of land by reforming the rural land expropriation system, industrial land use and its land management mechanism. The allocation of labour will be enhanced by deepening reforms to the household registration system by relaxing restrictions on residential registration. The market-based allocation of capital will be advanced by improving the issuance and delisting system of the stock market, accelerating the development of the bond market and opening up the financial industry to international markets.

- Following the principle of competitive neutrality so that enterprises under all forms of ownership are treated equally and resources are allocated efficiently between the state and private sectors (Li 2019). The OECD (2012) suggests that a competitive-neutrality framework should have some of the following elements: SOEs providing public services should be given adequate and transparent compensation while the commercial operations of SOEs should be separated from their responsibilities for public services; SOEs operating in a commercial and competitive environment should earn similar rates of return to comparable businesses; SOEs and private firms should enjoy equal tax, supervision and government procurement treatment; and debt neutrality. Mo Wangui (2019), Deputy Director General at the PBC, highlighted that gaps still exist between private firms and SOEs with regards to the protection of property rights, market access and equal access to factors of production including financial resources.

- Resolving zombie firms. The State Council mandated the closure or reorganisation of zombie companies, which are defined as firms operating in overcapacity industries that have experienced three consecutive years of losses (State Council 2015). The authorities hope to achieve these goals by improving the bankruptcy process, increasing financial support for mergers and strictly forbidding financial subsidies directed towards zombie enterprises. The State Council (2019) suggested it would dispose of zombie enterprises by the end of 2020.

Many of these reforms could be difficult to implement. In addition, the Chinese authorities have taken a number of steps in recent years that will increase the role of the state in the activities of the corporate sector, suggesting there may be limits to the extent that efficiency will be prioritised. For example, the authorities have sought to enhance their oversight of corporate decision-making (for both SOEs and private enterprises) and to channel more capital towards strategic industries (Naughton 2018). The ability of the Chinese authorities to direct the activities of the corporate sector has also been a factor in China's rapid economic recovery from COVID-19. The authorities may be more cautious about implementing reforms that weaken their ability to respond to future crises in this way.

Conclusion

The profitability of China's corporate sector has been trending lower alongside the broader moderation in economic momentum. In recent years, profitability has been weighed down by tighter domestic financial regulation, the slowdown in global trade and, in 2020, the imposition of domestic and international restrictions to contain COVID-19. The decline in profitability has been driven by labour-intensive private enterprises and has contributed to weak employment outcomes in the industrial sector.

Recent efforts by the authorities to reduce risks in the financial system have been successful in reducing leverage in China's corporate sector. However, financial conditions have tightened for smaller private enterprises, likely as a by-product of the greater regulatory scrutiny. The authorities have subsequently tried to ease financial conditions for smaller private firms but achieving this in practice could be challenging.

Risks remain elevated in the real estate sector, where tighter regulation of financing flows has led developers to rely increasingly on nondebt liabilities such as presales of apartments. The risk that developers encounter cash-flow difficulties and are unable to deliver presold homes has increased following the COVID-19 pandemic.

In the longer term, the efficiency of China's corporate sector can be supported by the effective implementation of a number of announced government measures including the liberalisation of factor markets, expanding competitive-neutrality policies and resolving zombie companies.

References

Boulter, J. (2018), China's supply-side structural reform, *RBA Bulletin*, December, Sydney: Reserve Bank of Australia. Available from: www.rba.gov.au/publications/bulletin/2018/dec/chinas-supply-side-structural-reform.html.

Bowman, J. (2019), Conditions in China's corporate sector, *RBA Bulletin*, December, Sydney: Reserve Bank of Australia. Available from: www.rba.gov.au/publications/bulletin/2019/dec/conditions-in-chinas-corporate-sector.html.

Bunny, M. (2020), Private sector financial conditions in China, *RBA Bulletin*, September, Sydney: Reserve Bank of Australia. Available from: www.rba.gov.au/publications/bulletin/2020/sep/private-sector-financial-conditions-in-china.html.

CEIC Data (2021), *CEIC: Global Economic Data, Indicators, Charts & Forecasts*, New York: CEIC Data.

Cui, E. (2019), *The emissions mess in autos*, Gavekal Research Note, July, Hong Kong: Gavekal.

Guo, S. (2018), Guo Shuqing answered questions on financial support for private enterprises, Press release, November, China Banking Insurance and Regulatory Commission, Beijing. Available from: www.cbrc.gov.cn/chinese/newShouDoc/7F7EDCDDD5A04396A00E8E23F8E2E813.html.

Guo, S. (2019), Opening remarks, 11th Lujiazui Forum, Shanghai, 14 June. Available from: www.bis.org/review/r190627n.htm.

International Monetary Fund (IMF) (2019), Box 1.1: China's share-collateralised lending and its financial stability implications, *Global Financial Stability Review* (April): 47–48.

Jahan, S. and Kang, K.H. (2019), Applying competitive neutrality in corporate financing in China, in K. Guo and A. Schipke (eds), *PBC and IMF Seventh Joint Conference: Opening Up and Competitive Neutrality—The international experience and insights for China*, 35–41, Washington, DC: IMF.

Kemp, J., Suthakar, A. and Williams, T. (2020), China's residential property sector, *RBA Bulletin*, June, Sydney: Reserve Bank of Australia. Available from: www.rba.gov.au/publications/bulletin/2020/jun/chinas-residential-property-sector.html#fn4.

Lam, R., Schipke, A., Tan, Y. and Tan, Z. (2017), *Resolving China's zombies: Tackling debt and raising productivity*, IMF Working Paper 17/266, Washington, DC: International Monetary Fund.

Laurenceson, J. and Ma, G. (2019), China's debt challenges: Stylised facts, drivers and policy implications, *Singapore Economic Review* 64(4): 815–37.

Li, K. (2018), Pay close attention to solving the problem of government departments and state-owned enterprises defaulting on private enterprise accounts, [In Chinese], State Council Executive Meeting, Beijing, 10 November. Available from: www.gov.cn/premier/2018-11/10/content_5339135.htm.

Li, K. (2019), Government work report, Delivered at the Second Session of the 13th National People's Congress of the People's Republic of China, Beijing, 5 March.

Li, K. (2020), Government work report, Delivered at the Third Session of the 13th National People's Congress of the People's Republic of China, Beijing, 22 May.

Mo, W. (2019), Competitive neutrality: A summary of the current conditions, in K. Guo and A. Schipke (eds), *PBC and IMF Seventh Joint Conference: Opening Up and Competitive Neutrality—The international experience and insights for China*, 23–25, Washington, DC: IMF.

Naughton, B. (2018), State enterprise reform today, in R. Garnaut, L. Song and F. Cai (eds), *China's 40 Years of Reform and Development: 1978–2018*, 375–91, Canberra: ANU Press. doi.org/10.22459/CYRD.07.2018.20.

Organisation for Economic Co-operation and Development (OECD) (2012), *Competitive Neutrality: Maintaining a level playing field between public and private business*, Paris: OECD Publishing.

People's Bank of China (PBC) and China Banking and Insurance Regulatory Commission (CBIRC) (2019), White paper on financial services for smaller businesses, Press release, 24 June, PBC, Beijing. Available from: www.pbc.gov.cn/en/3688110/3688172/3850272/index.html.

Read, C. (2017), Conditions in China's listed corporate sector, *RBA Bulletin*, June, 67–74, Sydney: Reserve Bank of Australia.

Roberts, I. and Zurawski, A. (2016), Changing patterns of corporate leverage in China: Evidence from listed companies, in L. Song, R. Garnaut, F. Cai and L. Johnston (eds), *China's New Sources of Economic Growth. Volume 1: Reform, resources and climate change*, 271–312, Canberra: ANU Press. doi.org/10.22459/CNSEG.07.2016.12.

State Council (2015), *State Council Cleans Up 'Zombie Enterprises' That Have Suffered Losses for More Than Three Years*, [In Chinese], 10 December, Beijing: State Council of the People's Republic of China. Available from: www.gov.cn/zhengce/2015-12/10/content_5022115.htm.

State Council (2018), *Guiding Opinions on Strengthening the Asset and Liability Constraints of State-Owned Enterprises*, [In Chinese], 13 September, Beijing: State Council of the People's Republic of China. Available from: www.gov.cn/zhengce/2018-09/13/content_5321717.htm.

State Council (2019), *Step Up Efforts to Properly Dispose of Zombie Enterprises*, [In Chinese], 30 January, Beijing: State Council of the People's Republic of China. Available from: www.gov.cn/xinwen/2019-01/30/content_5362166.htm.

State Council (2020), *Opinions of the Central Committee of the Communist Party of China and the State Council on Building a More Complete System and Mechanism for Market-Oriented Allocation of Factors*, [In Chinese], 9 April, Beijing: State Council of the People's Republic of China. Available from: www.gov.cn/zhengce/2020-04/09/content_5500622.htm.

State-Owned Assets Supervision and Administration Commission (SASAC) (2020), *Notice on supporting the development of small, medium and micro enterprises and individual industrial and commercial households to actively reduce or exempt operating house rent*, [In Chinese], SASAC Department Financial Review (2020) No. 42, 3 April, Beijing: SASAC. Available from: www.sasac.gov.cn/n2588030/n2588939/c14767666/content.html.

State Taxation Administration of the People's Republic of China (STA) (2020), Govt work report sends encouraging messages, Press release, 25 May, STA, Beijing. Available from: www.chinatax.gov.cn/eng/c101269/c5150281/content.html.

Tan, Y., Huang, Y. and Woo, W. (2016), Zombie firms and the crowding-out of private investment in China, *Asian Economic Papers* 15(3): 32–55.

Wind Information (1994–2021), *Wind Financial Terminal*, Shanghai: Wind Information Co. Ltd. Available from: www.wind.com.cn/en/wft.html.

Zhang, W., Han, G., Ng, B. and Chan, S. (2015), *Corporate leverage in China: Why has it increased fast in recent years and where do the risks lie?*, Working Paper 102015, Hong Kong: Hong Kong Institute for Monetary Research.

8

The transformation and upgrading of processing trade and its impact on firms' productivity

Kunwang Li and Haoran Hu

Introduction

Since the beginning of the reform and opening-up period, China's foreign trade has become one of the important drivers of economic growth. The proportion of exports in total gross domestic product (GDP) increased from less than 4 per cent in the initial period of opening up to its highest value, of 34.5 per cent, in 2007. China's export growth has been largely related to the rapid development of processing trade. Before the Global Financial Crisis (GFC), processing trade accounted for more than 50 per cent of China's exports. Processing trade has made great contributions to employment, industrialisation and foreign trade in China.

The processing trade policy was introduced in the late 1970s in China. Processing trade refers to the business activity of importing all or part of the raw materials, auxiliary materials, parts and components, accessories and packaging materials from abroad in bond and re-exporting the finished products after processing or assembly by enterprises within the mainland. China's processing trade is divided into two categories: processing with supplied materials and processing with imported materials. When processing with supplied materials, the imported materials and parts are supplied by foreign parties, who are also responsible for selling the finished products. The enterprises processing with supplied materials do not have to make foreign exchange payments for the imports and only charge the foreign party a processing fee. Under processing trade with imported materials, the enterprises make foreign exchange payments for those imported materials and parts and export the finished products after processing.

China's processing trade has developed in the context of economic globalisation and the deepening international division of labour, relying on factors such as low land and labour costs, and facilitated by international industrial transfers. However, China's processing trade has also faced problems—for instance, many processing trade enterprises remain at the low end of the global value chain, with lagging technology and low research and development (R&D) capabilities, and many are implicated in causing serious harm to the environment. As the costs of labour, land and resources grow and environmental pressures increase, China's processing trade faces more and more challenges.

Starting in 2003, China introduced a series of policies aimed at promoting the transformation and upgrading of processing trade. Primary examples of these measures include:

1. Attracting foreign direct investment in more advanced technology and greater value-added content in processing trade and encouraging multinational companies to transfer their R&D centres to China.
2. Adjusting the processing trade product catalogue of prohibited categories seven times between 2003 and 2005 to include 1,803 products, with the aim of optimising the structure of processing trade.
3. Encouraging labour-intensive processing enterprises in the eastern region to develop in the central and western regions, and successfully establishing 44 processing trade transfer bases in underdeveloped regions in China since 2006.
4. Reducing or abolishing export tax rebates for products related to energy-intensive, high-pollution and resource-based industries.
5. Establishing the national demonstration zone for the transformation and upgrading of processing trade in the Pearl River Delta and Suzhou Industrial Park in 2010.

The overall goal of these policies is to promote the adjustment of processing trade from low technology and low value added to high technology and high value added, and to lead the upgrading of domestic technology and economic development.

Figure 8.1 shows that, before 2006, the trends for processing trade and ordinary trade were basically the same, but after 2007, the proportion of processing trade in total exports began to decline sharply. The proportion of processing trade exports in 2004 was 55.3 per cent and was much the same the following year. The slight decline witnessed in 2006 was related to the Ministry of Commerce's significant adjustment of the export product catalogue for processing trade in 2005. Beginning in 2011, the proportion of processing trade was exceeded by that of ordinary trade.

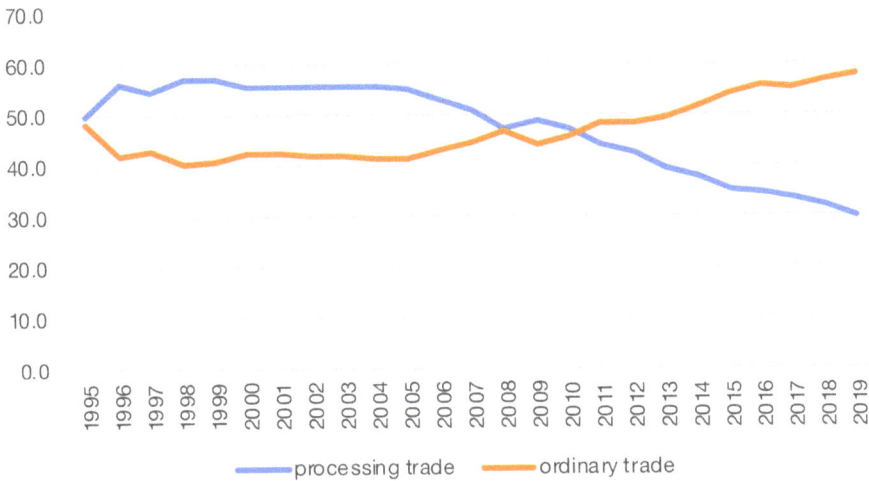

Figure 8.1 Proportions of processing trade and ordinary trade in total exports
Source: Chinese Monthly Customs Transactions, General Administration of Customs of China.

The strategy of transforming and upgrading processing trade involves the adjustment of business entities, product catalogues and production chains. At the microlevel, the impact of policies on processing trade enterprises takes effect through three main channels: first, enterprises shift from processing to ordinary trade or no longer engage in export; second, firms continue to engage in processing trade, but their product categories shift to products with higher technological content or higher value added; and third, processing trade enterprises move their processing bases from the coast to inland regions. The evaluation of industrial policy needs to look at its impact on resource allocation. Based on the theory of heterogeneous firms' trade, if a firm's average productivity increases after a policy is implemented, the policy improves the efficiency of resource allocation; otherwise, it leads to resource misallocation.

This chapter aims to investigate the impact of processing trade transformation and upgrading policies on China's resource allocation. We use Chinese customs and industrial panel data to empirically test the impact of these policies on enterprise productivity by using the double-difference method.

The rest of the chapter is arranged as follows: section two describes the data sources, section three is the econometric specification of the evaluating policy, section four is the empirical test and the final section provides concluding remarks.

Data and sources

The data used in this study are drawn from two large panel datasets of Chinese manufacturing firms. The first is the Chinese Monthly Customs Transactions from 2002 to 2006, which contain the value and quantity of all Chinese trade transactions at the six-digit product level. We supplement the trade data with information on manufacturing firms from the Annual Survey of Manufacturing—an extensive survey of Chinese manufacturing firms conducted each year by the National Bureau of Statistics of China (NBS). We merge the two datasets to create a sample set with 204,968 observations, accounting for 27.7 per cent of the customs database and 13.1 per cent of the manufacturing database. The customs database was constructed beginning in 2000, which is later than the manufacturing database. We therefore set the start of our empirical study as the year 2000 and opted to use 2000–06 as our research period. After 2007, a lot of blanks exist in the 'trade mode' column in the customs database and the label of 'ordinary trade' is missing. However, manual checking finds that these blanks are not equivalent to 'ordinary trade'. From another perspective, Chinese exports began to decline in February 2007, affected by the US subprime mortgage crisis, with processing trade exports declining even more rapidly. Therefore, the subprime mortgage crisis, together with the RMB4 trillion economic stimulus plan enacted in 2008 and the resulting European debt crisis, can generate an ambiguous effect on those corresponding observations.

Chinese Monthly Customs Transactions database

The customs database contains the product-level transaction data provided by the General Administration of Customs. It records all transaction data for import and export firms on a monthly basis, and we add up this data to obtain an annual value. Observed variables include firm name, telephone number, postal code, dollar-denominated import and export values, eight-digit Harmonised System (HS) code of imported and exported products, export destination, transportation method, trade mode and firm status. We use customs data to identify firms' trading patterns and status. Trade patterns include ordinary trade, processing trade and other trade modes. We classify firms marked as 'ordinary trade' as ordinary trade firms and classify firms labelled 'processing trade with imported materials' or 'processing trade with supplied materials' as processing trade firms. Together these two groups of firms account for about 98 per cent of the country's total exports. There is a deviation in the above classifications: since some firms are engaged in both ordinary trade and processing trade, we classify them as mixed-pattern firms. To eliminate the problem of sample selection bias, we will group the mixed-pattern firms according to the proportion of their processing trade export participation. We then incorporate them into the treatment and control groups as needed.

To get a direct measure of firms' productivity, more firm-level information is needed. The manufacturing database contains such information as firms' financial status, industry and region. To merge the customs and manufacturing databases, we follow the method of Tian and Yu (2012). First, we directly match the company name; then we conduct a second matching process for data that remain unmatched in the customs database. Both the customs database and the manufacturing database contain information on phone numbers and postal codes. We use the last seven digits of the phone numbers and the postal codes as related information to identify the same firm in the two databases.

Annual Survey of Manufacturing database

The observations of the manufacturing database can be refined to the county level with four-digit industries. We follow the method from existing research to process these observations (Brandt et al. 2012; Nie et al. 2012). The industry coding standard has changed over the course of our sample period: before 2002, the manufacturing database used the national economic industry classification (GB/T4754-1994); during the period 2003–06, the classification standard changed to GB/T4754-2002. To keep the industry code consistent, we unify the classification standard into the national economic industry classification (GB/T4754-2002). For the verification of area codes, we reconfirm the area codes according to the administrative division codes published on the website of the NBS. We delete observations with missing records for assets, value added and net value of fixed assets. We also delete observations that do not comply with accounting rules, dropping firms with total assets less than current assets, total assets less than net fixed assets or accumulated depreciation less than current depreciation. Firms with fewer than eight employees are also excluded.

The manufacturing database includes indicators such as a firm's output value, fixed assets and number of employees, which facilitate the calculation of total factor productivity (TFP). Currently, the mainstream econometric method for identifying the TFP value is Olley–Pakes' (1996) semiparametric estimation method (referred to as the OP method) and Levinsohn–Petrin's (2003) estimation method (referred to as the LP method). The Solow residual value is prone to endogeneity problems and sample selection bias, while the use of the OP and LP methods can solve these problems. This chapter uses the OP method as the basic regression method to construct a TFP index (TFP_OP), while using the LP method for mutual robustness tests. The data needed for calculating TFP are all from the manufacturing database.

Empirical model specification

When estimating the effect generated by a certain type of industrial policy, problems can potentially include: 1) the direct policy measure cannot be identified by constructing indexes as a regressor; 2) other exogenous shocks simultaneously involved in the phenomenon may be attenuated in our estimation methodology; and 3) it is critical to be able to specify the parallel trends in the pretreatment periods. To clarify these issues, we opted to use a difference-in-difference regression method, through which we are able to separate the observations into treatment and control groups. By introducing time dummy variables, we are able to control for pretreatment parallel trends. Given that policies aimed at the transformation and upgrading of processing trade were launched in 2003, we chose that year as the starting point for the treatment.

We argue that firms primarily involved in the export sector behave differently from those in non-export sectors. Export firms are affected by tariffs and other foreign trade policies, while non-export firms' product markets are not affected by these fluctuations. Foreign-invested firms and joint ventures undertake 85 per cent of processing trade in China (Lu et al. 2010). Previous studies have found that Chinese non-export firms tend to be more efficient than export companies (Dai et al. 2014). Therefore, we exclude non-exporting companies from our sample dataset. We chose to use firms primarily engaged in ordinary trade as a control group, leaving other firms primarily engaged in processing trade clustered in the treatment group. We then show the annual average TFP trend of the two groups of firms. From Figure 8.2, it can be seen that the assumption of parallel trends is met and there is little difference in the average annual productivity of the two groups before 2003, whereas after 2003, the productivity of processing trade firms declines markedly. We have conducted a parallel trend hypothesis test below, and the results are shown in Table 8.2.

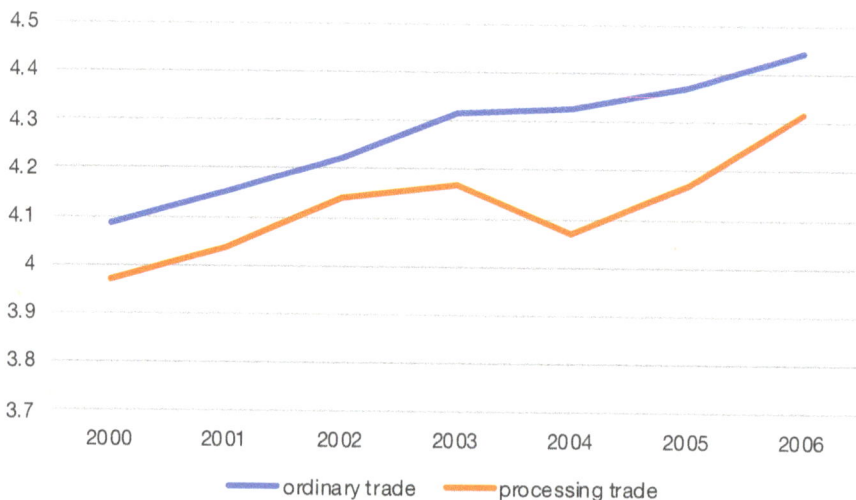

Figure 8.2 Productivity growth trend of different types of exporters: Processing trade versus ordinary trade (per cent)

Source: Annual Survey of Manufacturing, National Bureau of Statistics of China.

We use a fixed-effect regression model that controls for firm location, sector and time. The econometric model can be expressed as follows: the subscripts t, j, i and r represent year, firm, two-digit industry and location, respectively; X is the control variable; ε_{tj} is the error term. The dummy variable *treat* indicates whether the observation is affected by the policy. We use *treat*=1 to indicate the treatment group and *treat*=0 to indicate the control group unaffected by the policy. The term *time* represents the time dummy variable, indicating a period during which the policy has been implemented. After the policy is implemented, we have *time*=1, otherwise the dummy variable takes on the value of zero. The term *treat* × *time* represents the interaction effect of our treatment and time, representing the net effect before and after the policy is implemented. In the empirical section below, we use *tt* to represent the interaction term. To eliminate interference from other factors in the model, we introduce control variables at the firm, city, province and industry levels.

Equation 8.1

$$TFP_{tj} = a_r + a_i + a_t + \beta treat_{tj} \times time_{tj} + \sum_n \gamma_n X_{ntj} + \varepsilon_{tj}$$

In the benchmark regression model, we first add the control variables at the firm level and then gradually add the control variables at the city, province and industry level. Corporate capital intensity (capint) is calculated by dividing the annual average of net fixed assets by the annual average of all employees. We then take the logarithm value and deflate it using the fixed-asset price index based on the year 2000. The age of a firm is measured by the period the firm has actually existed, which we calculate by taking the logarithm of the difference between the current year and the year the firm was established. Wage payment ability (wage) is measured by taking the logarithm of the ratio of the firm's payable employee compensation to the annual average of all employees. Production capacity (output) is measured by taking the logarithm of the total industrial output per capita at constant prices. We then deflate the value using the industrial producer price index based on the year 2000. The scale of a firm is measured by the logarithm of the number of its employees. The level of firm profitability (prorate) is measured by the logarithm of total profit per capita, converting it using the industrial producer price index based on the year 2000. We identify the status of the firm via the sixth digit in the 10-digit customs enterprise code, classifying numbers '4' and '9' as foreign-funded firms and '2' and '3' as Chinese–foreign firms and Chinese–foreign joint ventures. The dummy variable (foe) is set for foreign-funded background firms, which takes the value of 1 when firms are foreign-funded or joint ventures and 0 otherwise. State-owned firms and collective firms are represented by the numbers '1' and '5', respectively. We set the dummy variable (soe), which takes the value of 1 for state-owned and collective firms. Private firms and individual businesses are represented by the numbers '6', '7' and '8' and we classify these observations as private enterprises. The technological intensity of export products differs in many ways, and we employ the classification method proposed by Lall, Weiss and Zhang (2006) to ascertain the level of technological intensity for each product from each company. We assign the technological level of a firm according to the technological intensity of its product with the largest export proportion. We then set the high technology-intensity dummy variable as htech, which takes the value of 1 for firms with high technology intensity. Similarly, the term mtech is for firms with a medium level of technological intensity.

In the following robustness test, to eliminate the interference of variance at the regional and industrial economic development levels, we introduce control variables at the city, province and industry level. The regional income level (lnwage) is measured by the per capita wage of the prefecture-level city, which is deflated by the consumer price index. Regional capital intensity (pcap) is measured by the per capita fixed assets of prefecture-level cities. The regional development level (pgdp) is measured by the per capita GDP of the prefecture-level city. We take the logarithm value and deflate it using the GDP deflator. Regional traffic conditions (pky) are measured by the ratio of the number of passengers transported in prefecture-level cities to the permanent population of the region. The degree of marketisation of each province (market) is measured by the comprehensive index of the marketisation process of each province proposed by Fan et al. (2011). The economic agglomeration degree (ecoag) of each province is constructed based on the method of Shi and Zhang (2016), which is measured according to the ratio of each province's GDP to its geographic area. The industrial structure (FGP) is measured by the proportion of agricultural output value in the total regional output value in the same city. Industry concentration (HHI) is used to reflect the degree of competition in industry i, $HHI_i = \Sigma_j (y_i^j)^2$, where y_i^j represents the proportion of the employed population of firm j in industry i. Here industry is defined at the two-digit level. The degree of industrial agglomeration (IDSAG) is constructed based on the method proposed by Ellison and Glaeser (1999), mainly taking into account differences in the composition of firms in the industry, with some industries constituted by large-scale firms and others by a large number of small firms. The corresponding subscripts are as follows: r refers to the city; refers to the proportion of employment in city r in the total employment in the country; refers to the proportion of the employment in city i in the total employment in industry i in the country. And the measure is similar to the former constructed industrial concentration measure. However, here we select industries at the four-digit level.

Equation 8.2

$$IDSAG_i = \frac{\Sigma_r (x_r - s_r^i)^2 - [1 - \Sigma_r (x_r)^2] H_i}{[1 - \Sigma_r (x_r)^2](1 - H_i)}$$

Results

Primary results

Since the random-effect model-fitting approach was rejected by the Hausman test, we choose the fixed-effect model in this study. In the benchmark model specification, the TFP heterogeneity mainly relies on across-firm differences in export patterns, controlling for firm location, sector and time effects. As the regression result displays, the interaction term coefficient is negative and statistically significant at the 1 per cent level. Since the export pattern choice could hinge on substantial firm heterogeneity, we cluster samples via the propensity score matching (PSM) method. The reported results in columns (5) and (6) are the regression model using the matched samples. Furthermore, the difference-in-difference (DID) method is proven to be robust across different sample sets.

As shown in Table 8.1, we find a negative effect on firms' TFP value caused by processing trade transformation and upgrading policies. Former research results shed light on the causal role of processing trade in the learning-by-exporting effect (Ge 1999), especially for those countries with firms primarily engaged in processing trade (Kandogan 2003). Previous research has also focused on the economic growth linked to this learning effect (Feenstra and Hanson 1995). On the other hand, in addition to potential positive prompting effects, these transformation and upgrading policies may exert a crowding-out effect in the short term (Shang and Zhu 2017), thereby increasing the costs of operating in the market. In the course of economic development, the industrial structure is constantly changing (Gan et al. 2011); to meet regulatory requirements, firms need to adjust their production strategies or introduce new production processes, which might in turn attenuate their original innovation intensity, restrict their innovation capabilities or reduce their profit margin and productivity (Blonigen 2016).

Table 8.1 Benchmark model regression

Variable	(1) TFP_OP	(2) TFP_OP	(3) TFP_LP	(4) TFP_LP	(5) TFP_OP	(6) TFP_LP
tt	−0.1260***	−0.1390***	−0.1180***	−0.1290***	−0.1730***	−0.1320***
	(0.0107)	(0.0133)	(0.0107)	(0.0133)	(0.0174)	(0.0171)
wage	0.3700***	0.3800***	0.4050***	0.4210***	0.4260***	0.4490***
	(0.0042)	(0.0075)	(0.0042)	(0.0076)	(0.0124)	(0.0124)
age	0.0780***	0.0590***	0.0310***	0.0130***	0.0650***	0.0120*
	(0.0041)	(0.0044)	(0.0041)	(0.0044)	(0.0068)	(0.0067)
scale	0.0370***	0.0460***	0.4760***	0.4850***	0.0720***	0.5200***
	(0.0030)	(0.0051)	(0.0030)	(0.0051)	(0.0069)	(0.0070)

Variable	(1) TFP_OP	(2) TFP_OP	(3) TFP_LP	(4) TFP_LP	(5) TFP_OP	(6) TFP_LP
capint	0.0140***	−0.0140***	0.0680***	0.0420***	0.0070	0.0710***
	(0.0023)	(0.0035)	(0.0023)	(0.0035)	(0.0053)	(0.0052)
output	0.0000***	0.0000***	0.0000***	0.0000***	0.0000***	0.0000***
	(0.0000)	(0.0000)	(0.0000)	(0.0000)	(0.0000)	(0.0000)
prorate	0.8530***	0.8470***	0.8520***	0.8470***	0.6700***	0.6680***
	(0.0117)	(0.2018)	(0.0117)	(0.2025)	(0.2329)	(0.2399)
htech	0.1160***	0.0440***	0.1120***	0.0430***	0.0350**	0.0530***
	(0.0083)	(0.0109)	(0.0083)	(0.0109)	(0.0162)	(0.0160)
mtech	0.0080	0.0150*	0.0030	0.0150*	0.0050	0.0240*
	(0.0070)	(0.0080)	(0.0070)	(0.0080)	(0.0129)	(0.0129)
foe	0.0100	0.0240***	−0.0030	0.0090	0.0180	−0.0120
	(0.0079)	(0.0079)	(0.0079)	(0.0079)	(0.0128)	(0.0125)
soe	−0.0020	−0.0400***	0.0050	−0.0420***	−0.0820***	−0.1080***
	(0.0115)	(0.0124)	(0.0115)	(0.0124)	(0.0178)	(0.0177)
cons	2.8100***	3.0370***	2.7720***	2.9590***	1.7640***	1.8600***
	(0.0212)	(0.2587)	(0.0212)	(0.2586)	(0.3406)	(0.3342)
City fixed effects	-	Yes	-	Yes	Yes	Yes
Industry fixed effects	-	Yes	-	Yes	Yes	Yes
Year fixed effects	-	Yes	-	Yes	Yes	Yes
Observations	135,264	135,264	135,002	135,002	53,088	53,020

*** $p < 0.01$

** $p < 0.05$

* $p < 0.1$

Notes: Standard errors in parentheses; model (1) and model (3) are random-effect regression models. Source: Authors' own estimation.

Parallel trend and robustness tests

We follow Alder et al.'s (2016) method to perform a parallel trend test, which consists of adding a year dummy variable (*year_dum*) for each year to the model. For example, for 2003, we let the corresponding dummy variable take the value of 1 with other observations taking the value of zero. In addition, we add the interaction term (*treat × year_dum*) for the identification of the effect generated by the time dummy variable (*year_dum*) and the policy dummy variable (*treat*) jointly. In the empirical part, *t_year* is used instead of *treat×year_dum*. For example, in 2003, it is expressed as *t_2003*. As shown in Equation 8.3, the regression results are displayed in Table 8.2.

Equation 8.3

$$TFP_{tj} = a_r + a_i + a_t + \beta treat_{tj} \times time_{tj} + \sum_n \lambda_n year\_dum_{tj}$$
$$+ \sum_n \mu_n treat_{tj} \times year\_dum_{tj} + \sum_n \gamma_n X_{ntj} + \varepsilon_{tj}$$

It can be seen that the interaction term coefficients from 2000 to 2002 are not statistically significant, but become significantly negative after 2003, showing that the test of the parallel trend hypothesis has been passed.

Table 8.2 Parallel trend test

Variable	(1)	(2)
	TFP_OP	TFP_LP
t_2000	–0.0440	–0.0580
	(0.0346)	(0.0353)
t_2001	–0.0320	–0.0380
	(0.0251)	(0.0256)
t_2002	0.0190	0.0140
	(0.0414)	(0.0414)
t_2003	–0.1150***	–0.1040***
	(0.0296)	(0.0282)
t_2004	–0.2150***	–0.2070***
	(0.0277)	(0.0274)
t_2005	–0.1580***	–0.1590***
	(0.0280)	(0.0270)
t_2006	–0.1340***	–0.1440***
	(0.0333)	(0.0337)
Observations	135,264	135,002

*** $p < 0.01$

** $p < 0.05$

* $p < 0.1$

Source: Authors' own estimation.

A sample selection bias may lie in the benchmark model, primarily caused by the fact that the sample of mixed-pattern firms is not considered. Mixed-pattern firms could engage in both ordinary trade and processing trade, and such firms are more or less affected by the policy. Hence it is difficult to identify the precise impact of the policy. We cluster different proportions of processing trade among the mixed-pattern firms, with firms with proportions above three-quarters used as the treatment group and those with proportions below one-quarter used as the control group. The results are displayed in Table 8.3. Models (1) and (2) only include mixed-pattern firms and we perform the regression according to the above grouping principle. The regression results show that, although the interaction term coefficient is negative, it does not pass the test for significance. Models (3) and (4) are placebo tests. We use samples between the three-quarters and the median of the mixed-pattern firm as the treatment group, and the one-quarter to the median as the control group. We can see that the regression results are not significant. Models (5) and (6) merge all mixed-pattern firms into the treatment group and the control group, and the regression results are consistent with the basic model. On the whole, it appears that adding a sample of mixed-pattern firms may interfere with the accurate assessment of policy effectiveness. In this section, we use the sample of mixed firms to perform a robustness test. The following estimation mainly makes use of samples of purely processing trade and purely ordinary trade enterprises.

Table 8.3 Regression with mixed-pattern firms

Variable	(1) TFP_OP	(2) TFP_LP	(3) TFP_OP	(4) TFP_LP	(5) TFP_OP	(6) TFP_LP
tt	−0.0570	−0.1200	0.1800	0.1840	−0.0730***	−0.0680***
	(0.1268)	(0.1276)	(0.1724)	(0.1769)	(0.0086)	(0.0087)
Observations	29,750	29,709	35,396	35,351	200,410	200,062

*** $p < 0.01$

** $p < 0.05$

* $p < 0.1$

Notes: Regression equations include control variables regarding firms. City, industry and time fixed effects have been controlled for unobserved variation.

Source: Authors' own estimation.

We controlled for firm-level characteristic variables as well as the fixed effects of city and industry, as well as adopting the PSM method to attenuate the endogeneity bias. However, there may be deviations in policy results caused by variances in regional and industrial development trends and we therefore need to further eliminate endogeneity problems caused by the pretreatment trends of regional and industrial development. To do this, we added regional-level and industry-level variables into the model to ensure the exogeneity of the policy. At the same time, we performed PSM on the variables of firm, region and industry to select more similar samples. Among them, the region and industry-level characteristics are controlled by newly added variables. The regression results are shown in Table 8.4. It can be seen that the interaction term coefficient is statistically significantly negative—consistent with the benchmark model. The control variables at the regional level are also statistically significant. Factors such as regional wage levels, economic development levels, capital density and economic accumulation are positively correlated with the production efficiency of firms, which is consistent with economic facts. At the same time, the control variables at the industry level vary in the opposite direction to productivity, which is consistent with the empirical fact that agricultural productivity is lower than that of manufacturing or service industries. By collecting observations from our dataset, we can identify the economic zone attributes of each city from the fifth digit of the customs code. For example, '4' and '5' represent the bonded area and export processing zone, respectively.[1] Each city corresponds to only one economy zone code, which shows that the distribution of firms may differ across cities. Therefore, on the basis of controlling the fixed effects of cities and industries, we further add all control variables at the city, province and industry level to ensure the exogeneity of policies.

Table 8.4 Robustness test for region and industry characteristics

Variable	(1) TFP_OP	(2) TFP_LP	(3) TFP_OP	(4) TFP_LP	(5) TFP_OP	(6) TFP_LP	(7) TFP_OP	(8) TFP_LP
	region		industry		Regional PSM		Industrial PSM	
tt	−0.1170***	−0.1040***	−0.1390***	−0.1290***	−0.1110***	−0.1080***	−0.1490***	−0.1470***
	(0.0140)	(0.0141)	(0.0133)	(0.0133)	(0.0204)	(0.0206)	(0.0189)	(0.0181)
lnwage	0.0430***	0.0460***			0.0710*	0.0820**		
	(0.0146)	(0.0147)			(0.0366)	(0.0387)		
pgdp	−0.0190	−0.0260			0.0430	0.0520*		
	(0.0173)	(0.0173)			(0.0281)	(0.0282)		
pcap	0.0510***	0.0560***			0.0310*	0.0390**		
	(0.0114)	(0.0114)			(0.0189)	(0.0194)		
pky	0.0060	0.0050			−0.0380*	−0.0540**		
	(0.0118)	(0.0118)			(0.0222)	(0.0225)		
market	0.0110	0.0130			0.0470***	0.0220		
	(0.0079)	(0.0079)			(0.0168)	(0.0173)		
ecoag	0.1450***	0.1500***			0.1870***	0.1740***		
	(0.0336)	(0.0335)			(0.0641)	(0.0656)		
FGP			−0.0030***	−0.0040***			−0.0070***	−0.0080***
			(0.0011)	(0.0011)			(0.0022)	(0.0023)
IDSAG			−0.0600	−0.1610			−0.0260	−0.0690
			(0.3047)	(0.3137)			(0.3411)	(0.3451)
HHI			0.0830	0.0440			1.0530	0.5310
			(0.2726)	(0.2781)			(0.6569)	(0.5516)
Observations	135,169	134,907	135,264	135,002	46,120	46,081	50,757	50,828

*** p < 0.01

** p < 0.05

* p < 0.1

Notes: Regression equations include control variables regarding firms. City, industry and time fixed effects have been controlled for unobserved variation.

Source: Authors' own estimation.

1   Among them, '1' stands for special economic zones; '2' is economic and technological development zones; '3' high-tech development zones; '4' bonded areas; '5' export processing zones; and '9' other unlisted areas. For the policies and regulations prohibiting ordinary trade, please refer to the *Interim Measures of the Customs of the People's Republic of China on the Supervision of Export Processing Zones* (The State Council of the People's Republic of China 2000).

The productivity of the treatment group and control group firms should have the same pretreatment trends. To eliminate the potential impact of different pretreatment trends, we add a time trend term for control (Jayachandran et al. 2010). Specifically, we add the corresponding year (t) to models (1) and (2) in Table 8.5. We take the logarithm to process it. We also add the interaction term (ts) to combine the year (t) with the policy grouping dummy variable (*treat*). The regression results are consistent with the benchmark model. In addition, interference from other potential policy factors may exist to cause differences in the productivity trends of processing trade and ordinary trade firms. We specifically used China's accession to the World Trade Organization (WTO) in 2001 as a potential policy shock. The time boundary for models (3) and (4) was changed to 2001, and the samples after 2004 are excluded. The interaction term is represented by tr. It can be seen that the regression result is not statistically significant. To further eliminate the interference of substantial policy factors, we randomly set the time dummy of 2005–06 to 1. The interaction term is represented by td, and the regression result is as model (5). As shown in model (6), the regression results did not pass the significance test. Therefore, we believe that the impact of other potential policies can be further excluded.

Table 8.5 Robustness test for pretreatment trend and other coexistent policies

Variable	(1) TFP_OP	(2) TFP_LP	(3) TFP_OP	(4) TFP_LP	(5) TFP_OP	(6) TFP_LP
tt	−0.1170***	−0.1040***				
	(0.0141)	(0.0141)				
t	35.1890***	18.3270*				
	(10.2110)	(10.2878)				
ts	−0.0050**	−0.0060***				
	(0.0020)	(0.0021)				
tr			0.0260	0.0280		
			(0.0175)	(0.0175)		
td					0.0140	0.0050
					(0.0126)	(0.0125)
Observations	13,5169	134,907	48,862	48,636	135,169	134,907

*** $p < 0.01$
** $p < 0.05$
* $p < 0.1$

Notes: Regression equations include control variables regarding firm, region and industry. City, industry and time fixed effects have been controlled for unobserved variation.

Source: Authors' own estimation.

Further heterogeneity tests

The distribution of China's processing trade between eastern and western regions and different types of enterprises is uneven. We further examine the different performance of the policy effects from the perspectives of region, enterprise and composition of processing trade.

Regarding the distribution of Chinese export companies, we make several assumptions. First, the productivity of firms in the eastern region is relatively higher than in other regions and most of the country's export firms are concentrated in the east. The firms in the eastern region are also more likely to become the focus of regulation, therefore policies may lower the average productivity of export firms in the eastern region and thereby reduce their overall level of efficiency. Second, the regression results in Table 8.1 show that the coefficient of *foe* is basically positive and the coefficient of *soe* is basically negative, indicating that the productivity of foreign-funded enterprises is relatively higher than that of state-owned and collective firms. At the same time, foreign-funded firms and joint ventures account for more than 80 per cent of the export sector, making them the potential focus of regulation. The effect generated by policies may therefore reduce the overall efficiency level by lowering the production efficiency of foreign-funded enterprises. From another perspective, the imported-material processing trade firms are characterised by having 'two ends outside', with both the import of raw materials and the export sales of products relying heavily on the international market. As such, the effect of domestic industrial policies could be relatively small. At the same time, ordinary trade firms are more likely to use domestic raw materials to replace imported raw materials under such policies, and as ordinary trade firms account for more than 95 per cent of processing trade, these may become an important target for regulation.

Heterogeneity test of regions and trade patterns

Economic development in China varies significantly by region. The eastern region is more developed and has a higher degree of industrial development than the others. Mature industries are faced with meeting the requirements of the transformation and upgrading policies and many labour-intensive and relatively mature industries have gradually relocated to the central and western regions. Foxconn, for instance, has invested in factories in Zhengzhou City in the central region and Chengdu City in the west. The regression results in Table 8.6 show that the net effect of these policies is not significant in the central and western regions, but has a significant, negative impact in the eastern region. This is because the eastern region is the main gathering area for processing trade, and the total export value of processing trade from the eastern region accounts for 98 per cent of the country's total processing exports. Although the policy proposes promoting the transfer of processing trade enterprises to the central and western regions, the eastern region retains certain geographical advantages and such transfers cannot be completed in one step. In addition, export enterprises in the eastern region face higher degrees of marketisation and have comparative advantages in location and transportation for processing trade. In the short term, transformation and upgrading policies may disrupt the original resource allocation conditions. The transfer of processing trade enterprises from the east to the central and western regions has resulted in a reduction in labour and land costs, but in the short term, this cannot compensate for the comparative advantages of the eastern region, thereby reducing the production efficiency of processing trade enterprises. As an extension, the central and western regions—as the main destinations for the transfer of processing trade—should actively undertake the transfer of enterprises and establish corresponding support facilities, as well as accept enterprises with higher development levels and higher production efficiencies, thereby improving the region's overall level of production efficiency.

Table 8.6 Heterogeneity test with location

Variable	(1)	(2)	(3)	(4)	(1)	(2)	(3)	(4)
	Eastern region			Central and western regions	Processing trade with imported materials		Processing trade with supplied materials	
	TFP_OP	TFP_LP	TFP_OP	TFP_LP	TFP_OP	TFP_LP	TFP_OP	TFP_LP
tt	−0.1010***	−0.0890***	−0.0230	−0.0210	−0.1280***	−0.1130***	−0.0580	−0.0540
	(0.0151)	(0.0151)	(0.0822)	(0.0843)	(0.0152)	(0.0152)	(0.0390)	(0.0398)
Observations	119,443	119,342	15,726	15,565	130,634	130,377	110,423	110,181

*** $p < 0.01$

** $p < 0.05$

* $p < 0.1$

Notes: Regression equations include control variables regarding firm, region and industry. City, industry and time fixed effects have been controlled for unobserved variation.

Source: Authors' own estimation.

The proportion of processing trade with supplied materials is below 5 per cent of total exports and this proportion has been on a downward trend since 2000, indicating that the importance of processing trade is also declining. It can be seen in Table 8.7 that the interaction term coefficient is significantly negative, which is consistent with the benchmark model. The interaction term coefficient in processing trade with supplied materials is negative, but not significant. The export value of processing trade with imported materials accounts for more than 95 per cent of all processing trade. Policies for the transformation and upgrading of processing trade are aimed at domestic firms, so firms engaged in processing trade with imported materials may be directly affected. Processing trade with supplied materials has the typical features of 'two ends outside'. In this case, the firm imports its raw materials from abroad, following which almost all of its product is sold on foreign markets. These firms maintain close ties with the country in which their parent company is located. Hence, firms engaged in processing trade with supplied materials are more susceptible to international market fluctuations and are relatively less affected by domestic industrial policies. In addition, firms engaged in processing trade with supplied materials are concentrated in simple processing and assembly businesses, most of which are labour-intensive industries characterised by low levels of production technology or low production efficiencies; as such, the crowding-out effects of these policies are likely to be negligible.

Heterogeneity test regarding the status of firms

The export value of joint ventures and foreign-funded enterprises accounts for more than 90 per cent of processing trade. The focus of policies for processing trade transformation and upgrading is on increasing the export proportion of private firms. As such, it is necessary to reconfirm the status of the sampled firms. The statistics indicate that the export value of joint-venture (cooperative) enterprises and wholly foreign-owned firms accounts for about 80 per cent of the total export value, although this declined in 2006. Meanwhile, the export value of private and state-owned firms has not changed much. We identify firms' status by the sixth digit of the firm customs code, employing the same grouping method previously stated. We divide the samples into four groups: private enterprises, state-owned enterprises, joint ventures and foreign-funded enterprises. The specifications of the treatment and control groups remain consistent. The regression results are displayed in Table 8.8. The results show that the interaction term coefficients for the joint ventures and foreign-funded enterprises are significantly negative, indicating that the net effect of the policy is significantly negative. Meanwhile, the interaction term coefficient for the private and state-owned enterprises is not significant.

Table 8.7 Heterogeneity test regarding firm status

Variable	(1)	(2)	(3)	(4)	(5)	(6)	(7)	(8)
	Private firms		soe		Joint ventures		foe	
	TFP_OP	TFP_LP	TFP_OP	TFP_LP	TFP_OP	TFP_LP	TFP_OP	TFP_LP
tt	−0.0230	−0.0230	0.0180	0.0060	−0.0820***	−0.0760***	−0.0910***	−0.0810***
	(0.0925)	(0.0907)	(0.0859)	(0.0867)	(0.0229)	(0.0229)	(0.0260)	(0.0262)
Observations	36,860	36,841	21,365	21,260	41,648	41,566	35,296	35,240

*** $p < 0.01$

** $p < 0.05$

* $p < 0.1$

Notes: Regression equations include control variables regarding firm, region and industry. City, industry and time fixed effects have been controlled for unobserved variation.

Source: Authors' own estimation.

The export value of foreign-funded enterprises (including joint ventures) has fluctuated greatly since 2005, while the export value of private and state-owned enterprises has not changed much in the same period, indicating that foreign-funded enterprises have experienced greater policy impacts. Private and state-owned enterprises account for a relatively small proportion of exports, while the impacts of transformation and upgrading policies are not obvious. At the same time, foreign-funded enterprises possess comparative advantages in terms of developing processing trade—for instance, compared with private and state-owned enterprises, foreign-funded firms are more familiar with the international market; moreover, they may receive management and even technical support from their parent company, as well as relatively mature development experience and an established international customer network. Private and state-owned enterprises, on the other hand, are at a relative disadvantage in the realm of international competition; as such, supportive policies may cause distortions and the misallocation of resources in the short term, thereby reducing firm productivity.

In addition, foreign-funded enterprises engaged in processing trade have the potential to generate more significant technological learning effects for the country (Kandogan 2003). However, one of the goals of the transformation and upgrading policies is to increase the diversification of business entities and increase the proportion of private and state-owned firms' exports as a share of total trade. Because of this, the direct impact of policies may serve to inhibit the transformation of foreign-funded enterprises' technological learning effects, thereby reducing their production efficiency. Private and state-owned enterprises have different priorities. In 1994, China promulgated the Foreign Trade Law to deepen the reform of the foreign trade system and gradually transfer foreign trade management rights from state-owned enterprises to private enterprises (Ping and Huang 2018).

Heterogeneity tests regarding region, trade mode and enterprise status

Region, trade mode and enterprise status are factors that cause variance in the net effectiveness of policies. The net effect of the policies is significantly negative when focusing on samples located in eastern China, which are primarily engaged in processing trade with imported materials and possess joint-venture or foreign-funded firm status. We will take these factors into further consideration and finish the heterogeneity tests.

We first consider the factors of region and trade mode, with the regression results displayed in Table 8.8. It can be seen from the table that the interaction term coefficient in the case of firms engaged in processing trade with imported materials in the eastern region is significantly negative, while the other results do not pass the significance test. It can be seen that the eastern region and processing trade with imported materials are the main factors influencing the policies' negative net effects.

On this basis, we retain the sample of firms in processing trade with imported materials in the eastern region to further investigate the differences in the status of firms. The results are shown in Table 8.9. The results are consistent with previous regressions: the interaction term coefficients of joint ventures and foreign-funded firms are significantly negative and the interaction term coefficients of private and state-owned enterprises are positive, failing to pass the significance test. The previous analysis shows that joint ventures and foreign-funded enterprises account for more than 80 per cent of processing trade exports and they are the key targets of the transformation and upgrading policies.

Table 8.8 Heterogeneity test by region and trade mode

Variable	(1)	(2)	(3)	(4)	(5)	(6)	(7)	(8)
	Processing trade with imported materials				Processing trade with supplied materials			
	Eastern		Central and western		Eastern		Central and western	
	TFP_OP	TFP_LP	TFP_OP	TFP_LP	TFP_OP	TFP_LP	TFP_OP	TFP_LP
tt	−0.1140***	−0.1000***	0.1520	0.1480	−0.0300	−0.0270	−0.2960	−0.2930
	(0.0163)	(0.0163)	(0.1066)	(0.1088)	(0.0306)	(0.0308)	(0.1251)	(0.1273)
Observations	115,134	115,034	15,500	15,343	95,114	95,025	15,309	15,156

*** p < 0.01

** p < 0.05

* p < 0.1

Notes: Regression equations include control variables regarding firm, region and industry. City, industry and time fixed effects have been controlled for unobserved variation.

Source: Authors' own estimation.

We argue, however, that the motivation for foreign-funded enterprises in processing trade to upgrade and improve their production efficiency may not be great, as the main purpose of these enterprises is to seek low-cost labour to reduce production costs and obtain higher profits. After being impacted by external policies, they have the flexibility to adjust their production strategies. Judging from the fact that a large number of foreign-funded firms have relocated their production bases to Southeast Asian countries in recent years, we believe foreign-funded enterprises have more flexibility in lowering costs. It can be seen from the regression results that the regression coefficients from model (1) to model (4) are positive but not significant, indicating that the crowding-out effect generated by these policies on private and state-owned enterprises is negligible. This is in line with the fact that the transformation and upgrading policies were intended to support private firms. Extending this further, we believe that the main focus of these transformation and upgrading policies should still be placed on private and state-owned enterprises. However, given that foreign-funded enterprises have suffered relatively greater policy crowding-out effects, appropriate subsidies could be provided during the initial stage of policy implementation to reduce their short-term negative impacts.

Table 8.9 Heterogeneity by firm status

Variable	(1)	(2)	(3)	(4)	(5)	(6)	(7)	(8)
	Private firms		soe		Joint ventures		foe	
	TFP_OP	TFP_LP	TFP_OP	TFP_LP	TFP_OP	TFP_LP	TFP_OP	TFP_LP
tt	0.1130	0.1100	0.1230	0.1150	−0.0880***	−0.0800***	−0.1040***	−0.0940***
	(0.1126)	(0.1098)	(0.1029)	(0.1028)	(0.0253)	(0.0253)	(0.0285)	(0.0286)
Observations	31,983	31,970	14,934	14,911	36,697	36,671	31,520	31,482

*** $p < 0.01$

** $p < 0.05$

* $p < 0.1$

Notes: Regression equations include control variables regarding firm, region and industry. City, industry and time fixed effects have been controlled for unobserved variation.

Source: Authors' own estimation.

In summary, transformation and upgrading policies have caused a decline in the productivity of processing trade firms, on average. We find the constructed DID model to be robust under different assumptions. Moreover, we considered the development trends of regions and industries to deal with the endogeneity problem and excluded the influence of other potential policy factors through a parallel trend test.

Conclusion

Since the implementation of the processing trade transformation and upgrading strategy in 2003, the proportion of China's processing trade in total exports has continued to decline, but the product structure has tended to improve in terms of technological content. This study uses the DID method to test the impact of processing trade transformation and upgrading policies on enterprise productivity. The study shows that such policies will reduce industry's average productivity and lead to resource misallocation.

Specifically, our empirical tests found that: first, the net effect of the transformation and upgrading policies on productivity has been negative, which means that, from the perspective of resource allocation efficiency, the policies have incurred distortions, indicating that, although the policy goal may have been achieved, it has been at the expense of efficiency. Innovation and profit factors may be microchannels through which policies affect enterprise productivity. The transformation and upgrading policies for processing trade reduce the level of innovation and profitability of enterprises, but enterprise innovation and profitability can increase enterprise productivity. Second, the misallocation of resources is concentrated in China's eastern region, while foreign-funded enterprises and firms engaged in processing trade with imported materials have been the most negatively affected by the policies.

China's processing trade is concentrated in the eastern region and is primarily labour intensive. Most processing trade companies have relatively high production efficiency in labour-intensive industries—a fact that is most obvious among foreign-funded companies. Additionally, labour-intensive processing trade enterprises are among those most negatively affected by the adoption of transformation and upgrading policies, leading to a loss of productivity, on average. Industrial policy must be efficiency-oriented or it will inevitably cause new distortions.

References

Alder, S., Shao, L. and Zilibotti, F. (2016), Economic reforms and industrial policy in a panel of Chinese cities, *Journal of Economic Growth* 21(4): 304–49. doi.org/10.1007/s10887-016-9131-x.

Blonigen, B.A. (2016), Industrial policy and downstream export performance, *The Economic Journal* 126(595): 1635–59. doi.org/10.1111/ecoj.12223.

Brandt, L., Van Biesebroeck, J. and Zhang, Y. (2012), Creative accounting or creative destruction? Firm-level productivity growth in Chinese manufacturing, *Journal of Development Economics* 97(2): 339–51. doi.org/10.1016/j.jdeveco.2011.02.002.

Dai, M., Yu, M. and Maitra, M. (2014), The mystery of the productivity of Chinese export companies: The role of processing trade, [In Chinese], *Economics (Quarterly)* 13(2): 675–98.

Ellison, G. and Glaeser, E.L. (1999), The geographic concentration of industry: Does natural advantage explain agglomeration?, *The American Economic Review* 89(2): 311–16. doi.org/10.1257/aer.89.2.311.

Fan, G., Wang, X. and Ma, G. (2011), Contribution of China's marketization process to economic growth, [In Chinese], *Economic Research* (9): 4–16.

Feenstra, R.C. and Hanson, G.H. (1995), *Foreign investment, outsourcing and relative wages*, NBER Working Papers 5121, Cambridge, MA: National Bureau of Economic Research. doi.org/10.3386/w5121.

Gan, C., Zheng, R. and Yu, D. (2011), The impact of China's industrial structure changes on economic growth and volatility, [In Chinese], *Economic Research* (5): 4–16, 31.

Ge, W. (1999), *The Dynamics of Export-Processing Zones*, Geneva: United Nations Conference on Trade and Development.

Jayachandran, S., Lleras-Muney, A. and Smith, K.V. (2010), Modern medicine and the twentieth century decline in mortality: Evidence on the impact of sulfa drugs, *American Economic Journal: Applied Economics* 2(2): 118–46. doi.org/10.1257/app.2.2.118.

Kandogan, Y. (2003), Intra-industry trade of transition countries: Trends and determinants, *Emerging Markets Review* 4(3): 273–86. doi.org/10.1016/S1566-0141(03)00040-2.

Lall, S., Weiss, J. and Zhang, J. (2006), The 'sophistication' of exports: A new trade measure, *World Development* 34(2): 222–37.

Levinsohn, J. and Petrin, A. (2003), Estimating production functions using inputs to control for unobservables, *The Review of Economic Studies* 70(2): 317–41. doi.org/10.1111/1467-937X.00246.

Lu, J., Lu, Y. and Tao, Z. (2010), Exporting behavior of foreign affiliates: Theory and evidence, *Journal of International Economics* 81(2): 197–205. doi.org/10.1016/j.jinteco.2010.03.002.

Nie, H., Jiang, T. and Yang, R. (2012), The current status and potential problems of the use of Chinese industrial enterprise database, [In Chinese], *World Economy* (5): 142–58.

Olley, S. and Pakes, A. (1996), The dynamics of productivity in the telecommunications equipment industry, *Econometrica* 64(6): 1263–97. doi.org/10.2307/2171831.

Ping, X. and Huang, X. (2018), Research on the heterogeneity of different ownership enterprises in various markets, [In Chinese], *Economic Aspect* (2): 35–48.

Shang, X. and Zhu, S. (2017), Analysis on the effect of agricultural land circulation subsidy policy: Based on crowding-out effect, government rent creation and target deviation perspective, [In Chinese], *China Rural Observation* (6): 43–56.

Shi, B. and Zhang, Y. (2016), Trade liberalization and the upgrade of imported intermediate quality of Chinese enterprises, [In Chinese], *Quantitative Economics and Technical Economic Research* (9): 3–21.

The State Council of the People's Republic of China (2000), *Interim Measures of the Customs of the People's Republic of China on the Supervision of Export Processing Zones*. General Administration of the People's Republic of China.

Tian, W. and Yu, M. (2012), Enterprise productivity and 'going global' foreign direct investment: An empirical study based on enterprise level data, [In Chinese], *Economics (Quarterly)* 11(2): 383–408.

9

The renminbi's status as a safe-haven currency

Liqing Zhang, Libo Yin and You Wu

Introduction

The *China Financial Stability Report* (Financial Stability Analysis Group of the People's Bank of China 2019) pointed out that the factors threatening global financial stability will likely persist into the future, especially as unilateralism and trade-protectionist sentiments have only intensified globally, while financial markets are highly sensitive to trade—all of which has led to growing uncertainty around the world. As such, global systemic risk prevention and control remain vital. Consequently, analysis of the demand for safe havens and the allocation of safe-haven assets appears extremely urgent. Traditionally, the main safe-haven currencies are the Swiss franc, the Japanese yen and the US dollar. However, these currencies do not exhibit the characteristics of a safe-haven asset all the time. Meanwhile, the large and concentrated demand for such assets is likely to lead to excessively high currency portfolio holding costs.

A highly topical research question is whether the renminbi (RMB) plays the role of a safe-haven currency. After two important reforms of the exchange rate system, the renminbi is striding towards greater marketisation. Currently, the value of the renminbi continues to be relatively stable, and the various monetary policies implemented and promoted by China's central bank are relatively independent and prudent. The renminbi has always maintained a stable position in the global monetary system. Since the renminbi is not yet fully convertible under the capital account, the onshore and offshore markets operate simultaneously and, compared with that onshore, the offshore renminbi market has a more flexible mechanism. After years of painstaking management and development, offshore renminbi market products have become more diversified. According to the *RMB Internationalisation*

Report 2020 issued by the People's Bank of China (PBC 2020), renminbi foreign exchange products in the offshore over-the-counter (OTC) market include spot, forward, swap, currency swap and option and a variety of renminbi-denominated investment products, such as renminbi currency futures, renminbi-traded open-end index funds (exchange-traded funds [ETF]) and renminbi real estate investment trusts (REITs). In addition, the implementation of financial innovation policies such as Shanghai–Hong Kong Stock Connect, Shenzhen–Hong Kong Stock Connect and Bond Connect has promoted the continuous expansion of the breadth and depth of the offshore renminbi market. To a certain extent, the renminbi already has the characteristics of a safe-haven currency.

Whether the renminbi—specifically, the offshore renminbi—has become a safe-haven currency has become a question among financial market observers and participants (Fatum et al. 2017). Habib and Stracca (2012) deemed the net foreign exchange asset position and the size of the stock market significant factors in measuring whether a country's currency can be regarded as a safe-haven currency. Currently, China holds the largest net foreign asset position in the world, reaching US$3.2 trillion, and its stock market is the second-largest in the world. Therefore, it is reasonable to include the renminbi when considering global safe-haven currencies. However, there is no consensus in the literature as to what constitutes a safe-haven currency or, for that matter, which currencies exhibit safe-haven features and when these emerge. Ranaldo and Söderlind (2010) found that, during episodes of elevated market uncertainty prior to the Global Financial Crisis (GFC), the Japanese yen, the Swiss franc, the euro and the British pound were all exhibiting safe-haven currency features. Coudert et al. (2014) offered a daily data analysis of the evolution of 26 currencies from both advanced and emerging economies. They found that only the Japanese yen and the US dollar exhibited safe-haven currency properties. Hossfeld and MacDonald (2015) defined a currency to be a safe-haven currency if its effective returns were significantly negatively related to global stock market returns in times of high financial stress. They hold the idea that the US dollar better qualifies as a safe-haven currency relative to the Swiss franc, but the euro and the yen are not safe-haven currencies. Grisse and Nitschka (2015) argue that a safe-haven currency is one that offers hedging value against global risk—on average and particularly during a crisis. They examined the hedging characteristics of the Swiss franc and found it exhibits safe-haven characteristics against most, but not all, other currencies. The results in Fatum and Yamamoto (2016) showed that, during the GFC, the Japanese yen appreciated significantly vis-a-vis all other possible safe-haven currencies, thereby implying that the yen was the 'safest' safe-haven currency during this recent period of extreme market turmoil. Moreover, the hedging characteristics of currencies are time-varying—that is, a currency may exhibit hedging characteristics only for a specific period.

It is worth noting that little scholarly attention has been given to whether the renminbi is a safe-haven currency, and what there has been has focused on the extent to which the renminbi has become the anchor of other local currencies. Currently, only Fatum et al. (2017) have discussed the risk aversion of the renminbi. They considered that, at the full sample level, the renminbi exhibited safe-haven asset characteristics against some currencies, including the pound and the euro, but not against other major currencies, such as the US dollar and the yen. Nevertheless, at the at the sub-sample level, the renminbi does not have risk-averse properties. Basically, the renminbi cannot yet be counted as a safe-haven currency, nor has it moved towards becoming one. Regarding the research into the renminbi's anchor-currency status, we list the following studies as representative examples. Ito (2010) quoted the method of studying currency anchors proposed by Frankel and Wei (1994) and found that the renminbi has played a de facto currency basket role in East Asian countries since China's implementation of a managed floating exchange rate system on 21 July 2005. Subramanian and Kessler (2013) believe the influence of the renminbi in East Asia has surpassed that of the dollar and the euro, and it is playing the role of an anchor currency. Ito (2017) pointed out that, in the post-GFC era, the weight of the renminbi in the recessive currency basket of Asian countries has surpassed that of the US dollar. The research of Pontines and Siregar (2012) and Shu et al. (2015) also supports the above conclusions. Chinese scholars have also carried out extensive research on this topic. Yang and Li (2017) consider that the renminbi has become an implicit currency anchor for most countries in the world, particularly those that have close economic and trade relations with China. Liu and Zhang (2018) point out that, with the advancement of the Belt and Road Initiative (BRI), the renminbi's anchor effect will gradually be amplified in inland regions such as Central Asia. Nevertheless, Jian and Zheng (2016) probed the dynamic spillover effects between the renminbi and East Asian currencies from the dual dimensions of space and time and found that the renminbi would not be able to shake the dominant position of the US dollar among East Asian currencies. Peng et al. (2015) also found that the renminbi is not currently the dominant currency in Asia. Although the renminbi may not have become the currency anchor in the region, this does not prevent it having increasing influence, especially the offshore renminbi (Yin and Wu 2017). Does this influence include the hedging properties of the renminbi—that is, in times of crisis, can the renminbi become a haven for various risk assets in the region? This point requires further investigation.

This raises some academic questions: Does the renminbi, especially the offshore renminbi, have the characteristics of a safe haven? Do these characteristics behave significantly differently due to the different monetary environment—that is, are there significant differences in the safe-haven characteristics of the offshore renminbi in different currency portfolios? Meanwhile, do these attributes have time-varying characteristics? In the context of renminbi internationalisation and the BRI, analysing these issues clearly assists us in exploring the hedging characteristics of the renminbi from a quantitative perspective and investigating the hedging value provided by the renminbi to investors when extreme events occur, which in turn provides support for renminbi internationalisation and the BRI. It also has critical reference value and practical significance for the security of the financial system and the reform of the exchange rate system under the 'New Normal'.

Starting from the extended uncovered interest rate parity (UIP), this chapter selects the bilateral exchange rates of the offshore renminbi relative to major currencies and those of countries along the BRI as its research objects. By observing the changes in the offshore renminbi when global risks are rising, and combining its differential performance in different currency environments, we are able to explore the safe-haven characteristics of the offshore renminbi, while simultaneously assessing the time-varying effects of safe-haven characteristics. This study contributes to the literature by providing evidence that the offshore renminbi is a safe-haven currency. We argue that the offshore renminbi exhibits safe-haven asset characteristics against some of the major currencies and those of countries along the BRI. It provides technical support and a demonstration of feasibility for promoting the development of the renminbi as a carrier of cross-border trade payments and settlements in countries along the BRI, and even as a denominated and reserve currency. To a certain extent, the exploration of the safe-haven value is an important manifestation of the offshore renminbi market's ability to perform its functions, which opens up new directions for subsequent research on the renminbi and its offshore markets. Based on the time-varying safe-haven characteristics of the offshore renminbi, export-oriented enterprises can reasonably plan their asset-allocation strategies, and financial regulatory authorities can carry out appropriate policy coordination and institutional arrangements.

Theoretical background

This section aims to employ an asset-pricing framework to interpret the changes in exchange rates. It first presents some conceptual background and then introduces recent advances in the currency risk models that create the foundation for our empirical analysis.

UIP regressions

With the assumption of rational expectations and risk neutrality, UIP declares that the expected changes in exchange rates reflect the interest rate differential between the home country and the foreign country in previous periods—that is, Equation 9.1.

Equation 9.1

$$E_t(s_{t+1}^k) - s_t^k = i_t^k - i_t + \delta_{t+1}$$

In Equation 9.1, s_{t+1}^{k} is the log spot exchange rate of the home country relative to country k at time $t+1$ and E indicates the expectation operator; i_t and i_t^k reflect the interest rates of the home country and country k, respectively; δ_{t+1} is a risk premium. An increase in s indicates an appreciation of the home currency and depreciation of the foreign (country k) currency.

According to the study by Akram et al. (2008), interest rate differentials are approximately equal to forward discounts at least at the monthly frequency—namely, Equation 9.2.

Equation 9.2

$$i_t^k - i_t \approx f_t^k - s_t^k$$

In Equation 9.2, f_t^k denotes the log forward exchange rate of the home country relative to country k at time t. Under the rational expectation, Equation 9.3 holds.

Equation 9.3

$$E_t(s_{t+1}^{k}) = s_{t+1}^{k} + e_{t+1}^{k}$$

In Equation 9.3, the forecast error, e_{t+1}^{k}, is white noise. In particular, e_{t+1}^{k} is unrelated to any information that is available in period t. Substituting Equation 9.3 into Equation 9.1, we have Equation 9.4.

Equation 9.4

$$\Delta s_{t+1}^{k} = (f_t^k - s_t^k) + \delta_{t+1} - e_{t+1}^{k}$$

We can then give the transformation form of the standard UIP regression for the bilateral exchange rate with country k, Equation 9.5.

Equation 9.5

$$\Delta s_{t+1}^{k} = \alpha^k + \beta^k (f_t^k - s_t^k) + \lambda_{t+1}^{k}$$

According to the UIP condition, the regression coefficient, β, should be equal to 1 and the constant term, α, should be equal to zero. The error term, λ_{t+1}^{k}, reflects both forecast errors and the risk premium. In other words, the forward exchange rate should be equal to the future spot exchange rate. However, there is little literature to support the UIP condition. In fact, most of the literature points out that the UIP condition is idealised. One potential explanation is that market participants have a demand for risk premiums in foreign currency investments—that is, the assumption of risk neutrality is too rigorous (for example, Ranaldo and Söderlind 2010; Lustig et al. 2011; Jin and Chen 2012; Menkhoff et al. 2012; Farhi and Gabaix 2016; Xiao and Liu 2016; Verdelhan 2018). According to this research, the ex post deviation from the UIP condition may be attributed to covariation of exchange rate returns with contemporaneous currency risk factors (Grisse and Nitschka 2015).

However, many studies employ survey-based expectations of exchange rates to illustrate that the UIP is reasonable ex ante. Recent representative literature includes Bacchetta et al. (2009) and Grisse and Nitschka (2015). Grisse and Nitschka (2015) used survey expectations data on Swiss franc exchange rates and found that the UIP basically holds ex ante. Generally, the findings indicate that the asset-pricing viewpoint for currency returns may not be the best or only explanation for the ex post deviation from the UIP condition.

However, for the assessment of currency investment strategies and the safe-haven characteristics of exchange rates, the asset-pricing models for currency returns still have a strong appeal. This is because a safe-haven currency can help investors to acquire hedging value against global risk (Grisse and Nitschka 2015). Adopting this model to evaluate the safe-haven characteristics of the offshore renminbi relative to some of the major currencies and those of countries along the BRI will be the contribution of this chapter.

Theoretical background to exchange rate return pricing models

The asset-pricing models of exchange rate returns regard the UIP condition as an investment strategy with zero net value. At time t, this strategy first claims borrowing in the home country with interest rate i and then converting the home currency at the spot exchange rate into $1/S$ foreign currency units (FCUs). Holding FCUs can obtain a certain foreign interest rate, i^k. At time $t+1$, the investor converts the FCUs into the home currency at the spot exchange rate, S_{t+1} (Burnside et al. 2011; Grisse and Nitschka 2015). This investment strategy yields the following payoff, χ_{t+1} (Equation 9.6).

Equation 9.6

$$\chi_{t+1} = \frac{1}{S_t} (1+i_t^k)S_{t+1} - (1+i_t)$$

We then directly employ the following asset-pricing equation for excess returns based on the above interpretation of the UIP condition (Cochrane 2005), such that we get Equation 9.7, which should hold and in which w_{t+1} indicates the stochastic discount factor.

Equation 9.7

$$E_t \left[\left(\frac{1}{S_t} (1+i_t^k)S_{t+1} - (1+i_t) \right) w_{t+1} \right] = 0$$

We can generate the 'risk-adjusted' form of the UIP condition by dividing $E_t(w_{t+1})$ and rearranging—namely, Equation 9.8.

Equation 9.8

$$(1+i_t) = (1+i_t^k)\left[E_t\left(\frac{S_{t+1}}{S_t}\right) + \frac{\text{cov}[(S_{t+1}/S_t),w_{t+1}]}{E_t(w_{t+1})}\right]$$

Meanwhile, the covered interest rate parity (CIP) condition is listed as Equation 9.9.

Equation 9.9

$$(1+i_t) = \frac{1}{S_t}(1+i_t^k)F_t$$

In Equation 9.9, F_t denotes the forward exchange rate of the home currency relative to the foreign currency at time t.

Combining Equations 9.8 and 9.9, we further obtain the alternative form of the 'risk-adjusted' UIP condition that constitutes the basis of most empirical studies of the link between risk factors and exchange rate returns—namely, Equation 9.10.

Equation 9.10

$$E_t\left(\frac{S_{t+1}-S_t}{S_t}\right) = \frac{F_t-S_t}{S_t} - \frac{\text{cov}[((S_{t+1}-S_t)/S_t),w_{t+1}]}{E_t(w_{t+1})}$$

According to Equation 9.10, expected exchange rate returns are influenced not only by the previous period's forward discount/interest rate differential but also by the stochastic discount factor. This rationale forms the backbone of asset-pricing models for exchange rate returns in recent studies. And we describe that in the next subsection, which guarantees follow-up empirical analysis work can be carried out smoothly.

Recent empirical advances in exchange rate return pricing models

The UIP regressions should be expanded by including currency risk factors in accordance with the asset-pricing viewpoint on exchange rate determination (Verdelhan 2018). The specific form is Equation 9.11.

Equation 9.11

$$\Delta s_{t+1}^k = \alpha^k + \beta_0^k(f_t^k - s_t^k) + \beta_1^k\theta_{t+1}^1 + \beta_2^k\theta_{t+1}^2 + \cdots + \beta_n^k\theta_{t+1}^n + \lambda_{t+1}^k$$

In Equation 9.11, n represents the number of risk factors in an augmented currency risk premium model, k denotes the currency and θ indicates a specific currency risk factor.

Note that Equation 9.11 additionally assumes that the investor's discount factor is a linear function of the risk factors, θ. The introduction of risk factors expands the UIP so as to be able to evaluate the impact of the risk factors on contemporaneous exchange rate returns. Therefore, it is crucial to explore favourable risk factors in empirical research.

Since traditional risk factors, such as those proposed by Fama and French (1993), fail to effectively depict exchange rate returns, we try to obtain information about currency risk factors directly from exchange rate data by following recent studies. By sorting currencies' forward discounts or interest rate differentials, Lustig et al. (2011) constructed two first-principle components in portfolios of foreign currency returns based on US investors' perspective, and they correspond to a country-specific and global risk factor of excess currency returns. The empirical results show that differences in the risk exposure to the global factor decide the average risk premium on the currency portfolios. Lustig et al. (2011) further pointed out that their empirical model embodied an extension of the two-country framework proposed by Backus et al. (2001) to a multi-country and even global context. In this model, the country-specific factors play no part in the determination of currency risk premiums.

Moreover, under the conditions of exchange rate changes and excess currency returns, Lustig et al. (2011) and Verdelhan (2018) show that the other risk factors that derive from portfolios of excess currency returns are also informative of both time-series and cross-sectional variations in terms of bilateral exchange rate changes as well as bilateral excess returns. Thus, we utilise this model as our benchmark to explore the specific characteristics of the offshore renminbi exchange rate returns in the following sections.

Data

In this chapter, we consider the offshore renminbi exchange rates relative to selected major currencies, as well as the currencies of countries along the BRI. Specifically, the major currencies selected are: the Australian dollar, the Canadian dollar, the Swiss franc, the euro, the British pound, the Japanese yen, the Norwegian krone, the New Zealand dollar, the Swedish krona, the Singaporean dollar, the US dollar and the South African rand. Most of these currencies are not only the main currencies in the foreign exchange market, but also maintain a high degree of correlation with the commodity market. Simultaneously, the selection of countries along the BRI is based mainly on the announcement of the 'Belt and Road Portal' at the end of August 2020. The sources of the spot exchange rate data and the one-month forward exchange rates are available from DataStream. Meanwhile, these are subject to daily data under the US dollar quotation. Considering the availability of data, 26 countries along the BRI were selected, as shown in the last two columns of Table 9.1. In the subsequent empirical analysis, this chapter will examine the safe-haven characteristics of the offshore renminbi relative to the major currencies and those of countries along the BRI to comparatively analyse whether the offshore renminbi possesses safe-haven properties.

Our sample period spans from 11 July 2011 to 31 August 2020—chosen because the forward exchange rate data for the offshore renminbi can only be traced back this far. It should also be noted that the data adopted in this chapter are all bilateral exchange rates on the offshore renminbi relative to other currencies, and we gain these rates from the cross-rates of US dollar exchange rates. For example, the bilateral exchange rate of the United Arab Emirates (UAE) dirham/offshore renminbi is obtained by cross calculation between the offshore renminbi/US dollar and UAE dirham/US dollar.

Last, this chapter employs changes in the VIX based on daily data as a proxy for global currency risk. The VIX denotes the Chicago Board Options Exchange (CBOE) option-implied volatility index of the S&P 500. The VIX is mainly used to indicate the turbulence of global financial markets and the risk aversion of investors. If the VIX rises, global financial market volatility and investor risk aversion will be exacerbated. The data for the VIX are acquired from the CBOE's website (www.cboe.com/). All the data mentioned above have been processed by logarithm.

Table 9.1 Currency names and their corresponding symbols

Currency name	Currency symbol
Australian dollar	AUD
Bahraini dinar	BHD
British pound	GBP
Bulgarian lev	BGN
Canadian dollar	CAD
Croatian kuna	HRK
Czech koruna	CZK
Egyptian pound	EGP
euro	EUR
Hungarian forint	HUF
Indonesian rupiah	IDR
Japanese yen	JPY
Kazakhstan tenge	KZT
Korean won	KRW

Currency name	Currency symbol
Kuwaiti dinar	KWD
Malaysian ringgit	MYR
Moroccan dirham	MAD
New Turkish lira	TRY
New Zealand dollar	NZD
Norwegian krone	NOK
Offshore renminbi	CNH
Omani rial	OMR
Pakistani rupee	PKR
Philippine peso	PHP
Polish zloty	PLN
Qatari rial	QAR
Romanian leu	RON
Russian rouble	RUB
Saudi riyal	SAR
Serbian dinar	RSD
Singaporean dollar	SGD
South African rand	ZAR
Sri Lankan rupee	LKR
Swedish krona	SEK
Swiss franc	CHF
Thai baht	THB
UAE dirham	AED
US dollar	USD
Vietnamese dong	VND

Empirical results and analysis

This chapter discusses the safe-haven properties of the offshore renminbi relative to some major currencies and those of countries along the BRI. First, it quantitatively analyses the safe-haven characteristics of the offshore renminbi in view of the UIP and augmented UIP regressions. Second, it adopts the rolling window regressions to obtain a comprehensive analysis of the offshore renminbi's safe-haven features and its time-varying state.

The analysis of UIP regressions

This subsection mainly elaborates whether the UIP is reasonable for explaining the bilateral exchange rate changes of the offshore renminbi relative to major currencies and those of countries along the BRI. The regression model is described by Equation 9.12.

Equation 9.12

$$\Delta s_{t+1}^k = \alpha^k + \beta_0^k \left(f_t^k - s_t^k \right) + \lambda_{t+1}^k$$

In Equation 9.12, k indicates one of the bilateral offshore renminbi exchange rates, and s and f are the changes in the log spot exchange rate and the one-month log forward exchange rate, respectively. If β_0 equals 1, it indicates that the UIP is applicable in explaining exchange rate changes. Otherwise, it is necessary to consider adding more risk factors to expand the regressions.

The results for the offshore renminbi relative to the major currencies and those of countries along the BRI under the UIP are summarised in Tables 9.2 and 9.3, respectively. We further report the Durbin–Watson (DW) statistic for checking the autocorrelation of the regression residuals. Combining the results in Tables 9.2 and 9.3, we find that: the UIP cannot well explain the exchange rate changes of the offshore renminbi. Depending on the estimation results of the coefficient β_0^k, we can test whether it rejects or accepts the null hypothesis that $\beta_0^k = 1$. Taking the offshore renminbi vis-à-vis the Australian dollar denoted by the AUD in Table 9.2 as an example, its estimation of β_0 is 0.061 with a standard error of 0.077. Then the corresponding t-statistic is $(0.061\text{-}1)/0.077 = -12.19$, and its absolute value is obviously larger than the threshold of t-statistic at 95 per cent confidence level. Hence, the UIP is not applicable in the explanation of the exchange rate changes of the offshore renminbi relative to the Australian dollar. This conclusion generally reflects in the bilateral exchange rates of the offshore renminbi relative to major currencies and the currencies of countries along the BRI. It means that the lagged forward discounts factors do not play a certain role in explaining the exchange rate changes of these currencies.

Obviously, it is necessary to expand the UIP by considering currency risk factors to better discuss the issue of the bilateral exchange rate changes of the offshore renminbi relative to other currencies. Therefore, this chapter will conduct a new analysis of the issue based on an augmented UIP with currency risk factors.

Table 9.2 UIP regressions for the offshore renminbi against major currencies

	α^k	β_0^k	R^2	DW
AUD	−0.015	0.061	0.0002	1.939
	(0.015)	(0.077)		
CAD	−0.011	0.004	0.0000	1.918
	(0.017)	(0.073)		
CHF	0.013	−0.032	0.0000	1.931
	(0.036)	(0.100)		
EUR	−0.006	0.014	0.0000	1.927
	(0.025)	(0.075)		
GBP	0.024	−0.136	0.0009	1.868
	(0.025)	(0.094)		
JPY	−0.028	0.076	0.0002	1.911
	(0.031)	(0.098)		
NOK	−0.027	0.075	0.0001	1.918
	(0.023)	(0.102)		
NZD	−0.009	0.079	0.0002	1.945
	(0.016)	(0.101)		
SEK	−0.013	0.022	0.0000	1.939
	(0.022)	(0.071)		
SGD	−0.004	0.014	0.0000	1.934
	(0.013)	(0.056)		
USD	0.006	−0.013	0.0001	1.929
	(0.009)	(0.040)		
ZAR	0.010	0.162	0.0004	1.900
	(0.059)	(0.184)		

Note: Standard errors are in parentheses.
Source: Authors' calculations.

Table 9.3 UIP regressions for the offshore renminbi against the currencies of countries along the BRI

	α^k	β_0^k	R^2	DW
AED	0.006	−0.014	0.0001	1.929
	(0.009)	(0.040)		
BGN	−0.008	0.021	0.0000	1.928
	(0.024)	(0.078)		
BHD	0.001	0.017	0.0002	1.943
	(0.008)	(0.035)		

	α^k	β_0^k	R^2	DW
CZK	−0.020	0.057	0.0002	1.928
	(0.025)	(0.077)		
EGP	0.111***	0.080***	0.0223	1.990
	(0.036)	(0.011)		
HRK	−0.015	0.061	0.0003	1.928
	(0.019)	(0.066)		
HUF	−0.020	0.049	0.0002	1.923
	(0.020)	(0.069)		
IDR	−0.042**	−0.098	0.0011	1.919
	(0.020)	(0.068)		
KRW	−0.000	−0.018	0.0000	1.951
	(0.014)	(0.065)		
KWD	0.003	−0.028	0.0002	1.944
	(0.008)	(0.039)		
KZT	−0.004	0.045***	0.0034	1.945
	(0.023)	(0.015)		
LKR	−0.012	0.020	0.0002	1.926
	(0.015)	(0.035)		
MAD	0.002	0.023	0.0001	1.930
	(0.012)	(0.047)		
MYR	−0.013	0.081	0.0007	1.935
	(0.010)	(0.068)		
OMR	0.006	−0.015	0.0001	1.930
	(0.008)	(0.038)		
PHP	0.004	−0.092**	0.0019	1.926
	(0.008)	(0.044)		
PKR	−0.033**	−0.028	0.0007	1.931
	(0.015)	(0.034)		
PLN	−0.011	0.080	0.0004	1.920
	(0.018)	(0.083)		
QAR	0.006	−0.014	0.0001	1.930
	(0.009)	(0.044)		
RON	−0.007	0.005	0.0000	1.928
	(0.014)	(0.053)		
RSD	0.005	0.069	0.0011	1.917
	(0.016)	(0.042)		
RUB	−0.086*	−0.101	0.0006	1.939
	(0.048)	(0.092)		

	a^k	β_0^k	R^2	DW
SAR	0.006	−0.016	0.0002	1.931
	(0.009)	(0.042)		
THB	−0.000	0.065	0.0011	1.893
	(0.008)	(0.042)		
TRY	−0.072*	−0.007	0.0004	1.826
	(0.040)	(0.045)		
VND	0.001	0.020	0.0003	1.941
	(0.006)	(0.021)		

*** significant at the 1 per cent level
** significant at the 5 per cent level
* significant at the 10 per cent level
Note: Standard errors are in parentheses.
Source: Authors' calculations.

The analysis of augmented UIP regressions

In this subsection, we observe whether potential currency risk factors can help us better understand the exchange rate dynamics of the offshore renminbi. In the subsequent analysis, we apply the asset-pricing models as used in studies by Lustig et al. (2011), Grisse and Nitschka (2015) and Verdelhan (2018) to the offshore renminbi exchange rate context.

The currency-pricing model used in this chapter contains two risk factors. The first is currency-specific and is expressed by the average exchange rate change of the offshore renminbi. In other words, the average bilateral exchange rate changes of different currencies relative to the offshore renminbi are not completely consistent. According to Lustig et al. (2011), this factor interprets most of the time variation in excess currency returns. When we calculate the currency-specific factor, we must exclude the exchange rate itself, as recommended by Verdelhan (2018). For example, we use the arithmetical average of the exchange rate changes of 11 major currencies as the first risk factor when computing the average exchange rate changes of the offshore renminbi relative to the Australian dollar in the augmented UIP regressions.

The second risk factor is the VIX, which is an effective measure of global risk on currency markets. Lustig et al. (2011) have shown that the empirical proxy of the global risk factors added to UIP regressions should be positively related to the volatility of global stock markets. Unlike Lustig et al. (2011), who adopted differences in the returns on high and low forward discount sorted currency baskets as the proxy for global risk factors, this chapter refers to the VIX proposed by Grisse and Nitschka (2015). The latter argue that VIX returns can be viewed as a significant measure of global equity market volatility and hence serve as an approximate proxy variable to estimate global risk factors in the model of Lustig et al. (2011). It should be pointed out that, although the VIX is derived from the US stock market, it maintains a highly positive correlation with the volatility indices of other equity markets. Thus, the employment of the VIX as a proxy of global risk factors is conducive to avoiding potential double counting in the augmented UIP regressions. Moreover, it will generate econometric issues by directly incorporating the global factor of Lustig et al. (2011) into a regression together with the forward discount rate of the bilateral exchange rate. The reason is that a particular currency pair or cross-rate is already contained in Lustig et al.'s (2011) global risk factor, which is derived from currency portfolios sorted on forward discounts/interest rate differentials. We thus tend to adopt a global risk factor proxy that is obtained neither from forward discounts/ interest rate differentials nor from exchange rate data.

As Lustig et al. (2011) report, differences in the sensitivities of the returns to the global risk factor account to a large extent for the cross-sectional differences in foreign currency returns. Thus, exposures to global risk factors should reflect the safe-haven characteristics of a currency—namely, a safe-haven currency should have negative exposure to global risk factors. This means the safe-haven currency should gain in value when global risk materialises and thus provide a hedge for all investors (Grisse and Nitschka 2015).

The augmented UIP regressions then adopt the specification form of Equation 9.13.

Equation 9.13

$$\Delta s_{t+1}^{k} = \alpha^{k} + \beta_{0}^{k}(f_{t}^{k} - s_{t}^{k}) + \beta_{1}^{k} AFX_{t+1} + \beta_{2}^{k} \Delta(VIX)_{t+1} + \lambda_{t+1}^{k}$$

In Equation 9.13, *AFX* refers to the average bilateral exchange rate changes of the offshore renminbi relative to all currencies excluding the currency of country k.

The results for the offshore renminbi relative to the major currencies and those of countries along the BRI under the augmented UIP regressions are summarised in Tables 9.4 and 9.5, respectively. A few observations are worth noting. First of all, the forward discount rate is still weak in explaining not only the bilateral exchange rate changes of offshore renminbi against major currencies, but also the exchange rate changes of countries along the BRI. Specifically, the situation where the coefficient, β_{0}^{k}, on the forward discount is significantly different from zero remains scarce. Second, the average exchange rate change of a specific currency has an extremely significant effect in explaining the bilateral exchange rate change of the offshore renminbi relative to the currency, and it is shown that the situation where the coefficient, β_{1}^{k}, on the AFX significantly differs from zero holds in all cases. In the analysis of the offshore renminbi relative to major currencies, the estimates of the coefficient, β_{1}^{k}, range from 0.072 for the US dollar to 1.264 for the Norwegian krone. One potential reason the coefficient of the offshore renminbi against the US dollar is smallest may be the fact that Chinese international trade is closely linked to the United States and hence the capital transactions behind it are relatively frequent. Although the bilateral trade volume between the European Union and China is higher, the former, as a common political economy, has a much larger membership than just those who use the euro. Third, in the analysis of the offshore renminbi relative to major currencies, the coefficients of β_2^k have distinct results. It should be noted that positive (or negative) coefficient estimates indicate that the offshore renminbi depreciates (or appreciates) against the respective currency when the VIX—that is, global risk—increases. On average, the Swiss franc, the euro, the yen and the US dollar provide a better safe haven against global risk than the offshore renminbi. In the context of increasing global risks, the risk hedging provided by these currencies is significantly better than that of the offshore renminbi. In fact, as the most vital currency in the world, the US dollar plays the role of the benchmark currency in international trade, financial markets and commodity markets, and its safe-haven properties are naturally stronger than those of the offshore renminbi. The Swiss franc, the euro and the yen are traditional safe-haven currencies. As for the other currencies, their safe-haven properties are notably weaker than the offshore renminbi's. Fourth, in the analysis of the offshore renminbi relative to the currencies of countries along the BRI, the coefficients of β_2^k also have distinct results and the proportions with positive coefficients are more than those with negative coefficients. Currently, a significant negative coefficient signal indicates the offshore renminbi appreciates against the respective currency when global risk increases. This is the case for the bilateral exchange rate changes of the offshore renminbi against the Czech koruna, Hungarian forint, South Korean won, Polish zloty, Russian rouble and New Turkish lira, which make the safe-haven features of the offshore renminbi more prominent. By contrast, the fact that half the coefficients of β_2^k appear to be significantly positive denotes the fact that the safe-haven features of the offshore renminbi are not yet prominent for the currencies of countries along the BRI. However, it is worth emphasising that the Korean won, the Russian rouble and the New Turkish lira are all regionally representative currencies, and the offshore renminbi has stronger hedging properties against global risk than these. To a certain extent, there may be a situation where the offshore renminbi has stronger safe-haven properties relative to the currencies of countries along the BRI than those revealed by the empirical results. In addition, insignificant coefficients of β_2^k demonstrate that the offshore renminbi relative to the Association of Southeast Asian Nations (ASEAN) currencies has not changed significantly under the rise in global risk factors. According to the thesis of Baur and Lucey (2010), this phenomenon to a certain extent reflects the fact that specific assets have safe-haven properties. Therefore, the offshore renminbi also has a safe-haven value relative to these currencies. In summary, the offshore renminbi holds safe-haven characteristics, which mostly exist for a few major currencies, while the safe-haven characteristics of the offshore renminbi relative to the currencies of countries along the BRI appear relatively weaker.

Table 9.4 Augmented UIP regressions for the offshore renminbi against major currencies

	α^k	β_0^k	β_1^k	β_2^k	R^2	DW
	(Constant)	$(f_t^k - s_t^k)$	(AFX_{t+1})	$(\Delta(VIX)_{t+1})$		
AUD	−0.003	0.005	1.109***	−0.604***	0.489	1.939
	(0.010)	(0.054)	(0.024)	(0.109)		
CAD	−0.000	−0.024	0.759***	−0.247***	0.390	1.906
	(0.013)	(0.057)	(0.020)	(0.093)		
CHF	0.028	−0.059	0.910***	1.082***	0.315	1.946
	(0.030)	(0.083)	(0.028)	(0.130)		
EUR	0.010	−0.015	0.998***	0.592***	0.546	1.942
	(0.017)	(0.051)	(0.019)	(0.087)		
GBP	0.039*	−0.172**	0.796***	−0.069	0.296	1.867
	(0.021)	(0.078)	(0.025)	(0.119)		
JPY	−0.026	0.078	0.485***	2.052***	0.161	1.916
	(0.028)	(0.087)	(0.029)	(0.140)		
NOK	−0.006	0.003	1.264***	−0.796***	0.490	1.939
	(0.016)	(0.070)	(0.027)	(0.123)		
NZD	0.006	−0.006	1.188***	−0.336***	0.445	1.962
	(0.012)	(0.072)	(0.027)	(0.126)		
SEK	0.006	−0.016	1.144***	−0.119	0.489	1.955
	(0.016)	(0.049)	(0.024)	(0.111)		
SGD	0.002	0.009	0.605***	−0.118**	0.582	1.942
	(0.008)	(0.035)	(0.011)	(0.051)		
USD	0.006	−0.011	0.072***	0.471***	0.036	1.930
	(0.009)	(0.039)	(0.012)	(0.061)		
ZAR	0.016	0.157	1.262***	−2.675***	0.290	1.903
	(0.050)	(0.158)	(0.045)	(0.203)		

*** significant at the 1 per cent level
** significant at the 5 per cent level
* significant at the 10 per cent level
Note: Standard errors are in parentheses.
Source: Authors' calculations.

Table 9.5 Augmented UIP regressions for the offshore renminbi against the currencies of countries along the BRI

	α^k	β_0^k	β_1^k	β_2^k	R^2	DW
	(Constant)	$(f_t^k - s_t^k)$	(AFX_{t+1})	$(\Delta(VIX)_{t+1})$		
AED	0.009	0.003	0.484***	0.484***	0.304	1.935
	(0.008)	(0.033)	(0.016)	(0.052)		
BGN	0.014	−0.001	1.447***	0.326***	0.545	1.930
	(0.016)	(0.053)	(0.027)	(0.087)		
BHD	0.003	0.038	0.484***	0.519***	0.297	1.950
	(0.007)	(0.029)	(0.016)	(0.053)		
CZK	−0.005	0.068	1.615***	−0.207*	0.444	1.942
	(0.018)	(0.056)	(0.037)	(0.119)		
EGP	0.116***	0.081***	0.477***	0.212	0.038	1.994
	(0.036)	(0.011)	(0.078)	(0.254)		
HRK	0.010	0.017	1.438***	0.237**	0.506	1.928
	(0.013)	(0.047)	(0.029)	(0.094)		
HUF	0.002	0.028	1.768***	−0.887***	0.385	1.929
	(0.015)	(0.053)	(0.046)	(0.147)		
IDR	−0.033*	−0.088	0.597***	0.073	0.136	1.925
	(0.018)	(0.061)	(0.031)	(0.102)		
KRW	0.008	−0.026	0.606***	−0.218*	0.105	1.965
	(0.013)	(0.059)	(0.037)	(0.123)		
KWD	0.007	−0.008	0.619***	0.458***	0.456	1.958
	(0.006)	(0.028)	(0.014)	(0.047)		
KZT	0.001	0.044***	0.592***	0.303	0.037	1.950
	(0.022)	(0.015)	(0.065)	(0.218)		
LKR	−0.005	0.026	0.489***	0.495***	0.155	1.924
	(0.014)	(0.033)	(0.024)	(0.081)		
MAD	0.016**	0.023	1.213***	0.263***	0.630	1.932
	(0.007)	(0.029)	(0.019)	(0.062)		
MYR	−0.005	0.072	0.665***	−0.024	0.180	1.951
	(0.009)	(0.059)	(0.029)	(0.097)		
OMR	0.009	−0.001	0.483***	0.491***	0.302	1.937
	(0.007)	(0.032)	(0.016)	(0.052)		
PHP	0.010	−0.078**	0.598***	0.102	0.237	1.933
	(0.007)	(0.037)	(0.022)	(0.074)		
PKR	−0.026*	−0.021	0.514***	0.444***	0.118	1.929
	(0.014)	(0.033)	(0.030)	(0.098)		

	α^k	β_0^k	β_1^k	β_2^k	R^2	DW
	(Constant)	$(f_t^k - s_t^k)$	(AFX_{t+1})	$(\Delta(VIX)_{t+1})$		
PLN	0.011	0.054	1.750***	−0.833***	0.426	1.935
	(0.013)	(0.062)	(0.042)	(0.134)		
QAR	0.010	−0.004	0.483***	0.481***	0.298	1.936
	(0.008)	(0.037)	(0.016)	(0.053)		
RON	0.010	0.007	1.527***	0.064	0.505	1.934
	(0.010)	(0.038)	(0.031)	(0.099)		
RSD	0.014	0.032	1.450***	0.334***	0.456	1.927
	(0.011)	(0.031)	(0.033)	(0.104)		
RUB	−0.072	−0.092	0.847***	−3.152***	0.099	1.948
	(0.044)	(0.084)	(0.079)	(0.259)		
SAR	0.008	0.009	0.484***	0.484***	0.303	1.938
	(0.008)	(0.034)	(0.016)	(0.052)		
THB	0.008	0.048	0.655***	0.000	0.330	1.886
	(0.007)	(0.034)	(0.019)	(0.063)		
TRY	−0.053	0.008	0.996***	−1.456***	0.111	1.823
	(0.037)	(0.042)	(0.063)	(0.205)		
VND	0.005	0.009	0.481***	0.460***	0.270	1.947
	(0.005)	(0.018)	(0.017)	(0.056)		

*** significant at the 1 per cent level

˙˙ significant at the 5 per cent level

˙ significant at the 10 per cent level

Note: Standard errors are in parentheses.

Source: Authors' calculations.

The time-varying relationship between exchange rate changes and global risk factors

Considering that there may have been structural breaks in the course of our sample period, the corresponding research conclusions may have changed substantially. Meanwhile, within this period, several reforms of the renminbi exchange rate system have also been carried out, which may have had a profound impact on the relationship between the exchange rate changes of the offshore renminbi and global risk factors. Therefore, this subsection enriches this chapter's research conclusions by further exploring the time-varying relationships between the bilateral exchange rate changes of the offshore renminbi against the major currencies and those of countries along the BRI and global risk factors.

Figures 9.1 and 9.2 show the dynamic evolution paths of the relationships between the bilateral exchange rate changes of the offshore renminbi against major currencies and those of countries along the BRI, respectively, and global risk factors. According to Figure 9.1, several observations are remarkable. First, during the sample period, the time variation between the bilateral exchange rate change of the offshore renminbi against the Swiss franc and global risk factors was consistent with that of the Japanese yen. Specifically, with an increase in global risks, the Swiss franc and the Japanese yen maintained an appreciative trend relative to the offshore renminbi, and the safe-haven characteristics of the two currencies tended to strengthen, while the Japanese yen possessed better safe-haven characteristics than the offshore renminbi. This may be due to the geographical proximity of and close international trade between China and Japan. Therefore, compared with traditional safe-haven currencies, the safe-haven characteristics of the offshore renminbi do not exist. Second, compared with the Swiss franc and the Japanese yen, the time variation fluctuations in the bilateral exchange rate changes of the offshore renminbi against the euro and the US dollar and global risk factors were relatively weak. The reason the euro fluctuated sharply in the first half of 2016 may be attributed to the vote for Brexit, during which risk-averse sentiments surged and assets priced in the euro were able to attract some of the pound's safe-haven inflows, causing the time-varying relationship to reach a peak state—that is, the hedging value of the euro relative to the offshore renminbi increased. As for the US dollar, it maintained a moderate appreciation status relative to the offshore renminbi. On the whole, the US dollar's safe-haven feature is not salient. Especially in the second half of 2017, the offshore renminbi was better able to withstand global risk fluctuations than the US dollar. This may be because the US dollar was affected by the dual impacts of the international and domestic situations in 2017 and was unable to extricate itself from a sluggish market. Counterposed to this, the value of the renminbi continued to be firm, thereby satisfying investors' hedging demands to a certain extent. However, it is noticeable that the safe-haven characteristics of the US dollar relative to the offshore renminbi have become more obvious since the China–US trade friction began and continue to present a growing trend. This to some extent reflects the fact that the offshore renminbi is not yet fully equipped with safe-haven characteristics. Third, the time variation between the exchange rate changes and global risk factors tended to be consistent in terms of the offshore renminbi against the Australian, Canadian and New Zealand dollars. Among them, the main variation was in the first half of 2016, when the offshore renminbi had stronger safe-haven properties than these three currencies. A potential reason for this is that these are all commodity currencies and their values are profoundly affected by international commodity prices. From 2015 until the first half of 2016, commodity prices were in a sluggish state of decline, hence the corresponding commodity-currency values remained relatively weak. However, for the renminbi, its currency value was relatively stable and the steady demand for commodities in the Chinese market meant the hedging value of the offshore renminbi was greatly increased. Fourth, the offshore renminbi has more prominent safe-haven characteristics than the Norwegian krone, the Singaporean dollar and the South African rand—a fact that is especially obvious relative to the South African rand. Specifically, the time variation between the exchange rate changes of the offshore renminbi against these three currencies and global risk factors is generally negative, and the time variation for the South African rand tended to decline overall, especially between 2015 and the first half of 2016, such that this negative time-variation relationship continued to strengthen.

According to Figure 9.2, we obtain several conclusions. First, the time variation between the bilateral exchange rate change of the offshore renminbi against the Hungarian forint and global risk factors is basically consistent with that of the Polish zloty. Although the time variation appears positive in some periods, its overall trend presented as dominantly negative. That is, the safe-haven properties of the offshore renminbi relative to these two currencies are persistent. However, it is worth noting that the safe-haven attributes after 2015 gradually weakened compared with their strength before 2015. It appears as a time-varying relationship that begins to wander up and down near zero. This may be due to the fact that global political and economic uncertainties have intensified, prompting investors to gradually focus on traditional safe-haven assets, and leading to the weakening of the offshore renminbi's safe-haven attributes. Second, the time variation between the bilateral exchange rate changes of the offshore renminbi against the Czech koruna and global risk factors is basically inverse to that of the Russian rouble. The safe-haven characteristics of the offshore renminbi relative to the Russian rouble persist, because the time variation between the bilateral exchange rate change of the offshore renminbi against the rouble and the global risk factors is below zero. In extreme cases, holding the offshore renminbi to hedge against exchange rate fluctuations in the rouble can yield higher returns. At the end of 2014, the rouble depreciated drastically due to the dual impacts of the plunge in oil prices and the crisis in Ukraine. At this time, the safe-haven value of the offshore renminbi was highlighted considerably. Under this circumstance, a 1 per cent increase in global risk factors, as measured by the VIX, will induce a 12 per cent appreciation of the offshore renminbi against the rouble—more than four times larger than the average effect. Obviously, to a certain extent, this reflects the fragility of Russia's economic and financial regime and the instability of the rouble. In bilateral trade with Russia or other international economic and financial activities, we must increase the awareness of risk aversion and make timely preparations to convert the rouble into the offshore renminbi or other safe-haven currencies. Currently, the safe-haven characteristics of the offshore renminbi relative to the Czech koruna are confused. In extreme cases, the time variation between the bilateral exchange rate change of the offshore renminbi against the Czech koruna and global risk factors has turned into a positive relationship. Third, the safe-haven characteristics of the offshore renminbi relative to the New Turkish lira persist and have become even more outstanding in extreme situations. From 2018 to 2019, affected by the political situation and uncertainty about monetary and fiscal policies, the New Turkish lira depreciated sharply and the safe-haven nature of the offshore renminbi was significantly enhanced. A 1 per cent increase in the VIX generated a 5 per cent appreciation in the offshore renminbi relative to the New Turkish lira. As for the hedging characteristic of the offshore renminbi relative to the Korean won, it is being strengthened. After 2016, the time variation between the bilateral exchange rate change of the offshore renminbi against the won and global risk factors has remained below zero. This may be because China and South Korea continuously carry out currency-swap mechanisms and actively promote economic and trade exchanges and financial market transactions, which have promoted the closer relationship between the renminbi and the won.

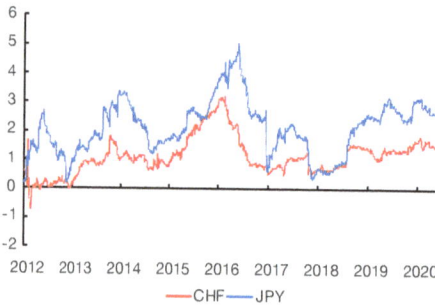

Figure 9.1a CHF and JPY

Figure 9.1b EUR and USD

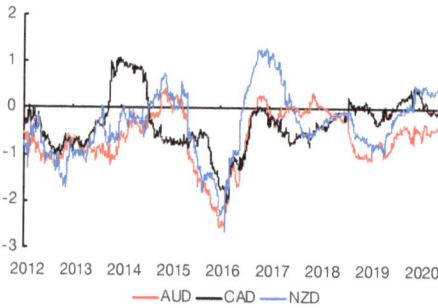

Figure 9.1c AUD, CAD and NZD

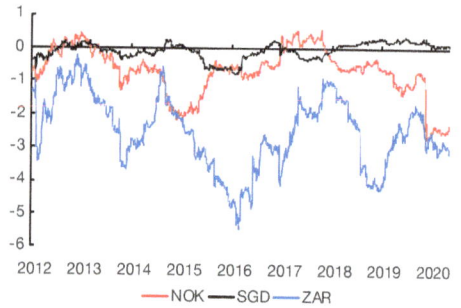

Figure 9.1d NOK, SGD and ZAR

Figure 9.1 The dynamic path of the relationship between the bilateral exchange rate changes of the offshore renminbi relative to major currencies and global risk factors

Source: Authors' calculations.

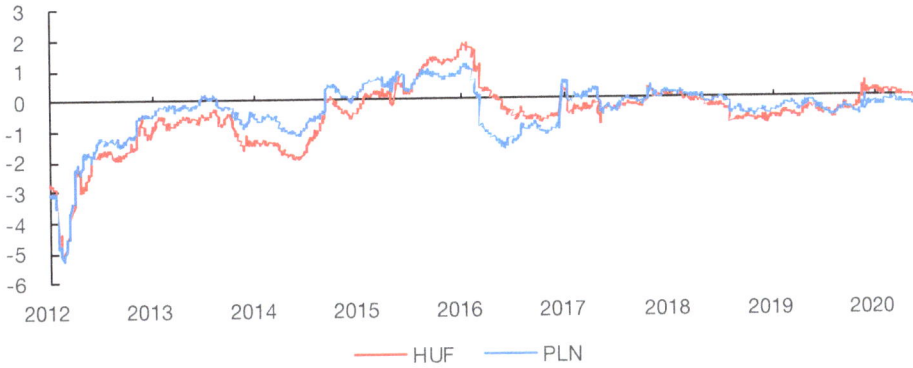

Figure 9.2a HUF and PLN

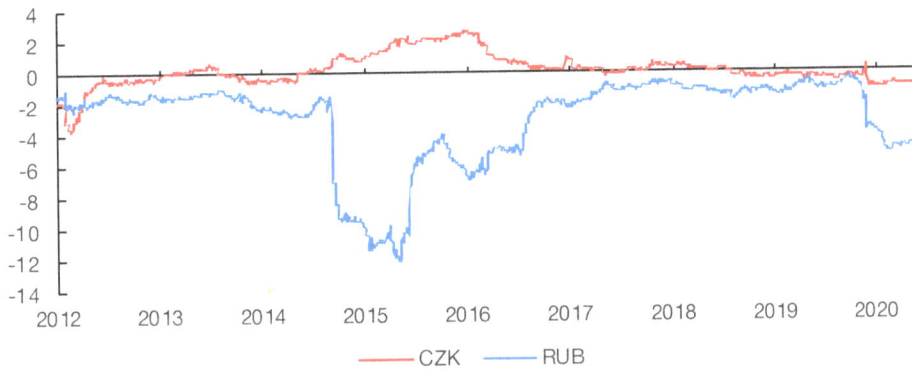

Figure 9.2b CZK and RUB

Figure 9.2c KRW and TRY

Figure 9.2 The dynamic path of the relationship between the bilateral exchange rate changes of the offshore renminbi relative to the currencies of the BRI countries and global risk factors

Source: Authors' calculations.

Conclusions and policy implications

Based on the classic asset-pricing framework, this chapter analyses the bilateral exchange rate changes of the offshore renminbi relative to some major currencies and those of countries along the BRI, before exploring whether the offshore renminbi possesses the characteristics of a safe-haven currency. Specifically, this chapter first introduces the augmented uncovered interest rate parity regressions including currency risk factors to obtain a basic understanding of the offshore renminbi's safe-haven characteristics. It then focuses on assessing the time variation between the bilateral exchange rate changes of the offshore renminbi relative to different currencies and global risk factors represented by the VIX to further examine the time-varying characteristics of the abovementioned safe-haven attributes.

This chapter draws some interesting conclusions. First, the offshore renminbi has safe-haven characteristics, which exist against some major currencies and some currencies along the BRI. Specifically, among major currencies, the offshore renminbi behaves like a safe-haven asset against partial currencies such as the Australian, Canadian, New Zealand and Singaporean dollars. Among the currencies of the countries along the BRI, the offshore renminbi also behaves like a safe-haven asset against partial currencies, including the Czech koruna, the Hungarian forint, the South Korean won, the Polish zloty, the Russian rouble and the New Turkish lira. Second, compared with major currencies, the safe-haven properties of the offshore renminbi are generally weaker in the currencies of the countries along the BRI. Taking into account the future growth trend of the Chinese economy, the continuous deepening of the renminbi's internationalisation and the advancement of the BRI, global recognition and acceptance of the renminbi will be greatly improved and the current status quo of weaker safe-haven properties for the offshore renminbi will also be ameliorated. Third, the traditional safe-haven currencies represented by the Swiss franc, the euro, the yen and the US dollar provided a better hedge against global risk than the offshore renminbi, and the hedging value of these currencies is significantly stronger than that of the offshore renminbi. In other words, the renminbi currently does not have enough power to compete with traditional safe-haven currencies in global financial markets and the rise of the renminbi has not completely subverted the global monetary system. Fourth, the safe-haven properties of the offshore renminbi possess time-varying characteristics. When extreme events occur, the hedging value of the offshore renminbi becomes more pronounced. For instance, during the financial crisis in Russia and the currency crisis in Turkey, the offshore renminbi's hedging performance against the rouble and the lira was outstanding. Obviously, to some extent this can provide new ideas for the arrangement of foreign exchange hedging strategies under situations of extreme risk.

In the process of advancing the internationalisation of the renminbi and the BRI, the renminbi's becoming a safe-haven currency is not among the primary strategic objectives, and yet it certainly remains a very important and meaningful attribute. On the one hand, it demonstrates the gradual formation of the renminbi's international status, while simultaneously guaranteeing the international community's recognition of China's identity as a responsible major country. On the other hand, it can help renminbi-denominated financial products gain wider market recognition in global foreign exchange asset allocations, especially when global markets are exposed to potential extreme risks.

To strengthen the renminbi's safe-haven characteristics, there are several areas in which China still needs to make significant progress. First, the reform of the renminbi exchange rate system should be steadily advanced to ensure that its flexibility better reflects market rules; second, the Hong Kong offshore renminbi market should be moved forward vigorously and given more scope for early and pilot implementation of financial innovation policies; third, the construction of renminbi internationalisation infrastructure should be promoted, and more useful attempts to support payment and settlement systems, accounting standards and rating systems should be made; fourth, economic and trade relations with countries along the BRI should continue to be strengthened and consideration should be given to placing the 'experimental field' of renminbi internationalisation in these countries.

References

Akram, Q.F., Rime, D. and Sarno, L. (2008), Arbitrage in the foreign exchange market: Turning on the microscope, *Journal of International Economics* 76(2): 237–53. doi.org/10.1016/j.jinteco.2008.07.004.

Bacchetta, P., Mertens, E. and Wincoop, E.V. (2009), Predictability in financial markets: What do survey expectations tell us?, *Journal of International Money & Finance* 28(3): 406–26. doi.org/10.1016/j.jimonfin.2008.09.001.

Backus, D.K., Foresi, S. and Telmer, C.I. 2001, Affine term structure models and the forward premium anomaly, *The Journal of Finance* 56(1): 279–304. doi.org/10.1111/0022-1082.00325.

Bank for International Settlements (BIS) (2019), *Triennial Central Bank Survey: Global Foreign Exchange Market Turnover in 2019*, Basel, Switzerland: Monetary and Economic Department of the Bank for International Settlements.

Baur, D.G. and Lucey, B.M. (2010), Is gold a hedge or a safe haven? An analysis of stocks, bonds and gold, *The Financial Review* 45(2): 217–29. doi.org/10.1111/j.1540-6288.2010.00244.x.

Burnside, C., Eichenbaum, M., Kleshchelski, I. and Rebelo, S. (2011), Do peso problems explain the returns to the carry trade?, *Review of Financial Studies* 24(3): 853–91. doi.org/10.1093/rfs/hhq138.

Cochrane, J.H. (2005), *Asset Pricing*, 2nd edn, Princeton, NJ: Princeton University Press.

Coudert, V., Guillaumin, C. and Raymond, H. (2014), *Looking at the Other Side of Carry Trades: Are There Any Safe Haven Currencies?*, CEPII Working Paper 2014-03, Paris: Centre d'Études Prospectives et d'Informations Internationales.

Fama, E.F. and French, K.R. (1993), Common risk factors in the returns on stocks and bonds, *Journal of Financial Economics* 33(1): 3–56. doi.org/10.1016/0304-405X(93)90023-5.

Farhi, E. and Gabaix, X. (2016), Rare disasters and exchange rates, *The Quarterly Journal of Economics* 131(1): 1–52. doi.org/10.1093/qje/qjv040.

Fatum, R. and Yamamoto, Y. (2016), Intra–safe haven currency behavior during the global financial crisis, *Journal of International Money and Finance* 66: 49–64. doi.org/10.1016/j.jimonfin.2015.12.007.

Fatum, R., Yamamoto, Y. and Zhu, G. (2017), Is the Renminbi a safe haven?, *Journal of International Money and Finance* 79: 189–202. doi.org/10.1016/j.jimonfin.2017.09.010.

Financial Stability Analysis Group of the People's Bank of China (2019), *China Financial Stability Report 2019*, [In Chinese], Beijing: China Financial Publishing House.

Frankel, J.A. and Wei, S.J. (1994), Yen bloc or dollar bloc? Exchange rate policies of the East Asian economies, in T. Ito and A.O. Krueger (eds), *Macroeconomic Linkage: Savings, Exchange Rates, and Capital Flows*, 295–355, Chicago: University of Chicago Press.

Grisse, C. and Nitschka, T. (2015), On financial risk and the safe haven characteristics of Swiss franc exchange rates, *Journal of Empirical Finance* 32: 153–64. doi.org/10.1016/j.jempfin.2015.03.006.

Habib, M.M. and Stracca, L. (2012), Getting beyond carry trade: What makes a safe haven currency?, *Journal of International Economics* 87(1): 50–64. doi.org/10.1016/j.jinteco.2011.12.005.

Hossfeld, O. and MacDonald, R. (2015), Carry funding and safe haven currencies: A threshold regression approach, *Journal of International Money and Finance* 59: 185–202. doi.org/10.1016/j.jimonfin.2015.07.005.

Ito, T. (2010), China as number one: How about the renminbi?, *Asian Economic Policy Review* 5: 249–76. doi.org/10.1111/j.1748-3131.2010.01169.x.

Ito, T. (2017), A new financial order in Asia: Will a RMB bloc emerge?, *Journal of International Money and Finance* 74: 232–57. doi.org/10.1016/j.jimonfin.2017.02.019.

Jian, Z. and Zheng, X. (2016), A study on the influence of RMB in Asia during the process of exchange rate reform: Based on the perspective of both time and space dimension, [In Chinese], *World Economy Studies* 3: 61–69.

Jin, Z. and Chen, H. (2012), The realisation of interest rate parity in China, [In Chinese], *Journal of Financial Research* 7: 63–74.

Liu, G. and Zhang, Y. (2018), Does the RMB play the role of anchor in the currency circle of 'the Belt and Road initiative'? Based on the comparative study of RMB and main international currencies, [In Chinese], *Studies of International Finance* 7: 32–41.

Lustig, H., Roussanov, N. and Verdelhan, A. (2011), Common risk factors in currency markets, *The Review of Financial Studies* 24(11): 3731–77. doi.org/10.1093/rfs/hhr068.

Menkhoff, L., Sarno L., Schmeling, M. and Schrimpf, A. (2012), Carry trades and global foreign exchange volatility, *The Journal of Finance* 67(2): 681–718. doi.org/10.1111/j.1540-6261.2012.01728.x.

Peng, H., Tan, X., Chen, W., Peng, H., Tan, X., Chen, W. and Li, Y. (2015), Asian monetary cooperation and RMB regionalisation process: An empirical research based on panel SURADF test with a Fourier function, [In Chinese], *World Economy Studies* 1: 36–47.

People's Bank of China (PBC) (2020), *RMB Internationalisation Report 2020*, 14 August, Beijing: PBC.

Pontines, V. and Siregar, R. (2012), Fear of appreciation in East and Southeast Asia: The role of the Chinese renminbi, *Journal of Asian Economics* 23(4): 324–34. doi.org/10.1016/j.asieco.2012.03.005.

Ranaldo, A. and Söderlind, P. (2010), Safe haven currencies, *Review of Finance* 14(3): 385–407. doi.org/10.1093/rof/rfq007.

Shu, C., He, D. and Cheng, X. (2015), One currency, two markets: The renminbi's growing influence in Asia-Pacific, *China Economic Review* 33: 163–78. doi.org/10.1016/j.chieco.2015.01.013.

Subramanian, A. and Kessler, M. (2013), The renminbi bloc is here: Asia down, rest of the world to go?, *Journal of Globalisation and Development* 4(1): 49–94. doi.org/10.1515/jgd-2013-0017.

Verdelhan, A. (2018), The share of systematic variation in bilateral exchange rates, *The Journal of Finance* 73(1): 375–418. doi.org/10.1111/jofi.12587.

Xiao, L. and Liu, Y. (2016), Uncovered interest rate parity puzzle: Four hypothesis tests, [In Chinese], *Management World* 7: 51–62.

Yang, R. and Li, Y. (2017), Capital account liberalisation and the anchor currency status of RMB during its globalisation process, [In Chinese], *Economic Research Journal* 52(1): 134–48.

Yin, L. and Wu, Y. (2017), The research of offshore RMB's regional influence: A perspective based on information spillover, [In Chinese], *Journal of Financial Research* 8: 1–18.

Index

A page number containing 'n.' indicates a reference appearing in a footnote on that page.

www.ingramcontent.com/pod-product-compliance
Lightning Source LLC
Chambersburg PA
CBHW050039220326
41599CB00041B/7211